P9-CCC-628

PLACE IN   t from

African American Children

Understanding Families

Series Editors: Bert N. Adams, University of Wisconsin
David M. Klein, University of Notre Dame

This book series examines a wide range of subjects relevant to studying families. Topics include, but are not limited to, theory and conceptual design, research methods on the family, racial/ethnic families, mate selection, marriage, family power dynamics, parenthood, divorce and remarriage, custody issues, and aging families.

The series is aimed primarily at scholars working in family studies, sociology, psychology, social work, ethnic studies, gender studies, cultural studies, and related fields as they focus on the family. Volumes will also be useful for graduate and undergraduate courses in sociology of the family, family relations, family and consumer sciences, social work and the family, family psychology, family history, cultural perspectives on the family, and others.

Books appearing in **Understanding Families** are either single- or multiple-authored volumes or concisely edited books of original chapters on focused topics within the broad interdisciplinary field of marriage and family.

The books are reports of significant research, innovations in methodology, treatises on family theory, syntheses of current knowledge in a family subfield, or advanced textbooks. Each volume meets the highest academic standards and makes a substantial contribution to our understanding of marriages and families.

Shirley A. Hill

African American Children

Socialization and Development in Families

UNDERSTANDING FAMILIES

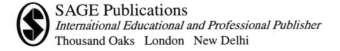

SAGE Publications
International Educational and Professional Publisher
Thousand Oaks   London   New Delhi

For information:

 SAGE Publications, Inc.
2455 Teller Road
Thousand Oaks, California 91320
E-mail: order@sagepub.com

SAGE Publications Ltd.
6 Bonhill Street
London EC2A 4PU
United Kingdom

SAGE Publications India Pvt. Ltd.
M-32 Market
Greater Kailash I
New Delhi 110 048 India

Printed in the United States of America

Library of Congress Cataloging-in-Publication Data

Hill, Shirley A. (Shirley Ann), 1947-
    African American children: Socialization and development in families / Shirley A. Hill.
        p. cm. — (Understanding families ; v. 14)
    Includes bibliographical references and index.
    ISBN 0-7619-0433-6 (cloth : acid-free paper)
    ISBN 0-7619-0434-4 (pbk. : acid-free paper)
    1. Afro-American children. 2. Socialization—United States. 3. Afro-American families. 4. Parenting—United States. I. Title. II. Series.
    E185.86 .H665 1998
    306.85'089'96073—ddc21   98-25352

This book is printed on acid-free paper.

99   00   01   02   03   04   05   7   6   5   4   3   2   1

Acquisition Editor:	Jim Nageotte
Editorial Assistant:	Heidi Van Middlesworth
Production Editor:	Denise Santoyo
Editorial Assistant:	Nevair Kabakian
Typesetter:	Christina M. Hill

Contents

Preface

Children:
Our Raison d'être

In terms of organizational purpose of the Black family, the family's reason for being can be considered childcenteredness. By this is meant that the purpose of the Black family focused on, if not required, the presence of children. The family unit exists for the growth and development of children, rather than for the self-actualization of the adult members of the unit.

Wade W. Nobles, *Africanity and the Black Family* (1985, p. 83)

African American family scholarship uniformly attests to the immense importance and centrality of children in black families (Anderson, 1991; Billingsley, 1968/1988, 1992; Burton, 1990; Collins, 1987; Hale, 1986; Nobles, 1985; Staples & Johnson, 1993). Yet, despite a proliferation of black family studies since the 1960s, very little research has been devoted to a systematic study of childhood socialization processes or the work that parents do in raising their children. Studies that emphasize the strengths of black families rarely examine the strengths and successes of parents, nor do they explore the child-rearing beliefs and strategies of black parents. Most research on child socialization and parent-child relations includes either no or very small numbers of African Americans, and, as Peters (1997) points out, studies that do include black parents, children, or both usually limit their analyses to problem populations and concentrate on interventions rather than on normal family socialization processes.

The growing socioeconomic diversity of African Americans makes the inordinate research emphasis on poor and low-income populations even more problematic, as the results generated by such studies fail to capture the life experiences of most blacks by presenting them as a monolithic group. The child-rearing practices of low-income black parents are then evaluated on the basis of white, middle-class norms and deemed defective. Popular theories of child development, many of them articulated in the early 1900s on the basis of a value system that emerged among affluent whites during industrialization, also unwittingly denigrate the cultural experiences of racial minority children (Taylor, 1994). For example, the emphasis on the importance of separation and individuation as crucial aspects of child development may not reflect the cultural experiences of black children, as they are often taught to value cooperation and interdependency. Child-rearing practices, values, and norms are best viewed in economic and cultural context, as these factors most frequently shape the risks, opportunities, and challenges of parenthood.

The paucity of research on child socialization in African American families, the focus on poor and/or problem populations, and the failure to acknowledge the incongruence between the class and cultural backgrounds of white and black Americans, all foster the notion that black parents are incapable of raising successful, well-adjusted children. The current social-political discourse on black families, which increasingly downplays the realities of racism and economic inequality, reinforces the notion that poor child socialization outcomes are attributable to incompetent, indifferent, or irresponsible parents. Black parents are stereotyped as poor and pathological, as more interested in governmental handouts than employment, and as failing to teach their children the value of hard work.

The culture versus structure controversy, which has raged for decades and has now been expanded to include the underclass concept, derives its energy from the persistent myth that African American families are generally defective, defined as welfare-dependent, fatherless, and female-headed. Under the rubric of individual responsibility, the cultural patterns of the poor are now rarely understood as adaptive responses to social structural forces but are seen as freely chosen lifestyles guided by a value system that promotes illegitimacy, poverty, and family instability. This resurgence of victim-blaming ideologies belies nearly three decades of family scholarship that has challenged depictions of black families as abnormal and dysfunctional (Allen, 1978, 1981; Billingsley, 1968/1988, 1992; Gutman, 1976; Staples & Johnson, 1993). The current debate over the declining status of African American families and its impact on children also highlights the importance of better understanding of child socialization processes.

Evolution of the Study

As a family sociology teacher at a large, predominantly white university, I have always been aware of the scarcity of research on the normal socialization of African American children and believed that major child development theories were less applicable to their experiences. I became more acutely aware of this a few years ago, however, as I was conducting research on family caregiving for children with sickle cell disease (Hill, 1994). In my interviews, I found a gendered pattern of caregiving whereby mothers of sons saw their children as more fragile and helpless than did mothers of daughters, and devoted more time, energy, and effort to caring for chronically ill sons (Hill & Zimmerman, 1995). Given the focus on gender studies in the past few decades, especially the vast literature on the differential socialization of boys and girls, I began to search for studies that would shed some light on how gender affected child rearing in black families. I found that few, if any, empirical studies had examined this issue, despite the immense popularity of gender studies.

My awareness of the void in research on the work parents do in socializing their children was also heightened as I prepared to teach a weekend seminar on the black family. There was a wealth of information available on African American families in general, but very little of it had explored child-rearing or socialization processes. Studies that did include or focus on black children most often addressed issues such as teenage pregnancy, substance abuse, or juvenile delinquency rather than normal patterns of child rearing. Moreover, researchers tended to address problem issues of black children in ways that omitted the voices, activities, and efforts of their parents. While I believe in the importance of social structural forces (e.g., race, class, family structure, schools, public policy) in shaping socialization patterns and the overall quality of family life, it seemed that too few scholars had considered the importance of human agency, or the energy, work, and social capital (Coleman, 1988) parents invest in their children. These are some of the central issues I hoped to address as I embarked upon a study of child socialization in African American families.

In 1992, I contacted the principal of a large, midwestern, predominantly black elementary school and gained permission to send letters home to the parents of fourth and fifth graders explaining my interest in child rearing and requesting an interview (see Appendix A for more details on the research methodology). I developed an interview guide based on an analysis of central issues identified in child-rearing and black family literature, and revised and expanded it as a result of my initial interviews (Appendix B). I then constructed a survey (Appendix C) of these relevant issues to be self-administered to a larger, more diverse group of parents. I had initially targeted the parents of fourth and fifth graders but later distributed the surveys more widely. Either parent (or primary caregiver) was free to complete the survey sent home with the child, but more than 80% of the surveys were completed by mothers. I continued to interview parents who responded to the interview request, and they sometimes referred me to other parents, creating a snowball sample. Over a three-year period, I interviewed a nonrandom sample of 35 African American parents (Table P.1) and collected surveys from 729 parents: 525 black parents and 204 white parents. Although this book focuses mostly on black parents, these data allowed me to examine the racial differences between blacks and whites in their child-rearing work as well as differences among blacks based on social class.

The black and white parents who completed the surveys were similar in most of their characteristics (Table P.2). The average age for both black and white parents was the midthirties. Black parents were more likely than white parents to have attended college (46% versus 33%), but fewer than 20% of blacks or whites had a four-year college education or more. This racial gap in education is probably due to the fact that these parents lived in predominantly black neighborhoods, and educated blacks are more likely than educated whites to remain in such neighborhoods. The majority of respondents were employed (61% of whites and 70% of blacks) with family incomes of less than $30,000 per year. In answering the surveys, parents were asked to identify and focus on just one child. Table P.2 profiles those children. Their ages ranged from 1 to 18 years for black parents and from 1 to 15 years for white parents, with an overall average age of 9½ years old. The average grade level is about the fourth grade. To these survey and interview data I added some of my own family experiences and the experiences of other black Americans gained through reading their biographical works.

Objective of the Book

My objective in writing this book is to provide a relatively comprehensive overview of parenting and child socialization in African American families. Previous studies have provided some insights into specific areas of socialization, but no one work has examined the broad array of parenting challenges, issues, and strategies in black families. This study also differs from other research in that it focuses on the everyday work that parents do in raising their children (e.g., the values they try to teach their children, their views of the parenting role, their gender and racial socialization

Table P.1 Characteristics of Parents Interviewed

Number	Name	Age	Marital Status	Occupation	Number of Children	Name of Focus Child	Age of Focus Child
1	Yadira Bright	33	Married	Housewife	3	David	11
2	Sonya Daniels	40	Married	Housewife	2	Tamara	10
3	Sherry Davis	27	Married	Tax Examiner	2	Harry	7
4	Carrie Gaines	41	Separated	Administrative Assistant	2	Tiera	13
5	Kelly Coleman	30	Married	Secretary	2	Van	11
6	Terry Carter	36	Divorced	Punch Press Operator	2	Taylor	13
7	Paula Jackson	41	Married	Insurance Agent	2	Manuel	12
8	Melba Brown	35	Separated	Social Worker	2	Darla	12
9	Betty Thompson	43	Married	Teacher	2	Mickey	14
10	Kassandra Barton	32	Single	Unemployed	2	Tosha	12
11	Shawn Branson	22	Single	Unemployed	4	LaToya	6
12	Laura Raymond	31	Married	Insurance Reviewer	2	Aaron	13
13	Shirley Becker	40	Widowed	Federal Employee	2	Jazmine	13
14	Jackie Brady	31	Single	Teacher	1	Johnny	7
15	Doris Gatson	37	Married	Housewife	2	Jordan	9
16	Mary Hanley	40	Married	Teacher	2	Maylon	7
17	Murray Haney	41	Married	Laborer	2	Maylon	7
18	Pamela Baker	35	Married	Clerical Worker	3	Antoine	16
19	Candy Corbin	26	Single	Sales Clerk	1	Evan	6
20	Elisha Martin	35	Single	Contract Officer	1	Evelyn	11
21	Vera Wesley	38	Divorced	Secretary	1	Donald	8
22	Timothy Shannon	42	Married	Teacher (High School)	3	Robert	11
23	Vickie Mellon	39	Divorced	Insurance Adjuster	1	Charles	9
24	Maggie Terrance	35	Married	Housewife	2	Mona	8
25	Phyllis Rodney	42	Married	Radiology Technician	2	Deitrich	9
26	Norman Rodney	52	Married	Counselor	2	Deitrich	9
27	Larry Todd	46	Married	Federal Employee	2	Melanie	14
28	Delores Champ	42	Married	Housewife	3	Clifton	13
29	Michael Beard	35	Married	Sales Representative	3	Brandon	11
30	Jake Houser	28	Single	Unemployed	3	Esther	7
31	Deron Donaldson	32	Married	Contract Officer	2	Eric	7
32	Joshua Davis	44	Married	Computer Programmer	2	Tara	10
33	Sam Taylor	24	Single	Unemployed	1	Christopher	2
34	Glen Walker	25	Married	Unemployed	3	George	10
35	Brenda Johnson	43	Married	Day Care Owner	3	Kristen	9

NOTE: All names are pseudonyms.

Table P.2 Characteristics of All Parents

	Black Parents (N = 525)		White Parents (N = 204)		All Parents (N = 729)	
	n	(%)	n	(%)	n	(%)
Marital status						
single, never married	189	(36.0)	29	(14.3)	218	(30.0)
married	184	(35.0)	113	(55.7)	297	(40.9)
divorced	97	(18.5)	39	(19.2)	136	(18.7)
separated	39	(7.4)	15	(7.4)	54	(7.4)
widowed	13	(2.5)	7	(3.4)	20	(2.8)
other/no response	3	(.6)	.5	(—)	1	(.1)
Education (highest level completed)						
grade school	4	(.8)	3	(1.5)	7	(1.0)
junior high school	26	(5.0)	24	(11.8)	50	(6.9)
senior high school	190	(36.2)	72	(35.3)	262	(36.4)
some college	241	(45.9)	68	(33.3)	309	(42.9)
college education	45	(8.6)	14	(6.9)	59	(8.2)
postgraduate education	14	(2.7)	19	(9.3)	33	(4.9)
other/no response	5	(1.0)	4	(2.0)	9	(1.2)
Employment status						
employed	368	(70.1)	124	(60.8)	484	(67.8)
unemployed	121	(23.1)	68	(33.4)	174	(24.4)
retired	6	(1.1)	2	(1.0)	8	(1.1)
other/no response	30	(5.7)	14	(6.9)	44	(16.6)
Family's yearly income						
less than $15,000	201	(38.3)	71	(34.8)	272	(38.5)
$15,000-30,000	190	(36.2)	56	(27.5)	246	(34.8)
$30,001-50,000	92	(17.5)	43	(21.1)	135	(19.1)
more than $50,000	25	(4.8)	28	(13.7)	53	(7.5)
no response	17	(3.2)	6	(2.9)	23	(3.1)
Relationship to focus child						
mother	447	(85.1)	167	(81.9)	614	(84.8)
father	37	(7.0)	22	(10.8)	59	(8.1)
other relatives	31	(5.9)	14	(6.8)	25	(3.5)
other/no response	10	(1.9)	1	(.5)	11	(1.6)
Number of children						
1-2	259	(49.3)	93	(45.6)	352	(48.3)
3-5	235	(44.7)	104	(50.9)	339	(46.5)
6-7	18	(3.4)	7	(3.5)	25	(3.4)
8-11	13	(2.6)	0	(—)	13	(1.8)

Table P.2 Continued

	Black Parents (N = 525)		White Parents (N = 204)		All Parents (N = 729)	
	n	(%)	n	(%)	n	(%)
Sex of the focus child						
boys	262	(49.9)	93	(45.6)	355	(49.2)
girls	257	(49.0)	109	(53.4)	366	(50.8)
no response	6	(1.1)	2	(1.0)	8	(1.0)
Satisfaction with overall growth and development of the focus child						
very satisfied	286	(54.5)	119	(58.9)	405	(56.3)
somewhat satisfied	206	(39.2)	76	(37.9)	282	(39.2)
not very satisfied	26	(5.0)	7	(3.5)	33	(4.6)
no response	7	(1.3)	2	(1.0)	9	(1.1)
Ages of the focus children						
age range	1-18		1-15		1-18	
average age	9.56		9.36		9.51	
Grade level of focus children						
grade range	0-12		1-9		0-12	
average grade	4.03		3.77		3.97	
Age of parents						
age range	19-75		23-72		19-72	
average age	34.18		34.95		34.47	

ideologies, their discipline strategies, and the support they receive from their extended families and the broader community) rather than focusing exclusively on the problems they experience. In examining the everyday work parents invest in socializing their children, I try to avoid the common tendencies to portray black families either as devastated victims of poverty and racism or as uniformly strong, successful, and effective. Instead, I acknowledge the impact of poverty and inequality and attempt to capture at least some of the tremendous diversity that exists among African Americans. The parents surveyed and interviewed for this study illustrate the social class diversity that exists among black people.

Although focusing primarily on contemporary black families, I contextualize my findings with an examination of both the cultural and the historical factors that have shaped African American parenting strategies, from their West African cultural origins to the modern postindustrial economy. To achieve this, I have consolidated and critically analyzed the sparse and scattered existing research on various aspects of child rearing and so-cialization in black families. I make no claim of being able to describe all black parents based on a few hundred surveys and a handful of personal interviews. Rather, I strengthen and analyze my findings by couching them in the context of extant research, biographies, and my own experiential knowledge.

Thus, this book provides a historical and contemporary overview of parenting and child socialization in African American families by drawing together what we already know and expanding on and updating that knowledge. It encompasses class, cultural, and structural approaches to understanding child rearing by acknowledging the interactive nature of these factors rather than debating the relative merits of each approach. African American scholars of the civil rights era, emphasizing the much neglected strengths and successes of black families, effectively revised the pathological view of black families produced by researchers during the early twentieth century. Their revisionist work has been invaluable in broadening our understanding of African American families, yet the strengths perspective they advanced often fails to capture the current re-alities and diversity of the black experience.

A few scholars have begun to "revise the revisionists" by rethinking assumptions about black families that emerged during the civil rights era—such as the strength of intergenerational ties, the nature of the black com-munity, the impact of single-parenthood—within the context of current socioeconomic realities, changing expectations, and new research findings. This study builds on that emerging revisionist literature in several ways. First, it illustrates the interplay between structure and culture, and shows that culture is an evolving rather than a static force, that is it differentiated and class-based in black America, and that the existence and validity of black cultural patterns are subject to continual revision. Second, this study facilitates a discussion of black people as active agents in their own lives rather than as passive victims of external forces. I see African Americans as continually engaged in the process of creating and assigning meaning to life events, and it is these meanings that shape their child-rearing work.

A Social Constructionist View of Childhood

The theoretical framework of this study is social constructionism, an approach that synthesizes the microanalysis of symbolic interactionism with a more structural analysis of social life (Brown, 1996). The basic as-sumption of symbolic interactionism is that reality is socially defined as people use their own reflective processes to make sense of the world around them. The ability to subjectively define reality is rooted in the unique capacities of human consciousness and the mind (Mead, 1962); still, those definitions must be sustained and validated by others, and are constantly subject to change. As Denzin (1978) has pointed out, social reality is emergent and negotiated, as definitions are "ever-changing [and] subject to redefinitions, relocations, and realignments" (p. 7). New social definitions often emerge with changes in social structural forces, such as economies, polities, and laws. Given the tremendous diversity in notions about children, it seems apparent that child-rearing strategies and developmental theories are linked to specific structural factors, which in turn shape cultural values and ideologies. The social constructionist framework validates the importance of structure in shaping life options yet also sees people as active agents in their own lives, continually creating social meanings and behaving in accordance with those meanings.

Family scholars studying the history of childhood have shown that child-rearing approaches have varied both cross-culturally and historically. Research on the history of parents and children did not become popular until the 1960s (French, 1995) and initially indicated that parents in Western societies neither identified with their children nor saw childhood as a special, significant stage in the life cycle. Support for this view was based not only on the dearth of information about and depictions of children prior to the seventeenth century (Aries, 1962) but also on considerable evidence that parents have historically sacrificed their children to the gods, maimed them to serve as beggars, or merely abandoned them to a life of starvation and early death. Examining this maltreatment of children from antiquity through the Middle Ages, deMause (1974) concluded that "the further back in history one goes, the lower the level of child care, and the more likely children are to be killed, abandoned, beaten, terrorized, and sexually abused" (p. 504).

More recently, however, this view has been refuted by research documenting immense variability in the historical treatment of children. In her historical account of parenting, Valerie French (1995) has shown that in many early societies, children were highly valued and seen as having unique characteristics and needs. Children were quite visible and important in ancient Egypt, where all births were systematically recorded and families were determined to rear children properly. That childhood outcomes were important and linked to social environmental forces was also apparent among the early Greeks, among whom children were seen as "plastic, shapeable, unformed, [and] impressionable" (French, 1995, p. 271)—quite distinct from adults and in need of proper socialization.

The sociology of childhood is a relatively new and underdeveloped field of study (Zelizer, 1985) and thus far has not produced a definitive understanding of the general nature of childhood and parenting in early societies. The recent debate over the historical treatment of children and the nature of childhood highlights the fact that societies have varied widely in their ideas about children and child rearing. More important, it demonstrates that a society's ideas and beliefs about the nature and needs of children are socially created and defined. Although practically all societies give families the primary responsibility for socializing children, the meaning of childhood and the values and ideologies that shape parenting strategies are historically and culturally variant. To a large extent, the social construction of childhood emerges as a result of social structural forces, such as economic needs, technologies, and religious ideologies. Within varying social contexts, societies try to create a balance between the labor required to create and sustain families and the labor necessary to ensure economic survival, as both are vital for the maintenance of societies.

But even within a single society, the nature of childhood and parenting work can vary based on the social status and resources of individual families. In the United States, race and class have been major factors in shaping differential access to status and resources and child-rearing ideals. Notions about children and child rearing have been constructed primarily by the dominant racial group—white, middle-class Americans—and variously appropriated to and embraced by subordinate racial groups. In this book, I examine parenthood in black America in both historical and contemporary perspective, often in parallel with parenthood in white American families.

Overview of the Book

In Chapter 1, I examine the social construction of childhood in America during three major economic periods: the agricultural economy established in the 1600s, the industrial economy that developed during the mid-1800s, and the postindustrial economy that began to evolve as early as the late 1960s. Each economic period has influenced patterns of family life, and each period has embodied its own distinctive ideas about children and child rearing—such as what children are like, how they are best socialized, and what risks they face. In this chapter, I essentially argue that African American and white families have unique cultural heritages and value systems, and that this was reinforced and perpetuated in early American society as they were exposed to a very different set of structural constraints and opportunities.

The family life, gender roles, and parent-child relationships of black families in early American society were shaped primarily by slavery, which frequently gave parents little control over their own children. Even after the abolition of slavery, the majority of black people continued to live in the South, mostly as sharecroppers in the agricultural economy. As a result, their ability to conform to the family changes wrought by industrialization was limited. Similarly, the postindustrial economic transition of the 1970s has disproportionately affected black people, many of whom were just securing well-paid jobs in the manufacturing sector of the economy. Unemployment, job loss, and lower salaries are now correlated with high rates of nonmarriage, delayed marriage, divorce, and single-mother families. Although this transition has affected many American families, its impact is more evident among blacks, especially young males.

There is much debate over the causes of and solutions to these problems. Many social scientists and welfare rights advocates suggest that the problems lie in the social and economic structure of society, which provides few opportunities for jobs, marriage, and family stability among blacks. Others, however, feel that curtailing welfare benefits and promoting traditional families will lead to decreases in single-mother families and poverty. Chapter 2 of this book deals with that controversy. I begin by discussing how caste, class, and culture affect child socialization in African American families, starting with child rearing during slavery, when the racial caste system was firmly intact in the United States, and then proceeding to discuss the evolution of family studies in the 1930s and 1940s. These studies typically focused on lower-class black families, as has most recent research, and they produced the social deficit perspective.

I argue that contemporary class analyses have reached similar conclusions about the structure of poor families but have managed to avoid the evaluative tone of earlier work. A similar trend emerged in the study of culture, with the notion of the black culture as rife with pathology gradually giving way to a more positive Afrocentric view. This cultural perspective highlights the fact that all black children, to a greater or lesser extent, undergo a process of dual socialization that involves learning to survive in both the black and the dominant culture. I conclude with a discussion of the underclass concept.

Chapter 3 employs a social capital view to focus on the actual work parents do in rearing their children. I examine a broad array of child socialization issues, such as the values parents are trying to teach their children, their views of the parenting role, their discipline strategies, and their future hopes and aspirations for their children. I also discuss early sexuality and pregnancy among black teenagers, issues that are often seen as the outcome of poverty, ineffective parenting, or both, and as one of the major obstacles to socioeconomic success. Parents shared about the sexual standards they have and try to teach their children as well as on some of the difficulties they face in their efforts. I also devote considerable attention to educational gains and obstacles. Education has always been of central importance among blacks, as it is seen as the route to economic mobility and as a way to elevate the status of all African Americans. I conclude with parents' views on intergenerational changes.

Chapter 4 looks at the racial socialization of black children, or what parents think and teach their children about being black in a predominantly white society. Racial socialization dates back to slavery, when black children had to learn to be subordinate to whites, as their lives often depended on it. Yet parents sought to give their children a sense of self-worth. Here I explore the racial socialization messages and strategies of parents as they cope with the denigration of blackness in the dominant culture and the need to instill in their children a positive self-concept. I also consider the issue of self-esteem, and how it has changed among blacks, and hypothesize that such changes may be due racial socialization messages.

Chapter 5 focuses on the gender socialization of children. Social science interest in the gender roles of blacks accelerated in 1965, when Moynihan asserted a connection between what he saw as gender role confusion and black people's lack of socioeconomic progress. Since then, literature on the nature, origins, and organization of gender and blacks has skyrocketed, yet rarely has this literature been based on systematic research. Moreover, the evidence of unconventional gender roles rests almost solely on the experiences of black women, with much less said about black males. Using survey data collected on parents' values, aspirations for their children, types of discipline, and views of the parenting role, I examine the extent of gender socialization in black families. My findings suggest that black parents make few direct gender distinctions in socializing their children as a group, although some gender distinctions do seem to emerge among more affluent black parents. I also examine less direct socialization mechanisms, such as the organization of gender in the family, and conclude with a discussion of the gender dilemma among blacks.

Chapter 6 investigates the extent to which parents receive assistance from the community, extended family, church, and state in rearing their children. Many African Americans who grew up in the pre-civil rights era and were highly supportive of racial integration now reflect on the loss of the community they once shared. Although their creation and maintenance was fostered by racial segregation and poverty, black communities were often places where residents knew and trusted each other and were collectively involved in caring for and supervising children. Many of these community resources have waned in recent years, and drugs and violence have reached epidemic proportions in some areas. I also consider changes in the extended family and critically analyze both its strengths and its weaknesses. Grandmothers, once the backbone of black extended families, are younger now than in previous generations; they have a broader array of competing activities and are often more reluctant to become involved in child-rearing work. However, while extended family ties among low-income blacks are often based on necessity, the ideological commitment to the importance of the family is strong. Religion is also a strong cultural value and, as discussed here, often forms the basis for what parents teach their children. I conclude with a look at public policy, especially historical and contemporary views about Aid to Families With Dependent Children, commonly known as "welfare."

The conclusions are discussed in Chapter 7, along with the implications of this study and suggestions for future research.

Acknowledgments

I would like to thank the University of Kansas for providing two summer research grants that helped me complete this book, and would also like to thank Robert Coplan for his financial assistance. Bert Adams and David Klein deserve a special thanks for giving me the opportunity to write this book and for their patience and kind reviews of earlier manuscripts. My friend and colleague Joey Sprague and I used a portion of the quantitative data from this study to coauthor a paper titled *Constructing Gender in Black and White Families: The Interaction of Gender With Race and Class*, which was presented at the American Sociological Association meeting in Toronto in August, 1997. I owe her a debt of gratitude for helping to shape some of the ideas in Chapter 5 on gender socialization and for the panel design of the tables, which was her inspiration. Edwin, my husband, has also provided me with tremendous support and assistance during this project. I would like to thank him for all of his help, encouragement, and patience, and for carefully reading each chapter and giving me feedback and ideas. Finally, a special thanks to all the parents who completed surveys and participated in interviews, as this book clearly could not have been written without their cooperation. I am honored to be able to share with others their child socialization stories.

1

Childhood in Transition

The universal testimony of travelers and missionaries [is] that the love of the African mother for her children is unsurpassed in any part of the world. . . . It is not surprising, then, to find that slave mothers, instead of viewing with indifference the sale, or loss otherwise, of their children, often put up a stubborn resistance and suffered cruel punishment to prevent separation from them.

E. Franklin Frazier,
The Negro Family in the United States
(1939/1949, pp. 33, 41)

The history of Africans in North America dates back nearly as far as that of white Europeans, yet racial status has been the basis for the dramatically different experiences for the two groups and, subsequently, for their children. Slavery, racism, and racial inequality have been the most salient factors in defining the African American experience, including family life and childhood experiences. For most of America's history, economic and educational opportunities available to black Americans have been severely circumscribed by racial segregation and exclusion. Since the civil rights era of the 1960s, many blacks have made significant socioeconomic advancements, yet a significant minority—nearly one-third—continue to live in poverty. The growth of poverty has been accompanied by high rates of unemployment, teenage pregnancy, nonmarriage, and hopelessness among blacks—all factors that have undermined the welfare of children. After examining the evolution of child-rearing norms and values over three distinct economic periods in the United States—the colonial era, the industrial era, and the postindustrial era—I focus on the diversity that now exists in black families and its impact on child rearing. My research reveals that although poverty has diminished the parenting abilities and resources of some, the majority of black parents are successful, capable, and confident parents who are proud of their children and invest heavily in their well-being.

1

Childhood in Colonial America

In early colonial America, the economic and ideological factors that shaped the nature of childhood were patriarchy, the labor demands of an agricultural economy, and the Christian belief system. During this era, both birth- and death rates were extremely high. Women commonly gave birth to 8 to 10 children, but as many as 50% died in infancy or childhood. Despite this high rate of death, children were needed as workers in an economy based heavily on farming, and they were relied on as old-age security for parents (Zelizer, 1985). As a result, children were viewed primarily as economic assets and as the property of their fathers, who were the legally defined heads of their families. Fathers had the primary responsibility for supervising their children's work, education, and religious activities (Berry, 1993). In this family-based economy (Tilly & Scott, 1978), which required the productive labor of all family members, children were expected to be contributing members of their families by the age of 7. Although some parents were emotionally attached to their children, most were aloof and accepted the deaths of children with resignation, if not indifference (Zelizer, 1985). The high rate of childhood mortality placed the overall emphasis more on childbearing than child rearing. There is little evidence that parents understood childhood as a significant developmental stage or, perhaps more important, that they were particularly concerned about the happiness or psychological well-being of children. No doubt, however, there were social class variations, with affluent parents less likely to rely on or emphasize the economic value of their children than other parents.

Colonial American parents, with the support of the broader community, were expected to train and socialize their children. Much of the training consisted of children learning the occupations of their parents, as geographic and social mobility were limited and children were typically expected to assume the occupational roles of their own parents. In addition, child socialization revolved around teaching children the virtues of repressing their sexual and aggressive urges, respecting parents, and living according to the moral standards espoused by Christianity (Adams, 1980). As early as the 1600s, some colonies had begun to require that parents teach their children to read, as reading the Bible was seen as essential to Christian salvation. Overall, children were to work hard, be deferential, respectful, and obedient to those in authority, and conform to the values and rules of their families and community. As indicated by a 1854 Massachusetts law, children could be severely punished for failing to respect and obey parents who had tried to teach them Christian virtues:

If any children above sixteen years old and of sufficient understanding shall curse or smite their natural father or mother, they shall be put to death, unless it can be sufficiently testified that the parents have been unchristianly negligent in the education of such children or so provoked them by extreme and cruel correction that they have been forced thereunto to preserve themselves from death or maiming. (Bremner, 1970, p. 68)

Despite recent advances in understanding the history of childhood, knowledge in this area is still quite limited. It is unclear, for example, the extent to which the norms and ideologies involving children affected the actual behaviors of parents, or how social class or race-ethnicity shaped the child-rearing strategies of parents. Until recently, most historical accounts of preindustrial families focused on white Americans, with much less analysis of the histories of people of color. As I teach my family students about what seems to be, by today's standards, the harsh treatment of children in colonial America, I often compare it with the treatment of the millions of African children and their parents who were enslaved in the United States during this period. How was childhood socially defined for them in their native cultures? And how did those African traditions differ from what they experienced in the United States?

As most of what has been written is decidedly Western and European in orientation, these questions are often difficult to answer. Although some Africans migrated to the United States in the 1600s and were never enslaved, the majority were brought to the colonies as slaves and were from an area not more than 200 miles inland from the coast of West Africa (Kitano, 1991, p. 99). There were many cultural similarities between these West Africans but also considerable diversity in their family systems, cultural expressions, and belief systems. Two of the most consistent observations about West African cultures, however, are that fertility was highly valued and that women gained a great deal of status from both their childbearing abilities and their contributions to the economy. West African ideas about children's nature were probably also linked to the economy and may have been more lenient toward children than those in the United States. Overall, the emphasis on the suppression and control of children is greater in societies that emphasize food production and accumulation, and such societies typically have child-rearing norms that focus on adherence to externally imposed rules and on instilling obedience and responsibility in children. In societies where the environment provides a more natural and abundant supply of food, which may have been the case in some areas of West Africa, child-rearing practices are often more lenient and indulgent.

Another factor that may have resulted in a more indulgent attitude about children in West Africa was the absence of a Christian tradition that emphasized the repression of sexuality, illegitimacy, and the innate sinfulness of every child.

Whatever ideologies about children the West Africans might have held, they were radically altered by slavery and its emphasis on black men, women, and children as property rather than people. It meant that important African traditions, values, and family relationships were ignored. Their status as property made procreation extremely important, thus reinforcing and denigrating the African tradition of valuing childbearing and motherhood. Slave women sometimes had as many as 20 children, but neither they nor slave fathers had much control over their offspring (Davis, 1993). Rather than the basis for a family, childbearing was now frequently an involuntary activity for the production of children who were defined as property and owned by white slave masters. Fathers were often not even acknowledged and, as Davis (1993) has explained, motherhood became a fragmented and alienating experience for black women:

> Birth mothers could not therefore expect to be mothers in the legal sense. Legally these children were chattel and therefore motherless. Slave states passed laws to the effect that children of slave women no more belonged to their biological mothers than the young of animals belonged to the females that birthed them. (p. 358)

In most cases, black parents had very little control over their children, and their concerns about their children's welfare were probably quite different from those of white parents. While white parents labored to instill in their children conformity and an appreciation for the virtues of hard work and Christianity, black parents probably grappled with more fundamental issues, such as how to protect their children from being sold, the cruel treatment of slave masters, or how to instill in them the strength and will to survive.

Childhood in Modern America

The forces of industrialization and modernization during the 1800s helped to reorganize families and to redefine the nature of childhood, although the impact of these forces was quite different for white and black American families and varied based on social class position. For affluent white families, industrialization gradually shifted the majority of paid employment from homes to factories, resulting in the development of the family-wage economy. Although women and children initially entered the industrial labor force, based largely on the economic needs of the family, they were gradually relegated to the home when advances in technology and productivity made their labor unnecessary. This new organization of productive labor coincided with the development of the nuclear breadwinner-homemaker family model, which, based on the doctrine of separate spheres for men and women, advocated a gender division of labor in families. In the modern nuclear family, men were to provide economically for their families while women were to care for children and the home.

This gender division of labor was further justified when organized labor successfully negotiated with capitalists to pay male workers a family wage, or a wage adequate to provide for the entire family. In reality, most men were unable to support their families singlehandedly and continued to rely on the contributions of women and children (Fraser & Gordon, 1994). Nevertheless, the labor efforts of women and children became more obscure, and the nuclear breadwinner-homemaker family, now more commonly known as the "traditional family," was idealized as the American norm. According to the theoretical assumptions of early functionalism, these families were best suited to meet the needs of family members and the demands of industrial capitalism.

Childhood was also redefined in modern America. Rates of childhood mortality declined during modernization, primarily as a result of sanitation, better nutrition, and more control over infectious diseases. This decline in childhood mortality gradually led to a decrease in the rate of fertility, as parents could now expect their children to live. The reduction in childbirth rates was also due to the fact that neither the industrial economy nor the family needed the labor of children to survive. This led to a greater emphasis on elevating the quality of childhood, as evidenced by the eugenics movement, than on the quantity of children. Parents were to have fewer children but to invest more heavily both economically and psychologically in their offspring.

White, middle-class families were the first to embrace the breadwinner-homemaker, child-centered family model. As men defined being a breadwinner as their central role, the responsibility for child rearing shifted almost entirely to mothers, who were now to devote their full-time energies to the care and nurturing of children. The transfer of child-rearing work meant that children were no longer the economic assets of their fathers but the emotional assets of their mothers, thus giving rise to the "precious child" (Zelizer, 1985). Children were exempt from productive labor, and childhood was defined as a distinct stage in life. This new concern over the welfare of children resulted in the first White House Conference on Children in 1909, which created a Children's Bureau to "advocate for children and the traditional family" (Berry, 1993, p. 96). It argued for the right of all mothers, even those who were poor, to stay home and care for their children. In its final resolution, it stated: "Home life is the highest and finest product of civilization. It is the great molding force of mind and character. Children should not be deprived of it except for urgent and compelling reasons" (Berry, 1993, p. 96).

The ideology of the traditional family defined the nuclear, breadwinner-homemaker family as optimal for the growth and development of children, and other families types as dysfunctional. Despite significant changes in families and the economy, this ideology continues to inform the thinking of many Americans, especially conservative religionists and policy makers. Children were defined as of central importance in the modern nuclear family, and two-parent families were seen as essential to their well-being. The child-rearing work of parents became important during the early twentieth century, as social scientists began to examine environmental factors that affected families and their children.

Theories of child development proliferated, as did child-rearing literature proffering advice to mothers on caring for their children. One of the earliest efforts to understand human development is found in the work of psychotherapists, such as Sigmund Freud and Erik Erikson. Their theories saw children as progressing through a series of developmental stages propelled by inborn, biological needs and instincts, and social-environmental demands. This view placed a great deal of emphasis on the child-rearing work of parents, as proper socialization hinged on channeling innate biological drives into acceptable social behaviors. John Watson's behaviorism presented an even more environmentally focused approach to child rearing. He and other behaviorists argued that a child's development was shaped solely by responses to stimuli or the reinforcement of certain behaviors. Social psychologists such as George Herbert Mead contributed to the understanding of how the social self was developed, making the notion of developing a positive self-concept an integral part of childhood socialization.

Because the ideology of the traditional, child-centered family eventually prevailed—although for many Americans not until the 1950s—it is easy to overstate the consensus surrounding its importance during the early twentieth century. In fact, many working- and middle-class parents fought against the construction of the "economically useless" child (Zelizer, 1985), which they saw as inimical to their own social and economic well-being. It was only gradually that the colonial American child-rearing value system, which emphasized the labor, control, and strict discipline of children, gave way to the view of children as a protected labor-free class and embraced a greater orientation toward developing independence, autonomy, and self-direction in children (Alwin, 1988). Authoritarian child-rearing practices and corporal punishment were replaced by more permissive child-rearing

strategies. Overall, childhood was redefined as a time of carefree inno-
cence, a stage of life when children should be allowed to grow and develop
while being provided for and protected by their parents. In modern families, parental care transcended simply meeting the basic material needs of
children and included the important roles parents were to play in socializing their children—teaching their children values, shaping their identities,
supporting their activities and interests, and preparing them for adult life.
Parental efforts also included guarding children from the potentially harmful aspects of the larger social environment, such as early exposure to violence, drugs, and sexuality.

Millions of poor and racial-ethnic minority families were unable to implement the ideology of the traditional family as they lacked the economic
resources or social power to do so. It was fundamentally based on the ability
of men to earn wages sufficient to exempt their wives from labor force
participation, and both slavery and discrimination precluded this ability
among black men. But the newly emerging industrial order did affect black
families: It challenged the slavery-agricultural system of the South. The
growing industrial economy helped to end more than 250 years of chattel
slavery and pave the way for the slow process of, when possible, reuniting
black families and giving them custody of their children. For the next several decades, however, most black people continued to live in the rural
South and many worked in the agricultural economy as sharecroppers, a
labor system that in many ways replicated slavery. For example, sharecropping usually required the labor of entire families, and they often earned no
more than subsistence pay.

White Americans did not see parenting as important work in black families; rather, they were quite concerned about the potential loss of cheap
black female and child labor. Berry (1993) has pointed out that southern
planters still owned the land and needed workers after slavery had ended,
so the decision not to work was nearly impossible for African Americans.
In some states, Black Codes were written to help guarantee an adequate
supply of workers and the Freemen's Bureau, seeing employment as essential to the transition from slavery to citizenship, helped enforce contracts
between blacks and their white employers. Although sharecropping led to
blacks embracing the nuclear, patriarchal family, the entire family continued to be the basic unit of labor, with economic roles typically usurping
family roles. By the end of the nineteenth century, 90% of African Americans still lived in the South (Jones, 1985, p. 80), and most were involved
in the agricultural labor system. Moreover, they were governed by legalized
racial segregation that severely restricted the types of work they could do.

During the early twentieth century, millions of blacks migrated from the
South to the North in response to the loss of agricultural jobs and the
limited opportunity system available to them in the South. Many moved

into the industrial labor force and, creating a formidable voting bloc in many urban areas, began to effectively challenge the long-standing system of racial segregation that had circumscribed their personal and civil rights and denied them access to an equal education or employment. The diversity of the black population grew substantially with northward migration. From emancipation through World War I, according to Landry (1987), blacks were characterized primarily by economic homogeneity: With the exception of a small group of middle-class blacks, most of whom were the direct and recognizable descendants of slave women and their white owners, blacks occupied the lower classes and were poor. The black middle-class began to expand at the close of World War I and more than doubled between 1960 and 1970, primarily due to gains in education (Landry, 1987).

While most blacks never embraced the traditional family model, as their increased socioeconomic status was typically based on the labor roles of husbands and wives, many of those in the middle class achieved the means to provide their children with stable families and to invest in their emotional and economic well-being. The successes of black families, whether poor or middle class, were widely noted in African American scholarship during the 1960s and the 1970s. During this era, researchers were able to challenge existing studies that depicted black families as inherently dysfunctional and pathological by describing the immense social structural barriers they had faced and enumerating the adaptive strategies that had allowed them to survive.

The Postindustrial Family Transition

The number of white Americans able to implement the ideology of the traditional family grew substantially during the postwar affluence of the 1950s; however, by the end of the 1960s, a changing economy and political and cultural revolutions were again redefining families and the nature of childhood. Advances in technology and the growth of an international market during the early 1970s fueled a transformation in the economy, from an industry-based to an information and services economy. The process of deindustrialization led to a substantial reduction in the number of industrial jobs available, especially blue-collar manufacturing jobs, many of which allowed workers to earn high pay with very little education or training. At the same time, it pulled women into the labor force by increasing the number of low-paying service jobs available—jobs that traditionally had been seen as female work.

The impact of the postindustrial economy has been similar for blacks and whites: a decrease in industrial employment opportunities, fewer high-paying jobs, an economic polarization of the haves and have-nots—with the wealthy getting richer and the poor more impoverished—and an overall increase in the economic hardships experienced by families. Yet the scope and intensity of this economic transition has been much more devastating for black people, especially black men, as they were overrepresented among those in the industrial sector of the economy (Wilson, 1978, 1987, 1991). In fact, during the short period of expanded opportunities wrought by the civil rights movement of the 1960s and the emergence of the postindustrial economy of the 1970s, many blacks never actually had the opportunity to escape poverty, while others had achieved only a tenuous grasp on middle-class status. This economic transition, with its high rates of male jobless-ness, diminished many of the gains that had been made by blacks during the civil rights era. Landry (1987) points out that by 1982, thousands of black middle-class jobs were lost, and by 1984, the number of blacks at-tending college declined to the 1969 level of 27%. It also had a devastating impact on African American families.

Postindustrialism, feminism, the massive entry of women into the labor force, the sexual revolution, and a growing emphasis on social equality began to radically alter families and family values during the 1970s. This decade saw the lowest rates of marriage and childbearing in American his-tory, and the highest rate of divorce, leading some theorists to predict (often quite happily) that the family had become an obsolete institution. Feminists challenged the fundamental structure of the family, describing it as inher-ently oppressive to women, and argued convincingly that sex roles were based more on socially constructed gender norms than the biologically driven interests or potentials of men and women. White women entered the workforce in large numbers during the 1970s, often achieving eco-nomic independence and diminishing the importance of the male bread-winner role. By the early 1990s, about 60% of American women worked for pay, including about half of all mothers with preschool children (Jones, Tepperman, & Wilson, 1995).

While the family clearly has not become an obsolete institution, as most people expect to marry and have children, the trends toward delayed mar-riage and childbearing have continued. The median ages of marriage are 27 and 25 for men and women, respectively, and unmarrieds now represent nearly 40% of the population over the age of 18 (Saluter, 1994). In 1990, only 17% of previously single brides were teenagers, a decrease of 42% since 1970 (Clarke, 1995). And the overall rate of fertility declined from 2.6 in 1970 to 1.8 in 1990 (Jones et al., 1995).

Delayed marriage and childbearing, and high rates of divorce, have led to more nonmarital sex and pregnancy, more single-mother families, and more poverty. The age at which males and females have their first sexual experience has decreased in the United States, with 16 as the average age of first coitus and a majority of people sexually active prior to marriage. Due to improved birth control, the overall rate of teenage pregnancy in the United States actually declined between 1960 and 1993; however, the rate of nonmarital teenage pregnancy grew (Harris, 1997). In 1994, 26% of all American children were born out of wedlock (Bachu, 1995). Nonmarital pregnancy, coupled with a high rate of divorce, led to increases in the number of single-parent families. The proportion of children living in single-mother homes in 1993 was 24%, compared with 8% in 1960, and 54% of children living in female-headed families are poor (Harris, 1997). Teen sexuality and childbearing and single-mother families are now seen by many family scholars as the key factors in the declining status of children.

The postindustrial family trends found in the dominant society are amplified among black Americans, most of whom have never experienced the affluence or security of white Americans. Despite the socioeconomic gains made by millions of black people since the 1960s, economic and educational parity with whites has never been achieved. As Landry (1987) has pointed out, the educational gains of blacks, even during the civil rights era, were not as great as those for whites, nor did they pay off as much in economic advancement. The postindustrial economy intensified economic inequality based on race by producing an urban underclass comprising mostly young black men who are unable to obtain employment, marry, or participate effectively in families. The early onset of sexuality, nonmarital pregnancy and childbirth, single-mother families, poverty, and divorce are all interconnected outcomes of the economic despair that has gripped so many black communities.

In 1994, two-thirds of all births to black women were to unmarried women, more than three times the rate for white women (Bachu, 1995). Nearly all (93%) black adolescent childbearing is nonmarital (Ventura, Martin, Taffell, Matthews, & Clarke, 1995), with significant declines in marriage among black teenagers, from 16.2% in 1960 to 1.4% in 1993, accounting for much of the growth of single-parent families (Harris, 1997). In 1990, the overall marriage rate for white women was 58.8 per 1,000, compared with 33.5 per 1,000 for black women (Clarke, 1995). Parental absence in black families rose from about 32% in 1960 (Ruggles, 1994) to 61% (Billingsley, 1992), with fathers much more likely to be absent than mothers. At the same time, many of the resources traditionally available to black families, such as extended kin networks (Roschelle, 1997), have diminished in recent decades.

Despite these recent changes in the black families, having and raising children continue to be important activities. Children make up a substantial portion of the 30-35 million black people living in the United States in 1992; more than one-third are under age 18 (Pinkney, 1993). As a result, black children constituted more than 16% of the 70.5 million children under the age of 18 living in the United States in 1995 (Hernandez, 1997). Their high representation in the general population is accounted for mostly by a generally younger black population and differences in the timing of childbirth. The value African Americans place on children and the common myth that single, welfare-dependent mothers tend to have numerous children, however, often lead to the erroneous conclusion that black women have much higher rates of fertility than do white women.

The overall historical pattern of fertility among blacks and whites is quite similar: It was highest in colonial America and during World War II, and lowest during modernization and the social activism of the 1970s. Today, the rate of fertility for white couples is 1.87, compared with 1.90 for black couples (Jones et al., 1995). The average number of children born to white and black women is also comparable: About 41% have either one or two children (Bachu, 1995). Black women have more babies than white women in their early reproductive years, but they have fewer in the later reproductive years. Overall rates of childlessness are also similar: In 1994, nearly 43% of white women in their childbearing years (15 to 44 years old) had never given birth, compared with 37% of black women (Bachu, 1995).

Many of the liberal scholars of the 1950s and 1960s who argued that racial integration and equal opportunity were the keys to creating strong, stable African American families were silenced by the rise in nonmarital pregnancy, single-parent households, crime, and poverty in the post-civil rights era. In 1978, Wilson, observing the growth of joblessness and poverty in many urban areas, sought to address the issue by shifting the focus from race to social class. He pointed out that while many black people had experienced a measure of socioeconomic mobility since the 1960s, changes in the economy had produced an urban underclass of poor blacks. Indeed, the rise of the underclass since the 1970s has led to a resurgence in research on the difficulties of black families and the resurrection of the myth of family pathology.

Public commentators and researchers often express alarm over the growing separation of parenthood and marriage among blacks and its negative impact on the well-being of children. Policy makers and the media follow their lead by portraying African American children in ways that universalize and pathologize the experiences of the poor, often lamenting their plight while advocating less public assistance and support for their families. Recent public policies typically devalue the family work of poor black mothers, while many conservatives leaders are often as adamant about forcing poor mothers to enter the labor force as they are ambivalent about the voluntary employment of affluent mothers.

Black Children: A Diversity of Experiences

Despite the inordinate focus on the poor, black children grow up in a variety of family settings and socioeconomic environments, and their family relationships, health, education, and well-being are shaped by those factors. African family scholarship, modern feminism, and cultural theories have all effectively challenged the myth of the monolithic family experience or the notion prevalent in early family research that all well-functioning families are alike. Although these challenges have affirmed the importance of racial background and ethnicity in shaping families, they have scarcely begun to grapple with the issue of diversity within broad racial categories, especially those based on social class. Addressing this issue, McAdoo asserted in 1990 that

> contrary to what many people seem to think, there is no such thing as "the" African-American family. African-American families are as diverse as white, Hispanic, Asian, and other families in the United States today. Black families are not all headed by single women. . . . Far too many black families are certainly poor, but the majority of black families are not poor. (p. 74)

Despite this challenge, existing research on black children and parenting focuses largely on social problems and is skewed toward low-income families, providing little analysis of the normal growth and development of African American children in diverse social backgrounds. It is important to note that this diversity is not fully captured by class distinctions or the variety of family structures that exist among blacks. There are qualitative differences in the experiences of parenting and childhood that cannot be systematically equated with social class or family structure. For example, while the link between single-mother families and poverty is strong, not all single mothers are poor. Similarly, poverty is highly correlated with a broad array of factors that undermine the well-being of children, as I discuss later in this chapter. Yet, many children who are poor grow up in stable families where they are loved, well cared for, and given an opportunity to succeed.

The interviews and surveys from parents in this study highlight the diversity of childhood experiences among African Americans. For the most part, however, parents are satisfied with the overall growth and development of their children. Parents who were interviewed described their children as having a positive self-concept and doing well in school, and they were optimistic about their children's futures. Murray and Mary Haney, ages 41 and 40, are typical of the successful two-parent families interviewed in this study. Murray did not finish high school and works as a laborer for the city, while Mary, an elementary school teacher, has a master's degree in education and has earned some hours toward her doctorate. They have been married for nine years and are the parents of two sons, ages 3 and 7, both of whom attend a Christian school. For them, religion, marriage, parenthood, and family ties clearly are top priorities, and they took pleasure in describing Maylon, their oldest son:

> [Father] Maylon is a young 7-year-old who refuses to be defeated in anything. . . . [Mother] Yeah, a very strong-willed person! [Father] . . . and we're just hoping that this is something that will be positive for him as he grows up. [Mother] And he's active, very athletic . . . [Father] and very competitive. [Mother] . . . He's a very loving and emotional little fellow. Academically, he does very well in school. But we've found that for behaviors, we always have to have some behavior mod program going on at home and school to keep him in check. A lot of it is because he goes to a Christian school [which is very strict], a predominantly white school. But he's doing real well this year; we're very much pleased. [Father] I think he feels pretty good about himself . . . when he comes home from school he likes to let me know that he threw the ball the farthest . . . was the best catcher, and things like that. He's really good in athletics and very hyper.

Murray and Mary are among the 39% of African American families currently headed by two parents (Billingsley, 1992). The two-parent family was the norm among African Americans until 1980, when the postindustrial economy's impact on employment and marriage became more apparent. Today, the majority of black children live in single-parent homes, yet there is a great deal of diversity among single-parent families. Single-parent black families are often seen as all being alike, typically as families headed by welfare-dependent teenage mothers, and marital status erroneously becomes the basis for viewing families as weak or stable, functional or dysfunctional. Yet there are single women who have freely chosen to become mothers, are devoted to the care of their children, and are doing an excellent job of parenting. Jackie Brady, 31 years old and the mother of 7-year-old Jason, is an example. Jackie is employed in the field of education and is currently working on a master's degree. She has the resources to provide a good home for Jason and, despite a heavy workload, manages to spend a great deal of time with him. Asked to describe her son, Jackie is clearly excited about his personality and development:

> He's curious, adventuresome—very adventuresome—somewhat independent. . . . I would say that's because I'm a single parent, not totally, but I attribute a lot of it to that. A lot of times he has to go along with me to school, like when I was doing the master's program . . . and I have explained to him that this is the situation we're in, and he's really a help to me. He's a hard worker. He's a real sweet little boy, I really love his sweet spirit, always

wanting to help—he's not perfect, by any means, but he's a sweetie. . . . And I would say, for the most part, he's all boy. . . . He is the type of child that hates to be inside, just gotta be outside, anything that's outside—riding his bike, going to the park—he loves it. He loves sports. He's very active.

Elisha Martin, a 35-year-old single mother of an 11-year-old daughter, was separated from her husband, who recently passed away. Elisha grew up in a poor family but her education and professional occupation now place her in the middle class. My interview with Elisha reveals that she has internalized some of the myths and stereotypes historically used to describe black people, and as a mother she works hard to instill values in her daughter that eschew the negative images of blacks. Christianity is her route for achieving a more respected lifestyle, and she defines the middle class more in terms of values than economics. Asked what values she was teaching her daughter Evelyn, she responded

> That she is to be a Christian lady, to present herself as a Christian lady. I guess I'm trying to instill—quote/unquote—a lot of middle-class values in her. And to me that means don't steal, don't destroy other people's property, you work for what you have, and you don't expect something for nothing, and you got to learn that every time you give you don't get something in return. Those are the kinds of things I consider middle-class values.

Despite the fact that millions of African American children grow up in solid, loving families, the economy has had a devastating impact on many families and communities. The impact of the current economy is greater among blacks, who have always had to contend with higher and more persistent forms of poverty.

Shawn Branson is most characteristic of the stereotypical single black mother: She is 22 years old, single, unemployed, and the mother of four children, the oldest a 6-year-old daughter, LaToya. Shawn clearly feels overwhelmed by the demands of being a single mother. Asked why she had chosen to have her children at such a young age, she was unable to explain but made it clear that she had not viewed it so much as a choice. She answered mostly by saying how "shocked" she was to see several young African American girls on television talk shows claiming they had actually wanted to become mothers, something she could not even imagine. She clearly had made no specific plan to have children. Although she could offer no plausible reason for having had four children in the past six years, she accepted the responsibility for her situation, seeing it as her own fault. Asked if she could see a link between race, racial inequality, and the high rate of teenage pregnancy among blacks, Shawn answered:

Not really, because you're going to run into some kind of prejudice, no matter what. That's just life. But as far as myself, I think if I wouldn't have started having kids so young I would have had my goals together and I could have become whatever I wanted to if I had strived for it. But as far as right now, yes, I am struggling, but that's because my kids are young, but I don't think it has anything to do with being black or white or anything [*Why did you decide to have your children so young?*] I don't know. I didn't want to have them young; it was just something that happened. . . . I know when I was 15, I didn't even want to be pregnant. [It was] just something that happened, not using protection like I should have . . . really not caring, and not being cautious. Something I brought on myself, because I could have been more cautious of what I was doing, but I made an awful lot of mistakes.

The counterpart of the young, welfare-dependent mother is the young single man who has never been able to find a niche in the labor market and thus lacks the resources to marry or support families. My interviews included three single black fathers who were currently in their twenties, thus having grown up in the 1970s. All had spent at least part of their childhood years in households headed by single mothers, and they had experienced many family hardships. They felt that their mothers had worked hard to rear them properly, yet they had trouble completing high school (two of them never did) and none of them had found a permanent place in the labor market.

Jake Houser is a 28-year-old single biological father of three children, although he freely claims to be father to the children of several women he has lived with over the years. He does not describe his parents' failing marriage in terms of a postindustrial economic transition, but he does remember the violence and trouble that seemed to occur after his father lost a high-paying job at an automobile assembly plant in the 1970s:

I don't remember a happy time. I'm trying to remember a good time—maybe all I can remember are the bad times. All I remember was when he used to beat up on my mother, and I just couldn't wait until I grew up, because I wanted to get him back. I wanted to show him how I felt. Because my mother was a good mother; not like these girls now.

Despite his family troubles, Jake was considered a good student during most of his grade and high school years. He described himself as "one of the leaders in his class" during elementary school and a good student through much of high school. His parents separated and reconciled many times before eventually divorcing during his early teenage years, and Jake, the oldest of three children and the only son, felt a particular responsibility to take care of his mother. Yet his family moved frequently after the divorce, finally ending up in a rough inner-city neighborhood where Jake found himself "doing stuff I never thought in my life I would do":

> When I graduated to the 11th grade, I started skipping school, smoking weed, drinking beer, trying to hang out with the boys. . . . When I was a leader [in school], I wasn't even thinking about nothing like that. I started smoking weed, selling weed—I don't know why I'm telling you all this! I was in deep, skipping school. The main reason for skipping school was girls. . . . [then] I got into dancing with this group [which performed locally] and it was like I was a superstar, like I was a celebrity. All the girls wanted to be with me, and I wanted to be with them. And the grades started dropping, because I wasn't there. My teachers were always trying to counsel me, sending notes to my mother. But there was too much fun in what I was doing.

By his late teenage years, Jake was subscribing to what is now frequently called the "hip-hop" culture of young urban blacks. Many young African Americans reject the integrationist/assimilationist ideologies of their parents and espouse the values found in popular music that denigrate women, disrespect the elderly, and glorify crime, drugs, and violence. Jake is among the many who in a sense have been doubly victimized by the postindustrial transition: It undermined the stability of his parents' marriage and now seems to have precluded his own opportunity to find employment that would enable him to marry and develop a consistent relationship with his children. Like many young African American men, Jake has had numerous short-term, temporary, low-paying jobs and frequent long spans of unemployment. Jake clearly fits into the concept of an underclass, with the postindustrial economy shaping both his childhood experiences and his adult life. At age 28, he finds himself in a lifestyle that he views as inconsistent with his values.

Poverty and Parenthood:
Single Mothers, Absent Fathers

Although not all single parents are poor and not all poor families undermine the welfare of children, there are strong positive correlations among single-mother families, poverty, welfare dependency, and an array of adverse social, psychological, and health factors for children. There was a clear relationship between marital status and income for the respondents in this study (see Table 1.1). The health of poor children (and their mothers) is jeopardized from the onset of pregnancy, as poor women have more chronic health problems and less access to medical care (Luker, 1996).

Table 1.1 Characteristics of Black Parents by Marital Status

	Singles (N = 189)		Marrieds (N = 184)	
	n	%	n	%
Educational level				
less than high school	15	8.0	12	6.5
high school or more	160	85.1	135	74.2
bachelor's degree or more	13	7.0	35	19.2
no response	1	0.5	2	1.4
Employment status				
employed	115	61.8	142	78.5
unemployed	65	34.9	30	16.6
retired	6	3.2	—	—
Family's yearly income				
less than $15,000	113	61.7	31	17.5
$15,000-29,999	60	32.8	66	37.3
$30,000-50,000	9	4.9	56	31.6
more than $50,000	1	0.5	24	13.6
The problems facing American families today are mostly caused by				
personal decisions	117	61.9	106	57.6
social forces	58	30.7	67	36.4
both, refuse to choose	7	3.7	6	3.3
no response	7	3.7	5	2.7
Age range	19-50		25-65	
Average age	33.09		38.6	

Black mothers, regardless of their educational level, are less likely than white mothers to receive early prenatal care. Census data for 1993 show that only 55% of black mothers with fewer than 12 years of education received first trimester care, compared with 65% of white mothers. Among those with more than 12 years of education, 79% of black mothers and 92% of white mothers received prenatal care during the first trimester (U.S. Department of Health and Human Services, 1996). Poor black women also live in more stressful environments, have a more limited diet, and experience more psychological distress and depression (Carrington, 1980; Pyant & Yanico, 1991). They are overrepresented among mothers who give birth to low-weight infants: More than 16% of black mothers have low-weight infants, compared with 7% of white mothers (Luker, 1996). Low birth weight is the greatest single damaging factor to infant health (Christmas, 1996), as low-weight babies are more likely to die and to experience myriad other health problems.

Most teenage pregnancies are not planned, and teenage mothers typically have neither the economic resources nor the parenting skills needed for child rearing. According to McLanahan and Sandefur (1994), income accounts for more than half of the disadvantage associated with living with a single mother, but the rest of the disadvantage comes from other sources, such as parenting styles. Poverty and distress lessen the ability of parents to invest economically or emotionally in their children. McLoyd (1990) has described the impact of psychological distress on poor single mothers:

> Because they are more emotionally distressed than their advantaged counterparts, it is not surprising that the capacity of poor parents for supportive, sensitive, and involved parenting is diminished. Numerous studies . . . report that mothers who are poor, as compared to their advantaged counterparts, are more likely to use power-assertive techniques in disciplinary encounters and are generally less supportive of their children. (p. 322)

There is substantial evidence that growing up in single-mother families, especially those headed by poor teenagers, can lead to poor socialization outcomes for children. Poor children experience high levels of depression, dependence, unhappiness, and anxiety, and low levels of self-confidence and social adaptation (McLeod & Shanahan, 1996). They are also more likely than affluent children to have impairments in their cognitive development, to engage in problem behaviors, and to perform less well in school (Luker, 1996). Children in single-mother families have lower academic test scores, have poorer attendance, and are about twice as likely to drop out of high school than are those in dual-parent families (McLanahan & Sandefur, 1994).

Young single mothers are especially likely to be inconsistent in their child-rearing and disciplinary strategies; they are sometimes harsh and authoritarian, and at other times overly permissive. McLeod and Shanahan point out that poor mothers spank their children significantly more often than do nonpoor mothers, and greater spankings contribute to the mental health problems of children. The extensive use of physical punishment often occurs because parents do not understand the developmental stages of their children, thus expecting behaviors that children are not capable of performing, and because of the distress and isolation of parenting. Although it is common to racialize the problems associated with poverty, McLeod and Shanahan point out that the impact of poverty on family and parenting styles does not vary by race but is correlated with race because poverty is greater and more persistent among blacks.

One of the major losses for children who grow up in single-mother families is the father, as they rarely have an opportunity to form a consistent, supportive relationship with him. Father absence is an important issue, as it has been shown to adversely affect children's emotional and economic well-being and general childhood outcomes (Thomson, Hanson, & McLanahan, 1994). Still, generalizing this finding to all races can be problematic. First, the absence of black fathers is often more assumed than empirically investigated (Cazenave, 1981; Dembo, 1988). Mott (1990) has pointed out that paternal involvement with children is rarely captured by clear dichotomies between father absence and father presence, as most nonmarried fathers probably fall somewhere on a continuum between the two. There is evidence that black fathers are more involved with their children than is shown by statistical data on residential patterns (Danziger & Radin, 1990; Hammons-Bryner, 1995), and that even young, unmarried fathers make an effort to become part of their children's lives (Sullivan, 1989). Moreover, the absence of a biological father does not mean that children are deprived of relationships with caring men or that they are without male role models. Mott also noted that the impact of father absence is mediated by whether the father has ever lived with the child, how often he visits his child, and the availability of other father figures in the home. In addition to these observations, it is important to note that when mother-headed families are the cultural norm, the absence of a father may carry less stigma and some of its negative impact may be mitigated. Also, the close relationship between single-motherhood and poverty makes it difficult to identify which factor produces poor childhood outcomes.

Despite numerous difficulties in the father-absence hypothesis, African Americans do seem increasingly to expect and desire greater paternal participation and to see themselves as especially deprived when that participation is minimal or absent. In recent years, popular black magazines such as *Ebony* and *Essence* have published numerous essays from adults, mostly men, who grew up in single-mother families. They have high praise for the work and efforts of their mothers, but they uniformly lament the absence of their fathers. They express a deep longing for a relationship with their fathers and an inability to understand their fathers' lack of interest and involvement in their lives. Many children in single-mother families are exposed to an array of other adult males and in some cases develop meaningful relationships with them. My experience suggests, however, that most children in single-parent families, especially those who are poor, do not have the chance to develop stable, consistent, intimate relationships with any one male figure; at best, they have a series of brief, superficial relationships with a variety of men who offer varying levels of support and companionship. Children express a deep desire to know their fathers, and that desire persists even into adulthood. In my interviews, Brenda Johnson, a successful day care owner who is married to a pediatrician, said,

I am 43 years old and not having a father still affects me, and it still hurts after all this time. And I don't even need him now. I haven't needed him since I was able to do things for myself, even as a child. But I still long for him . . . I still wish now that I could get to know him, but he was older than my mother. He's probably in his late 60s or 70s by now, so it's a real rare chance that I will ever get a chance to see him. *[How would you life have been different with him?]* I don't know. I think it's just the fact that it really would have been nice to know him, to get in touch with him. Just to have someone to share things with.

In her recent book on teenage motherhood among African Americans, Kaplan (1997) uses the term *father loss* instead of *father absence* to convey the depth of emotional rejection felt by many children. Daughters need the experience of being loved and cared for by their fathers, and sons clearly need role models they can identify with to teach them about the responsibilities and challenges of manhood. This need becomes especially acute during puberty, as children face myriad challenges and choices. The absence of fathers does not necessarily mean that children will experience behavior problems, rebellion, delinquency, or academic failure, nor does the presence of a father always protect children against these problems. Still, single mothers, especially those who are poor and raising multiple children, are commonly challenged by the demands of exerting appropriate social control over the behaviors of their children, especially during the teenage years. And, as Kaplan has pointed out, the authority of women in black communities has decreased remarkably in the past 20 years, with children and teenagers especially unlikely to show respect for them.

The despair felt by many African American parents in their efforts to cope with the stress of unemployment, poverty, and poor self-esteem is linked with an increasing number of behaviors that jeopardize the welfare of their children. For example, the rate of crack addiction is high among black Americans; it has been described by many black leaders as the "greatest scourge of the Black community" (Staples, 1994, p. 261), and it has had a devastating impact on families and the well-being of children. Drug use is associated with child neglect, abuse, and abandonment (Pinkney, 1993). Jones and Roberts (1994) found that African Americans represented 15% of the population under 19 years old but more than 24% of all substantiated cases of child abuse and neglect.

Drug dependency on the part of black parents has also meant that their children are more likely to be placed in foster care than are other children, and to stay there for a longer period of time. In 1990, 40% of children waiting to be adopted were black (Staples, 1994). Much of the increase in the racial gap in life expectancy between blacks and whites that occurred in the mid-1980s, according to Staples, is attributable to black drug use.

Because it offers a lucrative income and prestige in some neighborhoods, many children have become directly involved in selling drugs. The use and sale of drugs has also jeopardized the welfare of black children by promoting the spread of AIDS, which increasingly is transmitted heterosexually by IV drug users. In 1988, blacks composed about 55% of all AIDS cases among children under age 13 (Staples, 1994, p. 261).

Despite the hardships of poor families, black families clearly value their children and try to instill in them mainstream American cultural values, such as the importance of family, hard work, a good education, and economic independence. In addition to embracing the dominant American value system, African American parents also teach their children more distinctively African and African American-centered values. For example, racism and the continuing denigration of blackness have made racial issues a crucial aspect of childhood socialization for black parents. The majority of black parents engage in the racial socialization of their children as they try to teach them about racism, and how to cope with it, and make special efforts to bolster their children's sense of worth and racial esteem. The historical exclusion of black people from equal participation in American society has led to the retention, reinforcement, and social construction of black cultural values, such as gender equality, reliance on extended families, mutual support networks, respect for the elderly, and religious participation. Poor blacks often experience these cultural values simply as adaptive strategies that allow them to survive economically, while many middle-class blacks deliberately construct and cultivate African-centered values as a source of ethnic pride and meaning. The next chapter explores in more detail how black child rearing has been affected by both class and cultural forces.

2

Caste, Class, and Culture

The vestiges of the African heritage, the experiences of slavery, the mixture of cultures, the long shadow of the plantation, the transition to Northern urban communities, the persistence of racism, the impact of the civil rights movement and the public policy initiatives it produced . . . can be seen to play important roles in an understanding of contemporary Afro-American family patterns.

Andrew Billingsley,
Black Families in White America
(1968/1988, p. xiii)

Slavery, caste, and class are distinct social stratification systems, often undergirded by differing political ideologies, yet they existed simultaneously in preindustrial American society. The institutionalization of slavery during the 1600s was motivated by the need to establish a cheap pool of agricultural workers. After efforts to enslave poor whites and Native Americans failed, Africans were brought to the United States involuntarily for perpetual servitude, making race the basis of slavery. Culturally distinct from white Europeans, Africans were also judged to be intellectually and socially inferior people, and a rigid caste system evolved to restrict their freedoms and rights. Thus, even the small percentage of Africans who had freely migrated to the United States and managed to escape bondage found their status defined by skin color.

In his classic studies on stratification, Weber (1964) described social status as constructed on the basis of the subjective appraisals of group characteristics, especially ascribed characteristics such as race. He explained that after status positions have been "lived in" for a while, they can become the basis of a legal system of privileges, or a caste system. Caste systems are characterized by hereditary membership, social immobility, endogamous marriages and social relationships, and access to a narrowly prescribed range of occupations (Weber, 1964). Although no stratification system adheres strictly to the ideal-type characteristics delineated by Weber, the racial stratification system during slavery and its aftermath certainly had castelike qualities. Prior to the Civil War and the abolition of slavery, most states had laws prohibiting blacks from intermarrying with whites, testifying in court against whites, voting, owning property, owning firearms, and even learning how to read and write (Hurst, 1998).

John Ogbu (1978, 1997) has argued that the castelike status of black people separated them from other racial minorities who had voluntarily immigrated to the United States. Because the vast majority of blacks came as slaves, they were consigned to a permanently low status from birth and denied access to the societal resources needed for socioeconomic mobility. Although there were some status distinctions and hierarchical relationships among slaves, based mostly on skin color and work responsibilities, for all practical purposes they were excluded from the open class system available to other Americans. Elements of this caste system continued through the early twentieth century, when legalized racial segregation circumscribed where African Americans could live, work, and attend school and restricted their right to vote and exercise other freedoms. And, although blacks have made notable achievements in the past 30 years, the legacy of slavery and the caste system has fostered racial disparities in educational and economic standing of whites and blacks that continue to adversely affect the status and quality of life for black people. Data from the U.S. Department of Commerce (1996) show that in 1995, the median income for black families was $24,698 compared with $40,884 for white families. During that same year, 9% of white families and 27% of black families had incomes below the poverty level. In terms of education, 24% of whites had obtained a four-year college degree or more, compared with only 13% of blacks.

While acknowledging the interactive and overlapping nature of caste, class, and culture, I organize this chapter by examining each factor separately and tying each to a particular historical period. I begin the chapter by examining black parents and their children from slavery until the early twentieth century, when the racial caste system structured black-white relations. Little has been written explicitly about child rearing during slavery, but available evidence suggests that black parents, within the boundaries and limitations of the system imposed upon them, attempted to nurture and train their children.

Next, I review studies that began to emerge in the 1900s on the importance of social class in shaping child-rearing work. After slavery had ended, many blacks, especially those in the South, still endured a racial caste system that made family life difficult. As studies during this era started to include blacks, they usually acknowledged the devastating impact of slavery on black families and rejected the view that any significant aspect of the African culture could have survived. Because these studies focused mostly on poor blacks, their perspective contributed to the social deficit model of the black family. However, studies of child rearing that included poor and middle-class black families typically found the latter to be surprisingly similar to the dominant society in their value system and family organization. For the liberal scholars of the pre-civil rights era, this was powerful evidence that social and economic opportunities were the keys to ending most of the problems found among black people.

Class analyses became even more important with Melvin Kohn's work on child rearing during the 1950s (Kohn, 1963). Much of this research supported an assimilationist framework by suggesting that African Americans, given access to the necessary social and material resources, are very much like white Americans. Given the growing class diversity among black Americans, it is difficult to describe any aspect of black life without considering social class. Billingsley (1968/1988) has always contended that blacks were more stratified than commonly assumed, and that social class was the most powerful dimension in describing the conditions of black family life. In his 1992 book, Billingsley used census data on income to categorize 30% of black families as poor, 34% as working class, 27% as middle class, and 9% as upper class. Yet income does not provide a complete picture of social class background, especially when education and occupation are not considered. And, as Sigelman and Welch (1991) warn, class is a "murky" concept, even more nebulous among blacks, whose criteria for assigning class position may differ from those of white Americans.

Finally, I discuss cultural analyses of black families and child-rearing practices. Culture is commonly defined as the beliefs, values, behaviors, symbols, and products of a particular group of people. It provides the context for constructing identities and worldviews. The study of culture is a long-standing tradition in the social sciences. Sociologists, as observers and theorists of the link between macro and micro social processes, have carried the banner in explaining how social structural forces shape cultural patterns. The dominant theoretical perspective in family sociology prior to the 1960s, structural-functionalism, saw the structure, functions, and values of families being transformed by the social forces of industrialization, modernization, and urbanization. Within this tradition, I also view cultural values as related to structural forces, and culture and social class as similar rather than distinct; in fact, social classes are often very much like subcultures. I conclude with a discussion of the underclass concept, which illustrates the interactive nature of class and culture and has made the presumed link between cultural values and behaviors a contentious issue.

Caste Analysis

From the early 1600s until the abolition of slavery in 1865, the majority of Africans in the United States were forced immigrants brought to the country for the purpose of slavery. Slavery had been established in Virginia by 1640, and by the end of the seventeenth century, 90% of Africans in the United States were enduring a form of chattel slavery that defined them as the property of their white slave owners. Slaves were defined as less than human—as property or livestock—and were incorporated into the early economy with little regard for their previous social or family ties. Although not all blacks were slaves, the racial caste system that evolved between blacks and whites in colonial America extended beyond the relationships between slaves and their masters and severely circumscribed the freedoms of all blacks. Free blacks were not only often assumed to be slaves unless they could prove otherwise (Stack, 1974), but there were numerous restrictions on the occupations they could hold, the property they could own, and their right to vote (Kitano, 1991).

For most of the twentieth century, historians have debated the nature and stability of the black family under slavery. While an extensive discussion of this issue is beyond the scope of this research, it is important to have some idea of the social and family context of parents and their children during slavery. W. E. B. DuBois, in his 1908 work titled *The Negro American Family,* declared that the three essential features of American slavery for black people were no legal marriage, no legal family, and no legal control over children. His view that black families had been totally shattered by the experience of slavery, and thus had been of little significance during that era, was held by many scholars during the early twentieth century. Others, however, challenged that perspective.

In 1930, E. Franklin Frazier, one of the best known early African American family scholars, pointed out that neither structural forces nor the discretion of white slave owners had completely shaped the nature of the black family. He argued that

> to restrict the recognition of the Negro family to the individual judgement and caprice of the masters, is to overlook the influence of human relations that constantly tended to break down formal controls and legal definitions, and the force of traditions within the institution of slavery. (p. 199)

Although Frazier was later to assess the slave family as much weaker and more variable than he had earlier suggested (White, 1974), his view on the viability and importance of families among slaves has been reiterated in the work of others (Blassingame, 1972; Jones, 1985). Those who have argued that families did not exist during slavery may be narrowly defining the concept of family in terms of the Eurocentric model of a married couple living together with their children. The extent to which this type of family existed continues to be debated; some scholars (Gutman, 1976; Jones, 1985) have found extensive evidence that two-parent families and at least a modicum of family stability were the norm, while others (Davis, 1981) have argued that slaves rarely achieved nuclear families.

In all probability, there was great variability among the living arrangements of slaves based on historical period, geographic area, and labor demands. For example, early slaves were primarily young and male (Kitano, 1991), and their youth and lack of female partners probably diminished their opportunity to engage in African cultural or family practices. It was not until 1840, a few years before the end of slavery, that the sex ratio between males and females was relatively equal. Queen and Habenstein (1967) have documented differences in the slave system based on geography and economics. They pointed out that while slavery existed in the middle colonies, it was much more economically profitable in the South; thus the harshness of slave codes weakened from South to North.

Whatever form family life eventually took among slaves, white slave owners clearly controlled black families to their own advantage, deciding who could marry, dictating family roles, and asserting control over slave children (Blassingame, 1972). Still, it was to the advantage of slave owners to promote the formation of families among blacks as a way to control and discipline the slave labor force:

> By encouraging strong family attachments, slave owners reduced the danger that individual slaves would run away. By permitting families to have de facto ownership of houses, furniture, clothing, garden plots, and small livestock, planters created an economic stake for slaves in the system. (Fogel & Engerman, 1974, quoted in White, 1974, p. 388)

The family lives of Africans brought to the United States were transformed by the labor demands of the agricultural economy but, as will be discussed later, elements of their African heritage were retained. Although there was some cultural diversity among West Africans, the majority were from patriarchal and polygynous societies, where children were seen as a form of wealth and women were highly esteemed for their childbearing and child-rearing abilities. There was a way in which these African traits meshed with American family characteristics and the labor demands of slavery. For example, the fertility of slave women was highly valued in the southern agricultural economy, where child workers were needed but often scarce because of high rates of infant and childhood mortality. In addition to eventually becoming workers, black infants had an economic value at birth. Franklin and Moss (1988), who argue that slave breeding was common and popular, quote one slave owner as boasting that every black baby "was worth two hundred dollars . . . the moment it drew breath" (p. 106). They argue that it was common for female slaves to start having children by the age of 13 or 14.

The mothering skills of black women were highly touted: As Frazier (1939/1949) has noted, visitors to Africa often observed that "the love of the African mother for her children is unsurpassed in any part of the world" (p. 33). In the United States, these mothering skills met the demand for child care workers in affluent southern families, where slave women often nursed and nurtured white children, sometimes to the disadvantage or neglect of their own children. According to Frazier, it was the child care work that black women (as "mammies") were forced to provide to white children that led to the idealized picture of their selfless devotion to children. And, as was the case in Africa, slavery forced black women to hold both productive and reproductive roles. Similarly, slavery may have reinforced the African tradition of extended families, although such families were now based on necessity rather than cultural ideology. For white slave owners, one of the chief benefits of communal living was that it allowed the full exploitation of male and female slave labor.

Although there is a sense in which African cultural norms were reinforced by slavery, for the most part they were flagrantly and cruelly violated by white slave owners. For example, there were significantly more black men than women, thus making the tradition of polygyny impossible. Marriages between slaves had no legal basis and slaves working as field hands were often not allowed to marry at all (Queen & Habenstein, 1967), thus undermining the foundation for families. Moreover, black men were sometimes completely stripped of their family roles and the privileges of patriarchy, although many valiantly (and often at great risk) tried to protect and provide for their families. In the male-dominated society of colonial America, black women had less control over their lives than men, although their value as workers, mammies, and mistresses might have enhanced their status.

Female slaves worked as hard as their male counterparts, often as field hands, and had the bulk of the responsibility for child care and family work. Involuntary sexual liaisons between slave women and white men were common occurrences; in fact, Kardiner and Ovesey (1951) have noted that much of the white males' fear of black men was rooted in the former's extensive use of black women as sexual partners, mistresses, and nursemaids for their children. Similarly, Hymowitz and Weissman (1978, p. 51) add that opposing the rape of a black woman was tantamount to opposing slavery, as a black woman's body was not her own but the property of whoever held the bill of sale for her purchase. Thus, slavery violated the sanctity of childbearing by usurping the rights of black men and women to produce children in sexually exclusive, volitional relationships.

Childbearing under slavery probably provided some gratification for black parents, given the emphasis in their African cultural heritage on children and the fact that children often offered hope for racial survival and for a better future. Still, having and raising children under slavery was often involuntary, demeaning, and burdensome, as slaves often had very little control over their reproductive lives. The extent to which pregnancy and childbirth exempted women from field labor varied. Mothers and their newborns were valuable property and, to reduce the economic loss associated with their sickness and death, mothers sometimes gained relief from laborious fieldwork that would have undermined their physical welfare. In others cases, having the children of their white owners resulted in an improvement in the treatment and provisions for the mothers and their children. There were cases, however, when new mothers were forced to return to work almost immediately, either taking their babies with them or enlisting the child care help of older relatives. The conditions facing new mothers and their infants led to high rates of mortality. Based on available evidence, infant mortality rates for slaves were three times higher than for whites (Jones, 1985).

However long mothers were given to recover from the birth of a child, they eventually had to return to their productive labor roles, which took priority over caring for their own children. Children were often cared for communally, as Hymowitz and Weissman (1978) have pointed out:

> Most often children and toddlers spent the day in a children's house, where an elderly slave was in charge. She was helped by slightly older children who actually did most of the baby tending. The children's houses were not remembered with affection. One former slave recalled sleeping in the one-room house as well as spending his days there. The house was so crowded, he said, that "you couldn't stir us with a stick." . . . Children often ate out of the same dish . . . [and] until they were twelve years old girl and boy slaves wore the same clothing—a long shirt with nothing on underneath. Feeding slave children out of a common pot as though they were animals and ignoring their desire for modesty were common practices throughout the South. This treatment was part of the attempt to condition slave children to view themselves as less human than whites, and perhaps not human at all. (pp. 47-48)

Illegitimacy and single-parent families were the norms, a situation that made mothers the most reliable and readily available parents. In fact, slave families were often defined as comprising mothers and their children, thus ignoring the significance of fatherhood. Kardiner and Ovesey (1951) argue that the "mother-child family with the father either unknown, absent, or, if present, incapable of wielding influence, was the only type of family that could survive in the new environment" (p. 45). The fathering role was also diminished by the respect and authority slavery often accorded older black women, especially grandmothers, as the head of the family.

Despite the hardships they endured, most records indicate that slave parents valued their children, tried to protect them from the ravages of slavery, and loved them. Blassingame (1972) pointed out that the rearing of children was one of the most important family functions:

> Since slave parents were primarily responsible for training their children, they could cushion the shock of bondage for them, help them to understand their situation, teach them values different from those their masters tried to instill in them, and give them a referent for self-esteem other than their master. (p. 79)

Slave parents could also be harsh disciplinarians (Giddings, 1984), although it would be difficult to argue that their harshness exceeded that of other colonial American parents. Strict control of children and corporal punishment were clearly the cultural norms of the era and, given the severity of punishment doled out to slaves, black parents were probably especially likely to see their children's disobedience as threatening.

The age at which children were integrated into the slave labor force probably varied; in some cases, black children were apparently exempt from labor during their early childhood years, as the account of a North Carolina slave pointed out:

> My early boyhood [was spent] in playing with the other boys and girls, colored and white, in the yard, and occasionally doing such little matters of labor as one of so young years could. I knew no difference between myself and the white children; nor did they seem to know any in turn. Sometimes my master would come out and give a biscuit to me, and another to one of his own white boys; but I did not perceive the difference between myself and my master's white children. They began to order me about, and were told to do so by my master and mistress. (Frazier, 1939/1949, p. 28)

In other cases, relentless labor started at an early age, as children worked picking cotton or as house servants, and were widely abused. Slave children were often made to attend to the needs and obey the commands of white children, and sometimes even slept on the floor next to their young masters' beds (Comer & Poussaint, 1992). The relentless nature of their work was described in Booker T. Washington's (1924/1992) account of his own childhood years spent in slavery:

> From the time that I can remember anything, almost every day of my life has
> been occupied in some kind of labor. . . . During the period I spent in slavery
> I was not large enough to be of much service, still I was occupied most of
> the time in cleaning the yards, carrying water to men in the fields, or going
> to the mill to which I used to take the corn once a week, to be ground. The
> mill was about three miles from the plantation. This work I always dreaded.
> (p. 96)

The greatest threat to slave parents and their children was separation as
a result of sale. In his narrative account of slavery, Frederick Douglass
(1960) described being separated from his mother as an infant, a custom
that he noted was widespread during slavery in Maryland and probably
was intended to destroy mother-child bonds. His mother lived 12 miles
away, but his account testified to the intense devotion of many mothers to
their children, even when raising the child was not possible:

> I never saw my mother, to know her as such, more than four or five times in
> my life; and each of these times was very short in duration, and at night . . .
> She made her journeys to see me in the night, traveling the whole distance
> by foot, after the performance of her day's work. She was a field hand, and
> a whipping is the penalty of not being in the field at sunrise. . . . [so] She
> would lie down with me, and get me to sleep, but long before I waked she
> was gone. Very little communication ever took place between us. (p. 25)

Once slavery was abolished, black families struggled to emulate the patriarchal, nuclear family that was dominant among whites and, to some
extent, they succeeded. Black rates of illegitimacy declined dramatically
after slavery (Frazier, 1939/1949) and the two-parent nuclear family became the norm during Reconstruction (Gutman, 1976). Yet implementation of the breadwinner-homemaker system continued to elude black families, as southern landowners devised ways to continue their control over
black laborers. To survive, millions of black families became sharecroppers,
and thus were still tied to an agricultural economy that used the entire
family as the basic labor unit. And as Jones (1985) has pointed out, black
female sharecroppers who tried to exempt themselves from field labor, or
balance their time between work and family, were often accused of "female
loaferism." In some cases, black people could be forced to work for anyone
who wanted their labor. A black male stockyard worker during the 1930s
explained,

> Men and women had to work in the fields. A woman was not permitted to
> remain at home if she felt like it. If she was found at home, some of the white
> people would come and ask why she was not in the field and tell her she had

better get to the field or else abide by the consequences. After the summer crops were all in, any of the white people could send for any Negro woman to come and do the family washing at 75 cents to $1.00 a day. If she sent word she could not come she had to send an excuse why she could not come. They were never allowed to stay at home as long as they were able to go. Had to take whatever they paid you for your work. (Jones, 1985, p. 157)

Thus, full-time motherhood, prescribed in the dominant society as essential to the well-being of children, was never allowed for African American women. Even after slavery had ended, the labor needs of the South sometimes made it difficult for parents to keep their own children, as their labor was also sought by white landowners. Some black parents had to fight to gain or retain custody of their children, as some states passed laws allowing former slave owners to indenture (reenslave) those children who were under 21 years old and living with parents who were unmarried or unemployed. Scott (1985) has noted that in many cases "no money was specified to be given at the end of the term, children were bound without parental consent, no trades were specified, or children were bound beyond the legal age" (p. 196). Such laws clearly challenged the parental rights of blacks, who had been allowed neither to legally marry under slavery nor to obtain decent jobs afterward.

Finally, the implementation of the traditional family was also thwarted by the inability of black men to secure decent jobs—jobs paying the family wage—as well as the strong tradition of self-reliance African American women had developed under slavery. These economic and social factors made the subordination of women difficult to effect. Women continued to work outside of the home, and the tradition of relying on their own mothers for support continued.

Class Analyses:
The Social Deficit Model

With the rise of the modern family and the new importance being placed on child rearing, a plethora of studies emerged examining families and child rearing in the early twentieth century. In most cases, these studies were conducted using a white, middle-class orientation and guided by Eurocentric child-rearing theories. They tended to focus on low-income blacks and, while acknowledging the adverse impact of racism on their families, described them in ways that later gave credence to the pathological perspective of black families. African American families were stigmatized and stereotyped as a result of these early studies, as researchers were unable to shift their lens and evaluate blacks within the context of their own culture.

At the same time, it is important to point out that these were often ethnographic studies, based on interviews with blacks and reporting their experiences in their own words. Second, it must be noted that most of the researchers were liberal social scientists, and underlying their research was an assimilationist perspective that supported racial integration and greater opportunity for blacks. Thus, when black middle-class and lower-class families were included in the analyses, these researchers made it clear that poverty and deprivation, not racial inferiority, were the sources of so-called dysfunctional black families.

Pivotal in the early study of black families was Frazier's (1939/1949) work, which advanced the thesis of "the matriarchate"—the dominance of women in marriage and family relations—as one of the legacies of slavery. A more social psychological approach was found in the 1940 work of Allison Davis and John Dollard, *Children of Bondage,* which studied the personality development of adolescents in the South. They focused on the life histories of 30 black adolescents, ages 12 to 16, although they interviewed a much broader sample. Their book provided extensive documentation of the indignities experienced by all southern blacks living under the rigid racial caste system and the toll these indignities took on the psychological development of children. While noting that 75% of blacks were in the lower class, they found that social class was the major factor shaping black family patterns and child-rearing norms. They argued that although all blacks have the status of lower-caste people in the South, a "great divide" existed between those in the lower class and lower-middle class.

These class differences among blacks were nowhere more evident than in the child-rearing work of parents. Although lower-class parents were portrayed as violent and apathetic toward their children, blacks in the lower-middle class were seen as valuing marriage, fidelity, and white, middle-class child-rearing norms. Clearly, these researchers embraced such norms as superior:

> Lower-middle-class parents exert a powerful and continual pressure upon their children to study, to inhibit sexual impulses, to avoid lower-class playmates, to attend Sunday school regularly, and to avoid cabarets, night clubs, pool parlors, and gambling houses. They set before their children the goals of a high school education, a skilled or white collar occupation, and a "good" marriage. (Davis & Dollard, 1940, p. 265)

Davis and Havighurst (1946) also examined the role of social class in child-rearing strategies, although they argued that social class was an aspect of culture. They found few racial differences in early childhood training in white and black families but concluded that social class differences were quite striking:

The striking thing about this study is that Negro and white middle-class families are so much alike, and that white and Negro lower-class families are so much alike. The likenesses hold for such characteristics as number of children, ages of parents when married, as well as child-rearing practices and expectations of children. (p. 708)

In 1951, Abram Kardiner and Lionel Ovesey published *The Mark of Oppression,* another significant work on the family lives of black Americans. Like Frazier, they argued that the African culture of black people was completely destroyed by slavery and the racial caste system that evolved afterward. In an attempt to buffer their unflattering depiction of lower-class black families, the authors make it clear that they are not describing the innate racial characteristics of black people. Instead, they argued that the personality is acquired as the result of having to adapt to a particular set of environmental conditions—and for blacks, these conditions have been extremely harsh. Kardiner and Ovesey described lower-class black parents as basically inconsistent, demanding, and often lacking affection for their children. Mothers, most of whom are forced to work to help support their families, were seen often as cold, "loveless tyrants" who abused and exploited their children. According to these researchers, this type of mother typically is

ill-tempered, imposes severe and rigid discipline, demands immediate obedience, and offers only sporadic affection. In fact, this is the most common complaint, even by well-fed children, that the mothers in this group are often loveless tyrants. Coldness, scoldings, and frequent beatings are the rule. Exploitation of children by foster parents is extremely common. However, these features are not universal. (p. 65)

Low-income fathers were described by Kardiner and Ovesey (1951) as "seclusive, taciturn, violent, punitive, and without interest in their children" (pp. 65-66). They observed that among them "obedience [was] often enforced toward ends the child does not understand. . . . Beatings without provocation are common; severe punishment for minor infractions, likewise" (p. 67). From these studies arose a social deficit model of black child rearing in which parents were depicted as harsh, arbitrary, and controlling. While including at least some middle-income blacks in their studies, the emphasis was clearly on the nonconforming and potentially harmful behaviors of poor parents. The research of this era provided virtually no critical evaluation of white, middle-class families but accepted them as the model by which other families were to be judged. And, despite the emphasis on social class, there was little effort to capture the diversity of black families or, even more important, to acknowledge their strengths or successful cultural adaptations. Thus, these studies were later to be widely criticized for perpetuating myths and stereotypes about the black family. Still, they helped clarify the importance of social class in child rearing and shift the focus from racial inferiority to economics as the basis of viable families.

Class Analyses:
Contemporary Perspectives

During the early 1900s, the Middletown studies by Helen and Robert Lynd found class to be the most significant factor in shaping parental views about what was possible and desirable in child rearing (Alwin, 1988). They found a working-class focus on obedience in child rearing and a middle-class focus on autonomy—a value dichotomy that became the focus of more systematic research by Melvin Kohn during the 1950s. Kohn, who used education and occupation to define social class, established social class as a crucial factor in parental values and discipline strategies, arguing that it had an even greater impact on child rearing than did race. Kohn's work revealed that lower- and working-class parents, compared with their middle-class counterparts, were more likely to expect obedience and conformity from their children, more likely to use physical punishment, and less likely to be verbally expressive with their children. Middle-income parents, on the other hand, emphasized self-direction and autonomy, explained things to their children, and used more psychological forms of discipline. Maternal education had a major impact on child-rearing values: Educated mothers valued curiosity, consideration, self-control, and happiness in their children, while less educated mothers valued neatness, cleanliness, and obedience (Kohn, 1977, p. 31). Kohn explained these class differences by noting that educated mothers are more exposed to and likely to follow the advice of child-rearing experts. More important, he linked these values to the nature of working- and middle-class jobs, which he suggested differed on three main dimensions: routinization of activities, level of supervision, and complexity of work. Therefore, these class-based child-rearing values and discipline strategies embodied worldviews structured by occupations, and thus included characteristics parents saw as crucial for success in the varying occupational arenas.

Because Kohn's work lacked much of the evaluative tone of earlier research that had implicitly stigmatized poor families, it helped make class analyses more acceptable. The majority of contemporary research on child-rearing values and family patterns has found the family patterns and child-rearing strategies of black and white Americans to be quite similar, especially when social class is considered. In 1967, Kami and Radin documented social class variations in child rearing among blacks in the lower and middle classes. In this study, lower-class blacks, compared with their middle-class counterparts, were less likely to use a variety of child-rearing techniques, reward their children, or gratify their children's emotional needs. A 1972 study by Busse and Busse documented how social class affects the way parents interact with their children. They assigned black parents various tasks to teach their fifth-grade sons and observed how the parents interacted with their children. They found a direct positive correlation between parents' education and how they trained their children: Educated parents used more words and encouraged more autonomous behaviors.

Willie (1985) studied black and white parents from diverse social class backgrounds and found that they shared a common core of values, such as the priority of family, hard work, academic achievement, and social mobility, but they varied in access to these values and in adaptation strategies. For example, he notes that "poor whites emphasize the value of the group and the responsibility of the individual to the collectivity; poor blacks emphasize the value of the individual and responsibility of the collectivity for the individual" (p. 279). Other studies have shown that parents teach their children the norms of mainstream society (Taylor, Chatters, Tucker, & Lewis, 1990; Thornton, Chatters, Taylor, & Allen, 1990). For example, Allen (1981) found honesty was the number one child-rearing value of both black and white parents. McAdoo (1983) found that when black parents attain middle-class status, their value orientation and methods of discipline tend to conform to the patterns found among middle-class whites. The current research also found social class to be an important factor in child-rearing norms, in ways that will be discussed in more detail in the following chapters.

Cultural Analyses

Although the study of culture has always been important in the social sciences, it has also been one of the most conflictual aspects of scholarship on African American families. Debates over the relative impacts of biology, culture, and the social environment in shaping human behavior have waxed and waned in American society since its early origins. One issue has been the confluence of biology and culture, or the assumption that cultural values and norms reflect the biological potential of a given group. To a large extent, this notion stems from the ethnocentricity of Europeans who arrived in the New World convinced of the superiority of their own culture and religion and guided by ideologies of capitalism, manifest destiny, and social Darwinism. Their ideologies of white superiority made it easy for them to define people of color as innately inferior based on biology and culture—a view that proved handy in justifying slavery, land acquisition, and myriad other forms of social and economic exploitation. Although they no longer predominate in the social sciences, theories about the innate intellectual inferiority of racial minorities, especially African Americans, continue to surface periodically, creating controversy and even anger and hostility. Most social theorists today, however, are less interested in arguments about biological inferiority and more concerned about understanding the interplay of cultural and social structural forces in shaping opportunities, ideologies, family systems, and individual behaviors.

A second issue has been creating an exact definition of "culture" and how it relates to social class among blacks. Clearly, there is no one, unified, stagnant culture among African Americans, and this often means that children are exposed to contradictory ideologies and norms. The work of Boykin and Toms (1985) helps bring some clarity to the issue of culture among blacks. The authors have developed a conceptual framework that describes this complexity of the black culture in terms of a "triple quandary." They argue that black American children "must simultaneously negotiate through three distinctively different realms of experience . . . the mainstream, minority, and Black culture experience" (pp. 38-39). The mainstream culture is the dominant culture in America, often based on white, middle-class norms and values. Blacks are widely exposed to the dominant culture and vary in their interest and ability to embrace its value system. The legacy of slavery and the racial caste system, however, have left blacks disproportionately in the lower class and often unable to conform to mainstream values. The minority culture arises directly as a result of adaptations to racism and oppression, and it can be viewed either as pathological or as functional. Studies that focus on low-income families, such as that of Stack (1974), have used a minority culture approach. Although they overlap, the distinction between the minority and the black culture experience is primarily that the latter unifies the experiences of African Americans of various classes and views their cultural experiences as positive, legitimate, and arising from their African heritage.

Despite these differences in the meaning of culture, and the fact that culture and social class both have economic and behavioral components, there are some unifying themes and family patterns among African Americans that transcend class distinctions and are best seen as cultural. I think it is important to acknowledge the cultural heritage of African Americans, because failing to do so denies black people a collective identity based on more than skin color, pathologizes the socially adaptive family strategies of a significant segment of the population, and deprives blacks of agency in their own lives. And given that racial-ethnic interests and identities are constructed in part as symbols of culture (Smith & Seltzer, 1992), it diminishes a coherent articulation of African American political interests and issues. Even more relevant for this study, debates over culture have tremendous implications for black children, as nearly half of them are poor and live in families that are increasingly being depicted as neither embracing nor instilling in children cultural values that lead to economic success. Despite the growing recognition that social class, cultural values, and social forces all play a role in shaping human behavior, the debate in the larger polity over the causes of welfare dependency and poverty often juxtaposes cultural patterns against structural forces. Those who believe poverty is the result of particular cultural values often emphasize individual responsibility for social problems and support cutbacks in public assistance as a strategy to eliminate those problems.

Culture as Pathology

Historically, the handful of scholars studying black people routinely used race, caste, and social class to explain black family patterns. Prior to the civil rights era, the dominant argument was that slavery had completely destroyed the African culture; Kardiner and Ovesey (1951) stated, for example, that "the most conspicuous feature of the Negro in America is *that his aboriginal culture was smashed,* be it by design or accident" (p. 39, italics in original). Similarly, Queen and Habenstein (1967) argued that the "dispersion of social groups, separation of husbands from wives and families, [and] callous disregard for kindred relationships, all but destroyed the African cultural and social heritage" (p. 317). For these theorists, the behaviors of lower-class blacks did not constitute a culture as much as a set of dysfunctional behaviors, worldviews, and family patterns that grew out of slavery and racism. In his influential 1965 book *The Dark Ghetto,* Kenneth B. Clark seemed to agree: He wrote that "the dark ghetto is institutionalized pathology; it is chronic, self-perpetuating pathology" (p. 81), characterized by family instability, social disorganization, drugs, disease, and crime.

The pathological perspective on culture held that black families had failed to conform to the Euro-American family model, yet they were not particularly blamed for their shortcomings. Rather, the emphasis was on the racism and socioeconomic exclusion that had produced their nonconformity. In terms of their cultural values—their behavioral preferences, beliefs, and hopes—most of the major work done by liberal social scientists in the 1950s and early 1960s argued that black people held the same cultural values as white Americans. Indeed, Queen and Habenstein

(1967) posited that blacks were "purer" Americans culturally than were the majority of white immigrants in the United States, as the latter had managed to retain their European ties. Blacks, it was argued, had embraced American values but were simply prohibited from expressing them due to poverty and racial segregation. So, being deprived of their native African cultural traditions yet never able to fully assimilate into American society left black people virtually without a culture. Black people who were poor were simply mired in disorganized, disintegrating families and communities while middle-class blacks, pitiable caricatures of the whites, were still subject to the rigid caste system that forced them to dissimulate in the presence of whites.

Oscar Lewis tried to rescue the poor from this presumed absence of culture with his culture of poverty thesis. Based on research conducted among poor Puerto Ricans living in New York, Lewis (1959) noted that a certain set of values emerge when people live in persistent poverty, such as fatalism, hopelessness, nonmarital pregnancy, the absence of childhood, and nonmarriage. Although these values are initially adaptive, fostering psychological and economic coping in a social system that denied opportunities to certain groups, once institutionalized they actually perpetuate poverty. In other words, cultural values and behaviors have their origins in structural forces, but the link between the two diminishes over time. Structural forces (in this case, barriers to opportunity) change, but the poor remain poor because they continue to engage in a value system that is no longer necessary or adaptive. Although Lewis saw pathological cultural values as underlying the behaviors of the poor, he argued that only a relatively small segment of the poor population held such values. Clark (1965) rejected the culture of poverty thesis as seductive but seriously flawed, as it implied that personal values and cultural deprivation were the sources of black failure. He continued to focus on social institutions that disadvantaged black people. For example, his work found that the school performance of black children in ghetto schools was better explained by characteristics of the educational system, such as poor teacher training and inadequate equipment, than by family instability and poverty.

The culture of poverty thesis fell into even greater disrepute when reiterated in 1965 in the widely criticized Moynihan report on black families. In this study, Moynihan suggested that poverty, unemployment, poor housing, substandard education, and other social ills that plagued black communities were ultimately traceable to a pathological value system in families. This report sparked a 30-year controversy over the relative merits of culture, social structure, and the elements that constituted a functional family. The implication in Moynihan's work that the traditional, breadwinner-homemaker family was the only viable family form was criticized by feminists and African Americans, both of whom rejected the idea that female-headship made families inherently pathological. They saw female oppression and poverty as the real issues. Using cultural values to explain the hardships of black families seemed to overlook the social structural forces that created those hardships. Moreover, a cultural explanation advanced at the height of the civil rights movement was especially troublesome because it aimed to shift the focus from institutionalized racism and the policies that upheld it to the personal behaviors of African Americans.

Culture as Strength

The Moynihan report sparked a proliferation of African American family scholarship that challenged the notion of a dysfunctional family or value system as being at the root of black troubles. At the same time, these scholars reconceptualized the black culture as strong and adaptive, rooted in both the African and the American heritages of black people. Billingsley's (1968/1988) *Black Families in White America* was pivotal in the effort to refute myths of cultural pathology among black families while allowing them to claim their own unique culture. Using essentially a structural-functional analysis, Billingsley described the larger social forces that had shaped black families. In her study of black adolescent girls, Ladner (1971) drew parallels between the West African and black American notions of gender, thus reclaiming the importance of culture. Hill (1972) gave further credence to the cultural approach by articulating the positive cultural traditions found among blacks, such as a strong achievement orientation, adaptability of family roles, religiosity, and strong kinship bonds. A 1970 study by Virginia Heyer Young of a southern black community viewed parent-child relations as "aspects of an indigenous American Negro culture" (p. 269) rather than a pathologized version of white culture based on deprivation. She argued that many black family characteristics, such as the economic roles of women, the value of community over the individual, indulgence of young children and babies, were African retentions.

Carol Stack's anthropological account of extended patterns of exchange among urban black women saw the black culture as more of a social adaptation to poverty than an expression of African heritage but rejected the notion that it was disorganized or pathological. In *All Our Kin* (1974), based on two years of fieldwork in a poor black community, she described a complex network of relationships between family and nonfamily members based on specific cultural characteristics that fostered mutual trust and sharing. Gutman (1976) argued that even during slavery, black family patterns were not simply a reflection of the needs of their white owners.

Rather, drawing on their African traditions and their need to survive in the new setting, blacks actively constructed their culture. Based on these important works, the social deficit model of the black family was replaced with a strength-resiliency perspective, which portrayed families as having developed culturally unique but strong and viable families despite the adversities they had faced.

The cultural perspective gained momentum and further articulation in the 1970s and 1980s, especially with the increasing focus on multiculturalism in education. The strength-resiliency perspective had tied aspects of the black culture to its African origins, but Afrocentric theorists did so much more explicitly. Many drew on the early work of Melville J. Herskovits (e.g., 1958), one of the few theorists of the 1950s who had rejected the thesis that the African culture was weak, savage, and easily destroyed by slavery. Herskovits held that African traits were evident in the language, motor characteristics, dance, music, art, and religion of black people as well as in their family systems.

Asante (1987) has devoted a great deal of scholarly research to understanding the pervasive influence of African culture on black American language and modes of interacting. He defined Afrocentricity as "placing African ideals at the center of any analysis that involves African culture and behavior" (p. 6) and has argued that "human actions cannot be understood apart from the emotions, attitudes, and cultural definitions of a given context" (p. 164). Afrocentricity is thus also a method of establishing the worldviews of oppressed people, a view Asante sees as different from the emphasis on social Darwinism and capitalism that has dominated Eurocentric thinking. Still, the African American cultural system is often difficult to conceptualize, because it is less about specific rules and value-based behaviors and more about ways of thinking and styles of interacting (Young, 1974). To better capture the qualitative dimensions of the African American culture, Boykin outlined nine interrelated expressions of the African culture: spirituality, harmony, movement, verve (an affinity for variable and intense stimulation), affect (emotional expressiveness), expressive individualism (cultivating distinctive and spontaneous self-expression), orality, and a social time perspective (Boykin & Toms, 1985).

Wade W. Nobles (1985) has worked diligently to document continuities between African and black family systems, arguing that the "underlying principle and basic structure [and] functions of the Black family [are] ultimately traceable to its African value system and/or some modification thereof" (p. 74). Although black people are diverse in many ways, he saw a sense of Africanity as a common cultural theme. *Africanity* includes an ethos of survival of the group and a oneness of being, which are often manifested in patterns of collective responsibility and cooperative work (Nobles, 1974, pp. 12-15).

Child Socialization in Cultural Context

Cultural values affect the organization of family life and the child-rearing strategies of black Americans. Nobles considered child-centeredness the key characteristic of black families, as children symbolize the continuity of life. This value is an aspect of the ethos of group survival.

Other researchers have consistently noted the centrality of childbearing among black Americans. Stack pointed out that both men and women in her research saw having children as a "natural and highly desirable phenomenon." Ladner (1971) argued that the "one common standard for becoming a woman that was accepted by the majority of the people in the community" for young girls was giving birth to their first child (p. 215). The importance of childbearing describes the special status often attached to motherhood. For example, Nobles (1974) speaks of a special mother-child bond that cannot be explained by slavery but is "deeply rooted in our African heritage and philosophical orientation" (p. 15), an observation reinforced by many ethnographic researchers.

African-based norms are used to create the structures of families and notions about who has responsibility for caring for children. Nobles (1985) pointed out that in the black culture, multiple parent figures, interfamilial consensual adoptions, close family networking, gender flexibility role definition, and child-rearing norms are important traits:

> Generally child-rearing practices in Black families are characterized by an atmosphere of family orientation and unconditional love which place a special emphasis on strong family ties, respect for the elders and see the child as possessing a natural goodness. Within this concept the child's feelings of competence are confirmed through his participation in household activities. In Black families children are socialized to assume significant responsibilities and express mature social behavior at a young age. (p. 84)

Similarly, Asante described a sense of communalism, social interaction, and sharing that characterize so many black families by explaining their African origins:

> The African finds energy and life in the midst of persons; he or she does not escape to mountains, or the valleys, or the seashores in order to find energy. There is no "great tradition" of withdrawal in the African or African American traditions; ours is preeminently a tradition of remarkable encountering with others. (p. 187)

There is a strong communal aspect of child rearing in West African cultures, as children are seen as part of large extended family networks.

Caldwell (1996), in his observations on the West African family system, points out that children are taught to regard parents and other relatives as being alike, and to accept living with any of them as the natural thing to do. Thus, there is an intense social interaction with others that starts at the moment of birth. Young (1970), based on the time she spent observing and living in a southern community, described the unique ways in which black parents interacted with their babies, often attributing to the infant the assertive tendencies that are typically valued among blacks. She also explained that babies were always welcome and that they live in an almost wholly human environment: "Cribs, baby carriages, and highchairs are almost never seen. The baby is held and carried most of the time, and when it is laid down it is seldom without company" (pp. 275-276). Infants are exposed to constant stimulation from a broad array of people of all ages, and blacks value social adaptation and oral responsiveness in their children. Typically, parents take great pride in infants allowing themselves to be held and cuddled by an array of people without fussing or crying.

Janice E. Hale's (1986) extensive research on black children also cites evidence that the descendants of West Africa have some distinctive socialization values. Drawing on earlier research findings, she described mothers of West African descent as especially valuing three characteristics in their children: social breadth, autonomy, and expressionism (p. 55). Social breadth is seen in the special value mothers place on having their children interact with many rather than few people, and their tendency to frequently entrust their children to the care of other family members and nonrelatives. Collins (1987) has also pointed out that the West African tradition does not view mothering as "a privatized nurturing 'occupation' reserved for biological mothers" (p. 4) but as a responsibility shared by the community. Stack (1974) saw child sharing as an important aspect of the black culture, not only because it fostered mutual trust and sharing, but also as a strategy to deal with teenage pregnancy and poverty.

Autonomy means that mothers tend to encourage early self-care and self-reliance in their children. This observation has been supported in a study by Bartz and Levine (1978) comparing three ethnic groups. They observed that black parents "press most for acceleration of development, are the most concerned about a child wasting time, [and] exercise the most control over their children" (p. 715). Black parents often take pride in having a child weaned and toilet trained at an early age. In some cases, this emphasis on early development is motivated by the arrival of an additional child. Young (1970) pointed out that by age 3, children were often expected to join the "toddlers' gang," thus ending the extensive attention and care they once received from mothers. Caldwell's (1996) study of West African family systems pointed out a stark contrast between the lavish affection given infants and toddlers and the harsh treatment of older children.

According to his research, many older children are fostered out to relatives for whom they are forced to work like servants.

Expressionism is defined in terms of spontaneous behavior: Mothers place little emphasis on delayed gratification and denial of impulse (Hale, 1986). As children mature, the development of a distinctive style is also important, as black children usually derive little esteem from the dominant society's definitions of physical beauty or success. As Hale has pointed out, "style means not only what you do, but *how* you do it; it emphasizes verbal ability, personality, wit, strength, intelligence, speed" (p. 67). Asante, noting that black people expect the use of certain expressions and enjoy certain kinds of humor, describes *styling* as "the conscious or unconscious manipulation of language or mannerisms to influence favorably the hearers of a message" (p. 39). Among children, expression often takes the form of perfecting styles of walking and using distinctive language patterns.

Thus, children grow up exposed to the mainstream, the minority, and the black culture, creating some complexities in their socialization process. All children are not, however, equally immersed in these cultures; this varies based on social class and family background factors. For example, I found that parents who are newly middle class often try to dissociate themselves from the values that have been associated with low-income African Americans. Some parents are aware of and feel stigmatized by the stereotypes that have been attached to African Americans in general, and avoid engaging in particular cultural expressions. For others, however, the black culture affirms the ethnic identity of children and gives them an alternative source of pride and self-esteem. Although it does not necessarily conflict with the dominant culture, there are instances in which it creates difficulties for children. Children must sometimes learn to display the different behaviors in different social settings—they must act black around blacks but not around whites—and are sometimes penalized for not doing so. Their black peers may reinforce the value of speaking Black English and perfecting certain styles of dance, athletic prowess, and self-presentation to fit in, but they find these same behaviors negatively evaluated in the dominant culture and an obstacle to their success.

Children immersed in the African American culture may find themselves uncomfortable in predominantly white settings, while those immersed in the dominant culture are often criticized by their black peers for "acting white." Hale (1986) points out that for some black children, there is a conflict among the black cultural emphasis on survival of the group, interdependence, and cooperation and the dominant culture's emphasis on competition and individualism. Similarly, Holliday (1985), using an ecological approach to understanding the behaviors of black children, found that children relying on skills that are effective in their own homes and neighborhoods are often defined as intellectually or culturally deficient in schools.

The Underclass Controversy:
A Reemergence of Culture as Pathology

In this chapter, I have examined the impact of class and culture on child rearing separately, while arguing that there is a great deal of overlap between the two concepts. In recent decades, the underclass controversy has both reignited the historic debate over structure versus culture as the source of behavior and has shown their interactive nature. The traditional structural view in social science attributed racial differences in family organization and economic status to the barriers that blacks faced in American society. Despite the recent articulation of the culture as strength view, the primary message during the civil rights era was that racial integration and greater opportunity would result in greater family stability and conformity among African Americans. Since then, overt racism and discrimination (while still common in America) have diminished due to racial integration, equal opportunity, and affirmative action. Still, black families in many ways (e.g., unemployment, divorce) fare worse today than they did prior to the civil rights movement.

The extension of civil rights has allowed many blacks to advance their education, experience social class mobility, and move from inner-city to suburban neighborhoods. Yet the educational gains and economic progress that African Americans had begun to make in the 1960s were stagnating by the 1970s. This decline in status in the post-civil rights era challenged the claim that racial injustice was entirely responsible for the hardships African Americans were experiencing. Increases in crime, violence, gang behavior, teenage pregnancy, and child abuse also made it difficult to argue that black families were strong, functional, and culturally adaptive.

In a controversial book published in 1978, *The Declining Significance of Race,* Wilson shifted the analysis from race to class by arguing that the rise of the postindustrial economy was the key factor in the disadvantages now faced by African Americans. Wilson argued that historical racism had created a legacy of economic inequality between whites and blacks but that the loss of manufacturing jobs, which were disproportionately filled by black men, was now perpetuating that inequality. This economic transition undermined the ability of black men to marry, provide for their families, or both, and was fueling nonmarital pregnancy and single-mother households. Its impact on young black men was especially devastating: Rates of violence and homicide grew among the ranks of those who were unemployed, leading some to declare them an "endangered species." Between 1985 and 1990, homicide became the leading cause of death among young black men (Fulbright-Anderson, 1996). It seemed that an almost intractable black underclass had emerged displaying behaviors that contradicted the values of both the mainstream and the black culture.

The term *underclass* was coined in 1963 by Gunnar Myrdal, an economist who used the word to describe those persons experiencing job loss or unemployment as a result of deindustrialization. He defined the underclass as "an unprivileged class of unemployed, unemployables and underemployed who are more and more hopelessly set apart from the nation at large and do not share in its life, its ambitions and its achievements" (quoted in Gans, 1995, p. 28). By the late 1960s, many Western capitalist countries were experiencing the process of deindustrialization, leading to pronounced poverty and joblessness in urban areas, especially among young men. Wacquant (1993) compares deindustrialization in Chicago and the Red Belt of France, noting that what followed in each case was widespread unemployment and the development of xenophobic ideologies that stigmatize the poor. He points out, however, that in the United States, these ideologies are socially constructed on the basis of race and are especially likely to stigmatize and denigrate African Americans.

A recent book by Herbert Gans, *The War Against the Poor* (1995), describes how the notion of the underclass was transformed from an economic into a racial and behavioral concept. He tracks the increased usage of the concept, especially by journalists in popular magazines, as a way to describe the *behaviors* of urban blacks rather than their *economic* plight. In addition to labeling and stereotyping poor blacks in an ostensibly race-neutral manner, the concept is broad enough to include other groups, such as recent immigrants and the homeless, as part of the undeserving poor. Gans summarizes four aspects of the ideology of undeserving poor: (a) that they reject the values of the mainstream culture, (b) that men are lazy and unwilling to work, (c) that adolescent females have an "unhealthy and immoral taste for early sexual activity and having babies as adolescents," and (d) that they must be forced to change their values by policies that penalize these behaviors (pp. 6-7).

Conservative theorists who emphasize the behavioral aspects of the underclass argue that the problem lies not so much in an economic transition but in the fact that those in the underclass have rejected the value of work in favor of liberal welfare programs. Murray (1984), for example, strips the behaviors of the poor from the social-political context of job loss and growing racial inequality and defines the issue in terms of values and individual responsibility. He has argued that the underclass is a direct result of a proliferation of generous public assistance programs during the 1960s that actually increased poverty by creating disincentives for employment and marriage. His view of welfare policies as promoting nonmarital pregnancy and childbirth and single-parent families resonated well with the Reagan administration's contention that fraud and waste were prevalent in social welfare programs, and that the government should divest itself of responsibility for the poor.

The underclass debate has undermined the efforts of scholars who have labored to redeem, reconstruct, and validate the African American culture from a strength-resiliency perspective. As Jarrett (1994) has pointed out, the focus no longer seems to be on how poor black families have found the strength to adapt and survive. Instead, the notion of an underclass often assumes the presence of ghetto-specific cultural values that "positively [endorse] single motherhood, out-of-wedlock childbearing, welfare dependency, male irresponsibility, criminal behavior, low mobility aspirations, and more generally, family instability" (p. 32). This resurgence in research depicting the African American culture as consisting of a set of immoral and dysfunctional behaviors has made some researchers reluctant to discuss culture at all. As Sullivan (1989) has pointed out, however, this is "unfortunate because it leaves us in the dark as to how people deal collectively with economic disadvantage, prejudice, and the dilemmas of procreating and raising families under such conditions" (pp. 49-50).

At the heart of the underclass controversy is the issue of young single mothers who rely on the welfare system to care for their children. Despite the fact that the majority of those on welfare are not black, Fraser and Gordon (1994) point out that the concept of the welfare mother evokes the image of "young, unmarried, black women of uncontrolled sexuality" (p. 311). Conservative theorists have argued that nonmarital pregnancy and dependency are typical of the value system of the poor, an assertion challenged by most systematic research. Studies show that nonmarital pregnancy among adolescents is rarely the result of a personal decision or a cultural value. Still, those who grow up in poverty, in single-mother households, or both, consistently have a higher rate of nonmarital pregnancy. Wu and Martinson (1993) examined three possible explanations for this pattern. The child socialization hypothesis suggests girls are socialized to see single-parenthood as acceptable and desirable; the social control hypothesis, that two-parent families are capable of exercising greater control over their children's behavior; and the instability and change hypothesis, that major disruptions such as divorce, geographic moves, and so on create stress and damage the emotional security of children. Their findings supported the instability and change hypothesis: that for both black and Hispanic women, experiencing one or more changes in family situation significantly increased the risk of nonmarital birth.

Anderson's (1990) ethnographic research places the sexual conduct of poor young African Americans in social-political context by viewing it as "nothing less than the cultural manifestation of persistent poverty" (p. 113). Although their sexual urges and relations probably differ very little from their middle-class peers, with girls exchanging sex in the hope of obtaining love and marriage and boys seeking sexual gratification without responsibility or commitment, poor teenagers simply have less incentive to avoid pregnancy. Among the young men he interviewed, Anderson found that sexual prowess and babies are often evidence of manhood, especially in the absence of jobs or academic success. Thus, the results of sexuality are quite different for poor and middle-class youth. The difference is that "middle-class youths take a stronger interest in their future and know what a pregnancy can do to derail it . . . [while poor] adolescents see no future to derail—no hope for a tomorrow much different from today—hence they see little to lose by having a child out of wedlock" (p. 113).

In a recent book, Wilson (1996) shows how job loss and unemployment among young men help produce alternative cultural values and behaviors, which in turn reinforce negative stereotypes and perpetuate unemployment. He interviewed employers to determine the difficulties they have in hiring black males, and found that they described black males as lacking the basic social skills needed to successfully obtain work and as having numerous moral deficiencies. For example, employers pointed out that blacks dress inappropriately for job interviews and complain about their poor treatment and relations with previous employers. Black males were further described as frequently being tardy or absent from work and, perhaps more important, simply unreliable. One employer, asked why inner-city black men cannot find jobs, is quoted as saying,

> Number one . . . they're not dependable. They have never been taught that when you have a job you have to be there at a certain time and you're to stay there until the time is finished. They may not show up on time. They just disappear for an hour or two at a time. They'll call you up and say, "Ahhh, I'm not coming in today" and they don't even call you up. . . . And the second thing is theft. (Wilson, 1996, p. 120)

This work shows that employers highly stereotype young black men, often based on very few experiences. It also makes clear, however, that those lacking employment experience are often poorly informed about the requisites for obtaining and keeping employment.

Wilson's work complements that of other scholars who have sought to acknowledge the validity of culture while explaining it within the context of structural forces and the opportunities that are available to various groups. For example, contemporary cultural theorists challenge the as-

sumption that a consistent set of cultural values underlie and explain behaviors. Swidler (1986) describes the traditional classical approach as one
that "assumes that culture shapes action by supplying ultimate ends or
values . . . thus making values the central causal element in culture"
(p. 273). She suggests, however, that this is rarely the case. Rather, cultures
are merely "tool kits" from which people construct "strategies for action,"
more of a "style or a set of skills and habits than a set of preferences or
wants" (p. 275). Thus, the connection between what people value and how
they behave is often tenuous or nonexistent, especially during what Swidler
calls "unsettled periods."

Gambetta (1987) describes the behaviors of the poor from an extreme
"pushed from behind," or structural, perspective. He argues that the behaviors of individuals are often seen as propelled by external constraints
that leave little room for free choice. People are "pushed" to engage in
behaviors not by values but by "causes, either social or psychological, that
are opaque to the individual consciousness" (p. 11). Clearly, the majority
of poor people do not hold a set of values oppositional to those found in
the mainstream culture; rather, they struggle to manage their lives as well
as they can within the context of a quite limited opportunity system.

Conclusions

This chapter has provided the basic historical foundation for the book
by analyzing black families and, more specifically, their childbearing and
child-rearing behaviors within the contexts of slavery, social class, and culture. I have analyzed the system of slavery both as reinforcing and as vio-
lating the African cultural heritage. For example, the economic needs of
white slave owners may have reinforced African norms supporting procreation, motherhood, dual work-family roles for women, and extended families, yet slavery clearly violated African traditions of patriarchy, polygyny,
and the overall sanctity of marriage and family relationships. Slaves were
first and foremost workers and were forced to make their economic roles
eclipse their family roles. Although most studies have emphasized the importance of children to their slave parents, it is also the case that having
and rearing children was often a burden for slave mothers. They frequently
had no say in their own sexual and reproductive lives, and they were forced
to work long hours and to care for their own children as well as those of
their white owners with very little assistance from fathers. Moreover, the
sharecropping system that evolved after the abolition of slavery continued
to view black people primarily as workers and provided little support for
the creation of stable, breadwinner-homemaker families.

The massive migration of blacks to the North during the early 1900s increased their social class diversity, and these class distinctions became the focus of family studies during this era. For the most part, however, these studies still focused inordinately on low-income blacks, detailing the "pathologies" that plagued their families, such as abusive parents, single mothers, absent fathers, and parents' inability to teach their children sexual restraint. Researchers saw these problems as the result of slavery and the racial caste system rather than of cultural values; in fact, they argued that the African culture had been destroyed and that black people, when it was economically feasible, fully embraced the American cultural value system. During the civil rights era, however, both the notion of low-income black families as pathological and the view that the black culture had been destroyed by slavery were challenged. The strength-resiliency perspective was born as scholars documented the adaptative strategies of the poor, often undergirded by a retention of African-based values of family cooperation and mutual assistance. In this chapter, I have tried to document child- rearing attitudes and behaviors that capture the role of culture among blacks. Despite this revival of interest in culture, the underclass concept has caused the emphasis on culture to fall into disrepute among many scholars who view it as blaming the plight of the poor on their own behaviors and values.

Having provided the historical background of parenting among African Americans, in the next chapter I began to draw extensively on the data that were collected for this book through interviews and surveys. I examine how parents prioritize the values they teach their children, their future hopes for the children, and their views of the parenting role. I discuss their discipline strategies and the issue of child abuse. Drawing on the context of the class-culture overview that I have provided, I note the importance parents place on the values of responsibility, sexual restraint, and education.

3

Parenting Work

Black child socialization must necessarily be different from that of children reared in the white middle-class tradition, because of the sociohistorical differences that exist between the two groups . . . [The lower-class pattern] also differs to a great extent from the Black middle class, whose child-rearing practices are often similar to those of the white middle-class, but yet dissimilar in the sense that Black parents can never give their children the ultimate protection from racism which white parents exercise.

Joyce Ladner, *Tomorrow's Tomorrow* (1971, p. 96)

The sociological study of the family offers two interrelated approaches to understanding child socialization processes: general theories of child development and theories about effective child-rearing strategies. Child development theories, such as those proposed by Sigmund Freud, George Herbert Mead, and others, describe children as moving sequentially through specific stages of development, often propelled by a combination of biological and social forces. Theories about child rearing tend to be more prescriptive in nature, either overtly or implicitly, in that they analyze parenting strategies and the consequences of those strategies, and sometimes offer parental advice. Baumrind's (1968) classic conceptualization of three parenting styles—authoritative, authoritarian, and permissive—and their impact on children falls into this category, as does advice literature embracing a social psychological approach, such as that of Benjamin Spock and John Rosemond.

Developmental and child-rearing approaches to child socialization do overlap, of course, especially in the sense that they see nurture rather than nature as most important and place a great deal of emphasis on parenting work, that is, what parents actually think, do, and say as they rear their children. Neither the developmental nor the child-rearing theories, however, are particularly helpful in analyzing black parenting work. Created primarily on the basis of the work of white European scholars during the early 1900s, developmental theories emphasize culturally biased themes such as autonomy, separation, and individualism as the outcomes of successful child socialization. These concepts are less applicable to the cultural heritage of black people, who often try to instill in their children the values of unity, cooperation, and mutual support in families. Moreover, the values espoused by the dominant developmental approaches often assume that all parents have full access to societal resources and privileges, and that proper development cannot unfold outside of this context.

Child-rearing theories also often stigmatize black parents in various ways, such as by labeling them as having an authoritarian parenting style that is assumed to produce incompetent, discontented, withdrawn, and distrustful children (Berns, 1993). These assessments ignore the sociocultural meanings of child socialization practices and the social structural forces that shape those meanings. For example, black parents are often seen as overly harsh and restrictive with their children, yet many live in neighborhoods where children face substantial social-environmental risks. In that context, these same behaviors could be seen as responsible and protective. In many cases, parenting behaviors are neither inherently beneficial nor harmful but may be seen as either, depending on the cultural context of meanings and expectations. The recent focus on culturally diverse families has helped challenge the notion that the child-rearing values of middle-class white Americans are essential for optimal child development.

Although it is generally assumed that the family is the most important socialization agent and that parents have a profound impact on child socialization outcomes, much empirical research has focused almost exclusively on how social structural forces (e.g., socioeconomic inequality) and nonfamily institutions (e.g., the educational system) affect childhood socialization outcomes. This research is consistent with the traditional sociological approach to understanding families, which often casts the family as the dependent variable and views its structure, roles, and organization as shaped in response to other social processes. But it has led some recent theorists to assert that, in terms of its impact on childhood outcomes, the "family question" has been almost completely ignored (Lichter, Cornell, & Eggebeen, 1993). This is especially the case when studies of black families focus exclusively on social forces and public policies, and imply that they are solely responsible for shaping the viability of the families and the welfare of their children. Such a view renders human agency invisible and assumes that families are completely at the mercy of external forces. In this chapter, I address the "family question" by looking at parenting work—the values, attitudes, and child-rearing activities of parents. I do so using a social capital framework, which assumes that social relationships are resources for individuals (Coleman, 1988).

The Social Capital Perspective

In recent years, some theorists have begun to bring the family back into the analysis of child socialization, noting that there are numerous family background characteristics that shape childhood socialization outcomes. Coleman (1988) separated the family background factors that may affect children into three different components: financial capital (a family's wealth), human capital (parents' education and its impact on the cognitive environment of children), and social capital (the relationships between children and their parents and other important family members). The first two of the background components are included in analyses of social class. Perhaps the least amount of research on child socialization has been done on social capital, which includes the impact on children of social norms, reciprocal relationships, and information sharing. Coleman (1988) has asserted, however, that "human capital may be irrelevant to outcomes for children if parents are not an important part of their children's lives, if their human capital is employed exclusively at work or elsewhere outside the home" (p. S110).

The concept of social capital expands the narrow focus that links child socialization outcomes exclusively to family structure or poverty by creating a framework that views parents as active constructers of activities and experiences that affect the development of their children (Coleman 1988; Lichter et al., 1993; Parcel & Menaghan, 1993). It captures aspects of child rearing that transcend structural constraints and includes parents' value orientations and the time and energy they invest in raising their children, as well as the nature of the parent-child relationship.

Although the concept of social capital makes the child-rearing work that parents do important, it is a controversial concept that must be carefully examined and cautiously embraced. It is commendable in acknowledging the importance of the work parents do in rearing their children, yet it runs the risk of stripping child socialization outcomes from the larger social-environmental context. Such a view could ignore the broad array of non-family socialization forces that affect children and could imply that parents, regardless of their resources or circumstances, are completely responsible for effectively socializing their children. The idea of social capital can also be used to support conservative family ideologies, especially those that contend that two-parent families with nonemployed mothers are best able to invest in the social and emotional development of their children. Such notions can perpetuate the myth that black parents do a poor job of socializing their children and that single-parent families do an even poorer job, and resurrect victim-blaming approaches that pathologize black families. Although acknowledging the limitations of the social capital approach, I use it here not to ignore larger structural forces that no doubt influence childhood outcomes but to emphasize the fact that parents work hard to rear their children, and their efforts do make a difference.

Current Value Priorities

The surveys completed by the 729 parents in this study sought first to analyze parents' current value priorities for their children. To this end, parents were given three values and asked to rank these values in terms of their importance, from 1 (most important) to 3 (least important). Parental responses were then converted into dichotomous variables; that is, the value either was given top priority or it was not. In my analysis of findings, I examine overall racial differences between the parents surveyed and then look at the impact of social class, especially education and income, on the values of black parents. Because the sample of white parents (204) in this study is much smaller than the sample of black parents (525), I do not look at social class differences among whites.

As indicated by the percentages in Table 3.1, the overall prioritizing of the three values was the same for both black and white parents: Most ranked happiness and self-esteem as their top priority; a much smaller percentage ranked respect and obedience as their top priority; and an even smaller percentage said having the child do well in school was a top priority. Yet race was important in the extent to which parents embraced these values for their children: White parents (66%) were significantly more likely than black parents (56%) to give happiness and self-esteem their highest priority. Although the most common response of black parents was to rank happiness and self-esteem as their most important current value, social class influenced the overall ranking of this value. Three groups of black parents were less likely than others to rank this as their top priority: parents who were single, those with a household income of $15,000 or less, and those who had a high school education or less. This suggest that concern over the psychological well-being of children increases with socioeconomic status among blacks, perhaps because other issues, such as school performance, are less problematic among those who are more affluent.

The second most important priority for all parents is respect and obedience, with black parents (38%) significantly more likely than white parents (22%) to give this their top ranking. Among black parents, having a low income and less education, and being single, increased the importance placed on respect and obedience. An emphasis on respect and obedience based on age is characteristic of the traditional cultural value system of African Americans, with respect for elders being especially important. Of

Table 3.1 Current Values: Percentage of Parents Ranking Each Item as Their Top Priority for the Focus Child

	Comparison of black parents and white parents:		
	All (N = 729)	Blacks (N = 525)	Whites (N = 204)
Happiness and self-esteem	58.7	55.7	66.0***
Respect and obedience	33.7	38.4	22.4***
Doing well in school	26.1	29.6	17.9***
	Comparison of low-income and high-income black parents:		
	All (N = 318)	Low Income (N = 201)	High Income (N = 117)
Happiness and self-esteem	56.1	54.0	59.1
Respect and obedience	35.5	38.7	30.9
Doing well in school	29.2	37.5	15.7***
	Comparison of less educated and more educated black parents:		
	All (N = 520)	Less Educated (N = 220)	More Educated (N = 300)
Happiness and self-esteem	55.7	51.4	58.4
Respect and obedience	38.4	44.3	34.2*
Doing well in school	29.6	42.1	21.1***

$*p < .10; **p < .05; ***p < .01.$
NOTE: Tables do not necessarily equal 100% because a few parents chose more than one value as their top priority. *Low income* equals $15,000 per year or less, and *high income* equals more than $30,000 per year. *Less educated* means having a high school diploma or less, and *more educated* means having at least some college through postgraduate work.

interest, when parents who were interviewed were asked to describe the most important thing they were trying to teach their children, respect was the most frequently discussed issue: It was only when given a survey of preselected values that the category of happiness and self-esteem was ranked as number one. The increased importance of respect and obedience among low-income black parents may be due to their greater conformity to the traditional black value system or a greater perception that their children are rebellious or out of control. Their values may also, as Kohn (1977) has pointed out, be based on the fact that lower-income parents have occupations where conformity to authority is essential for success.

For African American parents, respect and obedience often go with other values, such as honesty. As indicated by the mother of a 7-year-old son,

Those are the main ones—honesty and respecting other people. Honesty is the one we deal with at least once a week. We tell him it's best to tell he truth up front, and he'll get into less trouble if he does, instead of having us find out later on.

Black parents emphasize respect as a sign of deference, especially when communicating with older people. A single mother of a 13-year-old daughter replied,

Most important is to be honest, and then to treat people the way she wants to be treated by others. To respect older people and that she has to realize that she cannot talk to adults the same way she talks to her friends, no matter who the adult is.

Despite the fact that respect for adults is one of the most frequently mentioned values of the parents in this study, there is evidence that some black parents are questioning the notion that children should automatically be expected to respect and obey all adults. Maggie Terrance, a 35-year-old mother of two children, sees respect as the product of a close relationship with a child:

A lot of times older people talk about kids not respecting them, but respect is earned. It's not given. And if you're going to go and tell a [child to respect you], but you don't have a relationship with them, they're not going to pay you any attention—if you're not spending any time with them, trying to find out what makes them tick, to find out what they're like.

Overall, parents were least likely to rank doing well in school as their number one priority, although black parents were significantly more likely than white parents to do so. The priority placed on education is strongest among low-income and less educated black parents (see Table 3.1): Parents in the lower social classes are not only more likely to have children already having academic problems, but they are especially likely to view education as their children's only route to a better life. The overall low priority ranking of education among parents stemmed from having to choose between three very important values. In interviews, parents often objected to having to prioritize these values, arguing that all three were important and interrelated. On the surveys, a few parents ranked more than one value as their top priority; some explained their choices in the margins of the survey by saying that children who are happy and have good self-esteem will naturally do well in school.

A subsample of respondents were asked how well their children were doing in school and how important it was to them to have the child attend

Table 3.2 Current Academic Performance and Parental Aspirations for College Attendance

	Comparison of black parents and white parents:		
	All (N = 483)	Blacks (N = 317)	Whites (N = 166)
Child is doing above average in school	40.4	37.2	46.4
Ranks attending college as very important	71.9	74.8	66.0
	Comparison of low-income and high-income black parents:		
	All (N = 118)	Low Income (N = 129)	High Income (N = 59)
Child is doing above average in school	33.0	29.4	40.7
Ranks attending college as very important	77.8	77.3	78.9
	Comparison of less educated and more educated black parents:		
	All (N = 317)	Less Educated (N = 128)	More Educated (N = 186)
Child is doing above average in school	37.2	34.4	39.2
Ranks attending college as very important	74.8	75.8	74.9

$*p < .10$; $**p < .05$; $***p < .01$.
NOTE: Only a subsample of respondents were asked these questions. For explanations of *low* and *high income* and *less* and *more educated,* see the note to Table 3.1.

college. The results are reported in Table 3.2. These data show that black parents (75%) are more likely than white parents (66%) to rank attending college as "very important" and, among black parents, neither education nor income influenced this desire. Academic preparation for college, however, is often influenced by success in the early years of schooling, and white parents, as a group, were significantly more likely than black parents to say that their children were doing above-average schoolwork. Socioeconomic status was positively correlated with the child's current school performance among blacks, but, even so, fewer black children were doing well in school than white children. This suggests that while blacks have very high educational aspirations for their children, these aspirations are not based on their current academic performance. Moreover, if children are not excelling at this young age, the probability that they will start doing so later in their academic careers is not great. Still, black parents were significantly more likely than white parents to say that they had discussed jobs or careers with their children, and to say that the child had a specific job/career interest

Table 3.3 Percentage of Parents Who Have Discussed Jobs/Careers With Their Children and Percentage of Parents Who Say Focus Child Has a Specific Job/Career Interest

	Comparison of black parents and white parents:		
	All (N = 729)	Blacks (N = 525)	Whites (N = 204)
Has discussed jobs/careers with child	78.1	79.4	74.5**
Child has specific job/career interest	61.6	62.7	58.8**

	Comparison of low-income and high-income black parents:		
	All (N = 318)	Low Income (N = 201)	High Income (N = 117)
Has discussed jobs/careers with child	79.4	78.6	80.3
Child has specific job/career interest	63.2	63.7	62.4

	Comparison of less educated and more educated black parents:		
	All (N = 525)	Less Educated (N = 220)	More Educated (N = 300)
Has discussed jobs/careers with child	79.4	74.1	83.0**
Child has specific job/career interest	62.7	62.3	63.0

*$p < .10$; **$p < .05$; ***$p < .01$.

NOTE: For explanations of *low* and *high income* and *less* and *more educated,* see the note to Table 3.1.

(see Table 3.3). African American parents do not simply expect their children to plan and think about their futures but are actually involved in helping their children do so.

My interview data reveal that parents in middle-income families start to stress the value of college at an early age. Laura Raymond, a 31-year-old married mother of two, pointed out that she and her husband invest a lot of time in helping 13-year-old Aaron shape his career ambitions. They want him to view going to college as the next logical step in his education, rather than an option. Like many black parents, they encourage Aaron to think beyond the possibility of being a star athlete—an image that often dominates the thinking of adolescent males:

> I think he has already made up his mind that he wants to be an architect—well, he's narrowed it down to two things . . . football player and an architect. . . . I said, "It's nice to be a football player, but don't put football player first. I don't want to kill that dream, because if you are good at football, that's

wonderful. But don't rely on football." So he's leaning toward architecture, he likes the engineer part because he likes math and all that. . . . A lot of people [tell their children] "When you get out of high school, you can do anything you want." But that's not what we say. We say, "Well, you don't have that far to go. You get out of high school, you go to college, maybe grad school, and then you're through." And we say that to him so much that he thinks . . . he's at least got eight years to go. Preferably ten, but we tell him at least eight years to go.

Vickie Mellon, the 39-year-old divorced mother of Charles, age 9, also makes an effort to shape and elevate her son's career aspirations:

He wants to play basketball, but we try to stress right now that he's going to Harvard, and he's going to be a doctor. I don't believe you can wait until a child gets in high school and then start talking about college. You have to start steering them towards college from the time they're in kindergarten. . . . It's a form of brainwashing, but they need that. And I had a brother who went to Harvard and became a doctor, so he has a good role model.

Education:
Obstacles and Opportunities

One of the most consistent findings in studies of African American families is that parents place a high value on their children's education and that they invest whatever resources they have in helping their children reach academic goals (Blau, 1981; Higginbotham, 1981; Scanzoni, 1977). Parents often feel that education is the most powerful way for their children to challenge racial stereotypes, overcome the racial barriers to success, and advance the cause of racial justice. Without a college education, blacks are even more likely than whites to end up in low- paying, dead-end jobs. Willie (1985, p. 33) studied a class-diversified sample of blacks and whites and found that 72% of young black workers without extensive educational preparation ended up in blue-collar jobs, compared with only 33% of young white workers.

Despite the emphasis placed on education, succeeding academically has always been a challenge for African Americans because of structural barriers and ideological factors. As slaves, black people were not allowed to learn how to read or write, yet many risked their lives to do so, and a significant minority were literate by the end of slavery. Once slavery ended, blacks quickly began to build their own educational institutions and to attend the public schools open to them, although the demands of work often made their school attendance sporadic. Billingsley (1992, p. 119) notes that less than two years after the end of the Civil War, more than 236 schools for black children had been established in the state of Georgia alone.

Most nineteenth-century Americans could not even imagine allowing blacks and whites to attend school together, and by the end of the century the informal separate but equal doctrine had received the legal sanction of the U.S. Supreme Court. In the field of education, it meant that black students were likely to attend racially segregated schools plagued with overcrowding, inadequate materials and supplies, and dilapidated facilities. Nearly a century after the abolition of slavery, the *Brown v. Topeka Board of Education* decision of 1954 mandated the end of segregation in schools, yet schools still have not been effectively desegregated (Baratz-Snowden, 1993). Poor children and children of color today still receive significantly fewer educational resources than do affluent white children, perpetuating historic inequities in educational opportunities (Darling-Hammond, 1995, p. 343). In addition to facing inferior public schools, African American children are less likely than white children (4% versus 10%) to receive an education at a private school chosen by their parents (U.S. Department of Education, 1996a).

These structural barriers to academic success are accentuated by the continuous recycling of ideologies arguing that blacks are innately intellectually inferior—ideologies that adversely affect the confidence of students and the willingness of teachers to invest in them. These notions are centuries old but gained their "scientific" grounding in the social Darwinism of the 1800s, which saw Europeans playing a superior role in processes of natural evolution and selection (Dennis, 1995). They have most recently been reignited by Hernstein and Murray's (1994) book *The Bell Curve*. According to Darling-Hammond (1995, p. 341), the bell-curve hypothesis rests primarily on the presumptions that intelligence is inherited and distributed unequally across groups, that intelligence is represented by a single measure of cognitive ability that predicts life success, and that intelligence is only minimally affected by environmental factors. One result of these theories is that black children have often been ignored and stigmatized by educators who have labeled them as unintelligent and, according to Holliday (1985), as children who generally are "unable to talk right, think right, act right, or feel right" (p. 53). Similarly, black parents have been described as uninterested or investing too little in their children's education.

Data from the U.S. Department of Education (1996b), however, indicate that black parents are more involved in some school-related activities than are white parents, often in an effort to supplement or compensate for the inadequate education their children receive in schools. African American parents of eighth graders were more likely than their white counterparts to say that they talked regularly with their child about school experiences and their plans for after high school, that they limited the number of hours of television their children watched on school days, and had rules about maintaining a certain grade point average. They were slightly less likely, however, to have helped with homework or attended parent-teacher meetings. Harry, Allen, and McLaughlin's (1995) research also challenges the assertion that African American parents are simply too passive in advocating for their children's education. Instead, studies that directly observe parent-teacher interactions show that black parents often become confused and resentful in an institutional setting where their own perspectives are delegitimized. In their study of parental involvement in a special education program, parents were initially actively involved but became disillusioned when they felt their children were inappropriately placed or given stigmatizing labels.

African American scholars and leaders have challenged the negative assessments of black children's intellectual ability by delineating the structural-cultural barriers that they face, studying the unique learning styles of black children, and creating alternative schools to meet their needs. Research has shown that academic achievement is higher when children feel a sense of control over their environment, and studies have shown that a low sense of control is more prevalent among black than white children (Blau, 1981). Other family variables also affect learning; for example, family size has the strongest negative effect on children's IQ and achievement scores, as it tends to depress mothers' valuation of and investment in education (Blau, 1981). Luster and McAdoo (1994), noting that numerous studies have identified family and social factors that are related to poor academic outcomes among African American children, devised an "advantage index" of factors related to success. They found that the family characteristics and processes of high-achieving black students included a supportive home environment, a small family, an income above the poverty level, and having educated mothers who scored high on intelligence and self-esteem measures.

Willis (1989) summarized extensive research showing that black students, because of their cultural background, have learning styles that are different from white students', although not deficient. She cites research showing that from birth until age 3, black children consistently score higher on tests of intelligence and development than do white children, yet they fall behind in the early years of school. African American children, according to Willis, have distinct ways of perceiving, conceptualizing, and problem-solving that are not incorporated in the dominant Eurocentric model of education. These learning styles essentially include a holistic perspective that includes social-affective experiences, harmony, and creative expression.

The black cultural values that stem from racial oppression may also be an obstacle to academic success for black children. Numerous observers have found that black students who perform well academically are often rejected and criticized by their peers, who have defined success in school as a "white thing." Fordham and Ogbu (1986) formalize this observation by using a cultural-ecological framework to explain the high rate of poor school performance among African Americans—a framework that has both instrumental and expressive components. They begin by acknowledging that black people differ from other immigrants who came to the United States: They were involuntary immigrants, incorporated into America through slavery, conquest, and caste relationships. Thus, from an instrumental standpoint, black children encounter substandard schools and learn that their academic talent is questioned and disregarded by teachers. They also learn that success does not give them equal access to jobs, wages, and prestige, a fact that diminishes their incentive to invest in education. In addition, an expressive component evolves that militates against black academic success: an oppositional collective or social identity. Many black students learn to denigrate the school experience and their peers who perform well in school, often accusing them of acting and talking white rather than being black. Fordham and Ogbu relate the experiences of Abdul-Jabbar, who was transferred from a predominantly white to an all-black school:

> It was my first time away from home, my first experience in an all-black situation, and I found myself being punished for doing everything I'd ever been taught was right. I got all A's and was hated for it; I spoke correctly and was called a punk. I had to learn a new language simply to be able to deal with the threats. I had good manners and was a good little boy and paid for it with my hide. (quoted in Fordham & Ogbu, 1986, p. 177)

In recent years, there has been much concern over the failure of African American males to achieve in traditional educational settings, as their rate of academic failure, behavioral problems, and apathy in schools is especially high. For example, Midgette and Glenn (1993) point out that black males constitute only 8.5% of all public school students but 36% of special education students and 37% of all school suspensions. They are more likely than other students to be placed in remedial programs and lower-track classes, and their high school dropout rate is as high as 60% in some cities. Black male students, according to Midgette and Glenn, are especially likely to experience the "Invisible Child Syndrome," where they are ignored and discouraged from learning. This concern about black males has led to widespread support among some for the development of all-male African American academies. Midgette and Glenn describe the advantages of these academies as promoting high academic standards, self-esteem, responsibility, and self-help.

Despite these barriers, there is evidence of black progress. For example, the Scholastic Aptitude Test scores of African Americans increased 54 points between 1976 and 1994, while those of white students remained stable (Darling-Hammond, 1995). Overall, black children from middle-income families have made outstanding gains in academic performance during the past two decades. Brooks-Gunn, Klebanov, and Duncan (1996) recently examined the differences in the intelligence test scores of black and white 5-year-olds and found that black children's scores were one standard deviation lower than those of white children. However, they found that when one adjusts for poverty, which black children were three times more likely to experience than white children, the differential in IQ score was reduced by 52%, and adjustments for home environment reduced it by an additional 28%. They concluded that controlling for social and economic differences all but eliminated racial differences in the IQ scores. Armor (1992) documented the gains made by African American 13-year-olds during the past 20 years in both reading and mathematics. After systematically examining several possible explanations for these gains, including desegregation and compensatory programs, he presented a compelling argument that these gains were linked mostly to the socio-economic advances of African American parents.

As Baratz-Snowden (1993) points out, America continues to grapple with the issue of equal opportunity, most recently under the "opportunity to learn" banner. The meaning of equal opportunity in education has shifted in the current sociopolitical context, with less support for racial integration and more support for investing in community schools and measuring educational achievement. As a result of much litigation, the legal definition of opportunity to learn now includes four important obligations: specifying what children must learn, undertaking periodic needs assessments, providing needed resources for children who are not succeeding, and training teachers in new methods for educating students who are not performing well (Baratz-Snowden, 1993, pp. 314-315).

Future Hopes of Parents

Parents were asked which of the following they would most like to see their child have or develop as he or she grows up: a strong, loving family, a good education and a good job, or a kind and compassionate personality. While all three are important hopes for parents, the survey question aimed to determine more generally how parents defined success in the long run: Was it based mostly on a satisfying family life, achieving in the socio-economic arena, or simply being a happy, well-adjusted human being? As

Table 3.4 Future Hopes: Percentage of Parents Ranking Each Item as Their Top Priority for the Focus Child

	Comparison of black parents and white parents:		
	All (N = 729)	Blacks (N = 525)	Whites (N = 204)
A good education and job	57.2	60.9	50.0***
A strong/loving family	34.4	34.7	34.0
Being nice and compassionate	17.7	16.0	21.5

	Comparison of low-income and high-income black parents:		
	All (N = 318)	Low Income (N = 201)	High Income (N = 117)
A good education and job	62.7	70.7	49.1***
A strong/loving family	33.0	30.6	36.7**
Being nice and compassionate	19.4	18.0	21.7*

	Comparison of less educated and more educated black parents:		
	All (N = 525)	Less Educated (N = 220)	More Educated (N = 300)
A good education and job	60.6	72.0	52.4***
A strong/loving family	35.9	35.0	35.9
Being nice and compassionate	20.6	20.9	20.4

*$p < .10$; **$p < .05$; ***$p < .01$.

NOTE: Tables do not necessarily equal 100% because a few parents chose more than one item as their top priority. For explanations of *low* and *high income* and *less* and *more educated*, see the note to Table 3.1.

indicated on Table 3.4, the single most common response for black (61%) and white (50%) parents was having a good education and a good job, with the difference between the two races being statistically significant. Low-income and less educated blacks are also significantly more likely than their more affluent counterparts to emphasize the importance of having their children get an education and a good job. Explaining why he chose education/career as a top future hope for his 9-year-old son, Norman Rodney said, "A good education and job have to come first, then a strong loving family. You have to have a job before you can even get married." Black parents who were single, less educated, or earning less than $15,000 were especially likely to rank a good education and a good job as their number one priority, perhaps because they are less likely to take achievements for granted.

Having a strong and loving family was ranked as a top priority by nearly one-third of all parents; race, income, education, or marital status did not affect this ranking. Finally, about 20% or fewer parents said that having the child develop a kind and compassionate personality was their top priority, with black parents as a group being less concerned about this as a future hope than white parents.

The Parenting Role

Asked to choose which they felt was their most important parenting role—being a teacher and guide, a disciplinarian, or a provider—the majority of black (61%) and white (74%) parents ranked being a teacher/guide as their most important role (see Table 3.5). Being a good provider was ranked as number one by 39% of black parents and 26% of white parents. Only a small percentage of parents ranked being a disciplinarian as their most important role, although African American parents were about three times more likely to give this a top ranking than were white parents.

Based on interview data, the most popular way in which parents teach and guide children revolves around teaching responsibility. This emphasis on responsibility usually means that parents teach their children how to care for themselves and to contribute to the family. These findings are consistent with studies showing that black children are quite integrated into the activities of the domestic arena, even in two-parent families, and that they are expected to care for themselves and to participate in domestic tasks (Billingsley, 1992; Goldscheiter & Waite, 1991). Responsibility is a major theme among African American parents, but social class shapes the direction of their teaching. For low-income parents, responsibility is often defined mostly in terms of self-care, especially early social, biological, and physical maturation. Research has indicated that parents want their children to be fairly self-sufficient at an early age, and that parents often measure this initially by their ability to get the child toilet trained and weaned from the bottle or breast. They also emphasize responsibility in their expectations that children participate in the care and supervision of their younger siblings. As Bartz and Levine (1978) have pointed out, lower-class black parents believe more in the "value of strictness, expecting early assumption of responsibility by a child for his or her own body functions and personal feelings [and] expecting that a child's time be used wisely and not wasted" (pp. 717-718). And black parents were twice as likely as other parents to actually enforce their strict rules and training. Overall, low-income, single mothers in this study had fewer activities they expected children to carry out independently on a daily basis. One 22-year-old

Table 3.5 Parenting Role: Percentage of Parents Ranking Each Item as Their Most Important Parenting Role

| | Comparison of black parents and white parents: | | |
	All (N = 729)	Blacks (N = 525)	Whites (N = 204)
Being a teacher and guide	65.3	60.7	74.2***
Being a good provider	35.1	39.8	26.3***
Being a disciplinarian	7.4	9.7	3.4**

| | Comparison of low-income and high-income black parents: | | |
	All (N = 318)	Low Income (N = 201)	High Income (N = 117)
Being a teacher and guide	64.0	59.0	71.9*
Being a good provider	37.5	45.8	24.3***
Being a disciplinarian	12.2	14.9	8.2*

| | Comparison of less educated and more educated black parents: | | |
	All (N = 525)	Less Educated (N = 220)	More Educated (N = 300)
Being a teacher and guide	64.2	62.2	65.5
Being a good provider	38.7	45.9	33.6**
Being a disciplinarian	12.2	17.3	9.0*

$*p < .10; **p < .05; ***p < .01.$
NOTE: Tables do not necessarily equal 100% because a few parents chose more than one role as their most important. For explanations of *low* and *high income* and *less* and *more educated,* see the note to Table 3.1.

mother could name few tasks she expected her 6-year-old daughter to carry out:

> After we get through eating, I have her clean up the kitchen, clean off the table, pick their stuff up after they mess up or something.

Middle-income parents, however, emphasize a broader array of self-care activities and, more significant, the fact that the child is to remember and carry out those activities without being reminded or told to do so. It is also clear that they invest more social capital, or time and effort, in supervising, monitoring, and trying to build a good relationship with the child. That parents expect autonomy in their children was especially apparent in the responses of Murray and Mary Haney when asked what they expected their 7-year-old son to do each day:

> Getting up in the morning—his clothes are already laid out for him. We want him to have the responsibility not to be told to put your shoes on now, put your pants on now. We want him to have that responsibility to get up, get washed up . . . brush your teeth, put everything on—don't just put your pants on and sit there and then Dad or Mom have to say put your shoes on now. That's your responsibility, to get yourself dressed—you're 7 years old now, big enough to dress yourself. And when he gets home from school every day he has homework, and he is to get his homework done. He knows that. He has to practice his piano lessons; he knows that. He has to come in and before he can go out to play, change his school clothes; he knows that. He's responsible for getting his backpack ready in the morning and getting his steno signed—that's our communication between home and school. And picking up his room.

Mary added another responsibility:

> Another responsibility is to make sure he brings his work from school. Make sure he brings home his spelling list, his reading book, everything he needs to bring home from school.

Notably, this father also expected his son to remember what needs to be done without being reminded. I asked what happens when his son doesn't follow this routine:

> If I should get home—that's when they really come out and play—but if for some reason or the other one is out there playing and he can't go out, he's sitting there trying to figure out why he can't go out. And I ask him, "Have you done everything you're supposed to do?" And I don't usually tell him what he hasn't done yet, even though we know what he hasn't done yet. We let him sit there and figure that out. And once he's figured it out, sometimes it's too late to go out. And next time he'll know.

They clearly provide a highly structured environment for their sons where self-reliance and responsibility are critical.

Discipline Strategies

Parents were asked which discipline strategy they used most often: reason and logic, loss of privileges, or spankings. Parents use a variety of

Table 3.6 Discipline: Percentage of Parents Ranking Each Item as Their Most Frequently Used Discipline Strategy

	Comparison of black parents and white parents:		
	All (N = 727)	Blacks (N = 525)	Whites (N = 204)
Reason and logic	52.0	50.2	55.5***
Loss of privileges	48.2	49.5	45.9***
Spankings	8.0	11.3	2.0***
	Comparison of low-income and high-income black parents:		
	All (N = 318)	Low Income (N = 201)	High Income (N = 117)
Reason and logic	51.9	52.2	51.4
Loss of privileges	50.3	54.1	44.8
Spankings	9.7	8.5	11.5
	Comparison of less educated and more educated black parents:		
	All (N = 525)	Less Educated (N = 220)	More Educated (N = 300)
Reason and logic	53.5	54.3	53.3
Loss of privileges	47.9	50.5	45.8
Spankings	10.6	14.3	8.1

*$p < .10$; **$p < .05$; ***$p < .01$.
NOTE: Tables do not necessarily equal 100% because a few parents chose more than one discipline strategy as their most frequently used strategy. For explanations of *low* and *high income* and *less* and *more educated*, see the note to Table 3.1.

discipline strategies but, as shown in Table 3.6, the single most common strategy for black (50%) and white (56%) parents was reason and logic. Paula Jackson, a 41-year-old married mother, explained how she manages the discipline of her 12-year-old son:

> He's a good child, and he really doesn't get into trouble very much. I always let him know that whatever he decides, there are consequences. So as far as discipline, he's hardly ever grounded. . . . Say he did something he wasn't supposed to do? First, we sit down and talk about it and say why it was right or why it was wrong. I want him to understand what he actually did. Once we get past that, we say, What do you think we should do about this? . . . I hardly ever spank, ever, even when they were little. Because to me spanking, when a parent spanks, they are almost at their last end—they've lost control.

Loss of privileges was ranked as the second most frequently used discipline strategy, and spanking was ranked by both racial groups as their least important discipline strategy. Still, black parents (11%) as a group were nearly three times more likely than white parents (3%) to say that spanking was their most frequently used method of discipline. Although spanking is a relatively low priority among black parents, none of those interviewed, even those with adolescent children, ruled out spanking as a possible discipline strategy. In my interviews, I asked parents how often they spanked the child and what kinds of behaviors usually warranted a spanking. Kelly Coleman, the 30-year-old mother of 11-year-old Van, said,

> Van is talked to the first time, and then spanked five licks the second time, and that usually does the job. *[What's likely to get him spanked?]* Not doing the things he expected to do, especially disobedience. *[How often do you spank him?]* Well, it just really varies . . . he has times when he doesn't get a spanking for months and months, and then if it's near Christmas, and he's excited about something, it can be once a week. Right now, with us having just moved, and we just got married in July, and he just started school, so he's going through a lot of transitions. And he's distracted from the things that are expected, and he's been getting spanked about once every two weeks.

Of interest, Kelly understands that her son's behavioral difficulties are often linked to significant family transitions and the excitement over upcoming events, yet she neither excuses his behavior nor exempts him for punishment.

Describing how she disciplines her 11-year-old son David, who is nearly as big as she is, Yadira Bright explained that she used a variety of techniques, with spanking as a last resort. The offense most likely to result in a spanking for her son is engaging in behaviors that indicate a lack of respect for his parents:

> I take something away that I know he doesn't want to lose. I'm trying to get better myself, because usually I used to holler, but I don't want to holler at them so much. Plus that it gets me nowhere. I try not to threaten him saying I'll punish him if he does it again. If I'm going to spank him, I go get the belt and spank him then. Because threats don't phase him. Usually, if I say I'm going to take away a television show, that upsets him. He really has to do something bad for me to whip him. *[How often does that happen?]* Once a month, if that often . . . everything doesn't require a spanking . . . [one thing] that will warrant a spanking is like [when] Van had an attitude problem. Every time we'd say something, he'd walk off and stomp and stare at us like we were crazy. Now that's an automatic whipping.

Like Yadira, Elisha Martin, a 35-year-old single mother of an 11-year-old daughter, suggests that if she feels disrespected, her daughter Evelyn will get a spanking. Yet she feels uncertain that she's being effective in disciplining her daughter:

> [*How do you handle discipline?*] Not very well. Not consistently. I might not have a good handle on that, but she does get whippings—not often and not as many as she should, so I believe in spanking and punishment. She's getting old enough now for punishments [rather than spankings]. But she gets away with too much. [*What's the last thing she did that resulted in her being punished or spanked?*] Being disrespectful—either answering me in a disrespectful tone or some kind of body language that indicated disrespect. These are the kinds of things that she gets spankings for more than almost anything else. Things that I detect as disrespectful, either the tone of voice or the body language.

Spanking and Child Abuse

Although the majority of American parents at least occasionally spank or hit their children, and such behavior is condoned by most adults and legal in every state (Straus, 1994), the physical punishment of children continues to be a controversial issue. Some argue that hitting children is simply ineffective as a discipline strategy; others see it as linked to childhood outcomes such as aggressiveness, violence, and criminal behavior. Additionally, it may be easy for parents who use physical punishment to cross the ambiguous line between acceptable discipline and child abuse.

The earliest studies of African American families (see Chapter 2) suggested that parents, at least by emerging white, middle-class standards, were excessively abusive with their children. In recent decades, family violence has reemerged as an important issue, and one that is quite common in American families. Still, there is evidence that rates of virtually all kinds of violence are higher among blacks than other racial groups (Hampton & Gelles, 1991; Straus, Gelles, & Steinmetz, 1980), although statistical data on family violence are faulty; for example, class and race may be conflated, and those who come to the attention of public authorities are more likely to be included in these data. The link between poverty and family violence is clear, as poverty is correlated with an array of factors that promote the abuse and neglect of children, such as social isolation, stress, poor self-esteem, and inadequate parenting skills. African Americans are overrepresented among those living in poverty, and the rates of physical and sexual abuse are six times higher for children in poor families than for other children (Reiss & Roth, 1993). Poverty often increases parental concern over the well-being of children, especially when it means that parents are unable to meet their children's needs, yet that concern ironically can manifest itself as abuse. Poor parents have higher rates of depression and stress; they are therefore less vocal, affectionate, and spontaneous in their interactions with children. Similarly, they are less able to be nurturing, kind, and patient with children, and they punish children more frequently, severely, and inconsistently (Tower, 1996).

Although not all spanking constitutes physical abuse, there appears to be a stronger advocacy among blacks for corporal punishment, which can sometimes lead to child abuse. Straus points out race and class differences in how people talk about physical punishment; for example, middle-class Americans use the word *spanking* more, which often means slapping or hitting any part of the body. Racial minorities and poor people most frequently speak of *whippings* and *beatings,* both of which are more severe forms of physical punishment. Still, what constitutes violence is socially constructed and varies from one culture to the next. An important distinction between corporal punishment and abuse, according to Straus, is whether the child is psychologically damaged. Thus, behaviors that may be psychologically harmful to some children may be accepted by others as appropriate. At least some research suggests that corporal punishment among blacks may not be linked with greater aggression. A study by Deater-Deckard, Dodge, Bates, and Pettit (1996) compared European American and black elementary school age children. They found that although children who were black, male, poor, and living with single mothers were more likely to have received physical discipline, they were not more likely to display externalizing or aggressive behaviors at school. These researchers suggest that the sociocultural meaning of physical punishment may vary based on ethnicity.

Sexual Socialization

A long-standing myth about African Americans has been that their beliefs about sexuality are considerably more lenient than the beliefs of other Americans. In the past, this myth has been used to justify the sexual exploitation of black women and the oppression of black men; today, however, it seems fueled by the high rate of sexual activity and pregnancy among black American teenagers. Despite this myth, recent studies show that blacks and whites are quite similar in their attitudes about issues of sexuality, with low-income blacks often even more conservative than their middle-income counterparts (Smith & Seltzer, 1992).

Parents are especially likely to hold conservative views about sexuality when it comes to their expectations for their own children. Among the parents in this study, more than 80% of blacks and whites indicated that they wanted or expected their children to get married before having sex, and the majority of blacks (92%) and whites (97%) said they expected their children to marry before having children.

Despite the fairly conservative sexual expectations parents have for their own children, studies have shown that the sexual revolution of the 1960s and 1970s radically altered American sexual ideologies and behaviors in a relatively short period of time. The percentage of Americans approving of premarital sex rose between 1969 and 1973 from about 20% to 50% (Luker, 1996). In 1972, 35% of Americans believed it was always wrong for a man and woman to have sex before marriage, but by 1989, only 27% felt that way (Smith, 1990). The liberalization of sexual attitudes that occurred during this era was sparked by the political and cultural revolutions on college campuses, the advent of the birth control pill, and the divorce revolution. Yet teenagers were not insulated from this sexualization of American culture, nor was it easy to teach them the standards of sexual abstinence and fidelity that were being challenged in the larger culture. Thus, although nearly 86% of adults say that sexual relations among persons in their early teens (14-16 years old) is always or almost always wrong (Smith, 1990), the number of sexually active teenagers doubled between 1970 and 1990 (Luker, 1996). The average age for first sexual intercourse among Americans is 16 or 17 years old (Reinisch, 1990), and in 1988 about 60% of males and 53% of females who were single and between the ages of 15-19 were sexually active (Sonenstein, Pleck, & Ku, 1991).

The sexual revolution increased acceptance of premarital sex for both black and white teenagers. Despite this similarity in the sexual ideologies of blacks and whites, black teenagers are still three times more likely to be sexually active than white teenagers, and they initiate sexual activity at an earlier age (Furstenberg, 1987). Black adolescent males are especially likely to initiate sexual activity earlier than their white counterparts do, and they have more sexual partners, according to research by Sonenstein et al. (1991). By age 13, 20% of black and 3% of white males have had sexual intercourse, and this percentage increases to 63% of blacks and 33% of whites by age 16. Between the ages of 15 and 19, black males have an average of eight sexual partners, compared with four for white males. These racial gaps in sexual behaviors are not reflective of the values parents are trying to teach but of other factors that enhance blacks' early participation in sexuality.

Reasons for Teen Sexuality

Although teenage sexuality is now the norm rather than the exception, numerous studies, most of them motivated by concern over teenage pregnancy, have sought to delineate the social factors linked to teenage sexuality. Most studies have found that some aspect of socioeconomic status accounts for most of the racial variation in teenage sexuality. Anderson (1991) has written extensively on how neighborhood context affects sexual norms, arguing that poor teenagers create an "ideology about their circumstances" that links sexuality with prestige and adult status. Similarly, Brewster (1994) found that premarital sexual activity for whites and blacks was linked to the socioeconomic status of the neighborhoods and the labor market experiences of women, with the overall opportunity structure shaping sexual behaviors. Examining data on sexuality from a life-course perspective, Murry (1994) found that African American females have consistently delayed their initiation of sexual activity when other life opportunities are available, and that intellectual ability, academic achievement, and career aspirations all militate against early sexual intercourse. Comparing patterns of sexuality among black Americans who entered and completed adolescence during the 1950s, 1960s, 1970s, and 1980s, she found a decline in adolescent sexuality during the 1960s—a period when ethnic pride was being emphasized and opportunities were increasing. This rate had increased significantly by the 1980s, despite greater parental efforts to teach children about sex.

The impact of family factors on teenage sexuality has also been examined. Scott (1993) has argued that there is more mother-daughter conflict in black single-parent than two-parent families, and that the sexual behavior of teenage girls may be a way of challenging maternal authority. Haurin and Mott (1990) hypothesized that older siblings influenced adolescent sexual activity but found that there was no direct sibling effect for blacks. Black adolescent female sexuality was tied to other class-related family factors; for example, there was a significant negative association between maternal education and sexual initiation, suggesting that educated mothers either exerted more control or provided better sex education. Less sexual activity among female adolescents was also tied to having two biological parents in the home and to church attendance. Haurin and Mott (1990) reported, however, that for black male adolescents, there were "virtually no significant predictors of first sexual activity, suggesting that the sexual behavior of these youths almost completely reflects forces from outside the family" (p. 550). A recent article in *Family Planning Perspectives* ("Age at Which," 1994), however, found that the age at which young men initiate sexual intercourse is tied to maternal characteristics and sex education. The sons of mothers who gave birth as teenagers or worked outside of the home, and, for African Americans, those who received instruction in sexual biology, had an elevated risk of early first intercourse.

Involvement in religion would seem to militate against early sexual activity. However, as Anderson (1991) notes, a fundamentalist religious orientation so characteristic of the poor usually emphasizes the role of fate in life: "If something happens, it happens; if something was meant to be, then let it be, and 'God will find a way' " (p. 383). Additionally, those with a strong religious orientation are less likely to actually plan to have sex, and thus are less likely to use contraceptives. Overall, studies differ in their assessment of the impact of religion on adolescent premarital sex.

Issues of gender, coercive sex, and rape are also frequently overlooked as factors in the early onset of sexuality and pregnancy among teenage girls. Luker (1996) reminds us that teenage girls may not always be involved in consensual sex. Asked if there was ever a time when they were forced to have sex against their will or raped, 13% of white and 8% of black women answered affirmatively. As many as 74% of women who had sex under age 14 reported they had been coerced, as did 60% of those who had sex before the age of 15 (p. 145).

Sex Education and Birth Control

Although many factors that promote teenage sex and pregnancy appear outside of their control, parents do try to exert control by providing sex education at home and supporting sex education in the schools. Parents have difficulty, however, deciding when and how to discuss sexuality with their children. Studies have found that parents in general are notoriously ineffective in providing sex education for their children. For example, one study of more than 8,000 college students with college-educated parents found that fewer than 15% had received meaningful sexual information from their parents (Gordon, 1986). The survey data that were collected in this study reveal that the majority of black parents (73%) have already discussed sexuality with their children, and most (85%) feel that children should be told about sexuality at least by age 12 (see Table 3.7). In response to the survey, most parents indicate they have talked with their children about sexuality. The interviews, however, reveal that parents provide sexual information primarily when they feel the child is interested in the opposite sex, and then in a rather limited and reactive manner. Asked if she had talked with her 9-year-old son about sex, one mother said:

> No, not yet. *[What about sexually transmitted diseases?]* Well, we did, because they sent papers home from school talking about AIDS, and . . . we discussed it when Magic Johnson [got the disease]. So we went to the library and got a book on how to talk to your kids about sex, and we went over that. We just basically went over the parts of the body—the technical terms. . . . *[When do you plan to really talk to him about sex?]* I don't think you really set an age. If you know your kid well enough, so that you'll know if something is puzzling them . . . I always try to stress with them that no matter what,

Table 3.7 Sex and Sexuality: Percentage of Parents Agreeing With Each Statement

	All	Blacks	Whites
	Comparison of black parents and white parents:		
Expects child to marry before having sex	82.4	83.1	80.4
Expects child to marry before having children	93.3	92.0	96.5*
Has already discussed sexuality with child	70.9	72.5	67.0
Child should be told about sex by age 12	85.1	84.9	85.8
Schools should teach child more about sex	64.2	65.7	60.

	Low Income (N = 129)	High Income (N = 59)
	Comparison of low-income and high-income black parents:	
Expects child to marry before having sex	82.1	79.1
Expects child to marry before having children	89.5	97.3**
Has already discussed sexuality with child	72.6	66.6
Child should be told about sex by age 12	86.9	81.4
Schools should teach child more about sex	73.8	70.4

	Less Educated (N = 128)	More Educated (N = 186)
	Comparison of less educated and more educated black parents:	
Expects child to marry before having sex	85.6	81.0
Expects child to marry before having childre	88.6	94.3
Has already discussed sexuality with child	72.6	66.4
Child should be told about sex by age 12	83.6	84.4
Schools should teach child more about sex	64.8	71.5

they can always come and talk to me . . . hopefully, he will make some kind of first move. [*So you don't have any age in mind?*] Just when his interest turns toward girls; that's what I'm thinking, but I could be wrong.

The majority of parents in this study (about 80%) believed that schools should teach their children more about sex, with only a few expressing concern about the content of that education. Americans' support for sex education in public schools has grown steadily over the years and now stands at about 85% (Smith, 1990), despite the presence of a vocal minority that insists that parents should be responsible for teaching children about sex. More than 90% of public high schools do offer some form of sex, AIDS education, or both, although most of it centers on "family life education" or reproductive biology (Luker, 1996; Ward & Taylor, 1994). Many of these programs are outdated or ineffective, according to Ward and Taylor (1994), because they are grounded in a Eurocentric framework that views central adolescent issues in terms of separation and independence, thus ignoring the increasing cultural diversity among students. Sex education programs are also sexist and racist in that they focus on females exerting control and perpetuate myths about the sexuality of racial minorities. Luker (1996) notes that the sex education programs that do exist in schools often are offered too late, especially considering the early onset of sexuality and the high rate of high school dropouts in some areas. For example, she cites a study showing that 81% of black males and 61% of white males were already sexually active before receiving formal sex education at school.

African American teenagers have been found to be less likely than whites to use birth control at first intercourse or on a regular basis thereafter (Furstenberg, 1987). The demand for contraceptives doubled between 1970 and 1990, paralleling the rise in sexual activity among teenagers. According to Luker (1996, p. 184), the majority of teens using contraceptives received them from a family planning clinic, with even higher rates of blacks than whites using this source. In 1983, more than 80% of teenagers using contraceptives lived in families below the poverty level and 13% were from families on public assistance.

In 1993, the Alan Guttmacher Institute conducted a series of focus groups composed of young, unmarried, racially diverse groups of males and females to discuss their contraceptive practices. Focusing especially on the role of men in contraceptive use, this research found that fear of AIDS, more than concern about pregnancy, inspired the use of condoms among men; thus, males were more likely to use condoms in casual sexual relationships than in long-term relationships, as greater familiarity with their partner made them feel safer (Landry & Camelo, 1994). Although they had many complaints about condoms, as one 16-year-old black male said, "The one-night stands—I would never go without a condom" (p. 224). For the most part, these males used contraceptives without even discussing it with casual partners, and were suspicious when their partners brought it up. There was more discussion of contraceptives in long-term relationships, although the responsibility was usually then given to the female and actual use was more sporadic. Perhaps because of the socioeconomic homogeneity of the participants in this study, there were few racial-ethnic differences in use or attitudes.

The parents interviewed in this study clearly wanted to teach their children abstinence, but single mothers seemed more receptive to the idea that their teenagers may need birth control. Elisha Miller, speaking of her 11-year-old daughter, said,

> I've asked her and am praying that she remains a virgin, and I've told her that I expected her to, although I don't know how realistic that is. Although I said that's an expectation, I don't know how strong it is, because I don't know who does anymore. But I don't lay heavy on it. *[Have you discussed birth control?]* Yes, we've discussed that, but probably not in a lot of detail. The one I speak to most is abstinence. *[How would you respond if she told you she wanted to get birth control?]* I would be broken-hearted, and receptive.

Being "broken-hearted" yet "receptive" describes most parents' responses to the discovery of sexual activity and pregnancy in their children.

Intergenerational Changes

I concluded my interviews with parents by asking how they thought their children would describe them, and how different they were from their own parents in their child-rearing views.

Asked how she thought her 13-year-old son would describe her, 32-year-old Laura Raymond said, "He'll say that I'm tough . . . and that I expect too much, and that I give him too much work to do."

Parents, who were interviewed in their own homes, most typically said that I should ask their children how they felt. Kelly Coleman called 11-year-old Van into the living room, and I asked him to describe his mother:

> Ummm . . . my mama's nice, and she's pretty. [Mother: I think I need to leave the room, so we can get an honest answer!] She teaches me a lot of things. If I make a mistake she'll help me fix it. She helps me understand things. *[Is there anything else?]* She washes my clothes, and she always gives me credit when I make a good tackle [in football].

Asked how their own child-rearing work differed from that of their own parents, four themes emerged: less corporal punishment, more communication and open affection, more freedom, and greater paternal involvement. A 26-year-old mother of a 6-year-old said,

> My mother—well, we got more whippings. I don't whip him as much; that's the big difference. It's hard for me to whip him . . . because either he runs, and the look on his face is like I'm going to kill him or something. . . . Mostly he don't do anything severe enough to call for a whipping; I just take away

some privilege or something. . . . I guess I let him make more decisions, like
what he wants to eat. Because when I was little, you ate what was cooked,
and you ate all of it, no choice. So he has more freedom. And he goes more
places, especially spending nights with people. I let him go and do more
things without me. But my mother was always like, "No, you can't go!"

Vickie Mellon's father died when she was age 12, leaving her mother
with numerous children to raise alone. She sees herself as more overtly
affectionate and loving with her son, at least in part because she does not
have nearly as many children as her mother had:

My child-rearing methods are really different, because my mother ruled with
a strong hand—and that's basically what I try to do—but there were 13 of
us, so she had a lot to try to spread around, while I just have one child. She
wasn't able to rock all of us at the same time, but I'm there to cradle him, to
tell him I love him. But we knew we were loved, but I'm able to show more
affection. Because my mother was always pregnant. It seemed there was
always a baby to take the last baby's place, but we loved each other.

Although only a few black fathers were interviewed, I was extremely
impressed by their eagerness to be involved in the lives of their children.
Those who were single, unemployed, or both accepted as many father
responsibilities as they could, even for children who were not biologically
their own. Those who were married and employed were especially proud
to have the opportunity to father their own children, often becoming the
type of father they wanted but never had. Noting that both his own and
his wife's parents were divorced, Timothy Shannon said,

Probably much different . . . I didn't have much contact with my father; he
had another family. We had some contact, but it wasn't frequent. But I think
that's the reason I emphasize so much the family and staying with each other
and supporting each other, because it wasn't there when I was growing up.
We had a lot of laughter in our house, but as far as communicating, as sitting
down talking, it just wasn't there. . . . I do a lot more talking to my kids. . . .
I think that as parents we need to listen more, to hear what our kids are
saying to us. If we did, we wouldn't have to use corporal punishment.

Fathering is an obvious priority and privilege for Murray, who grew up in
a single-mother home:

With me, as a black father, it's really a challenge to me because I didn't have
a father in my home. I came up with older brothers, but we never had that
father image as an example. We never used the word *daddy* in my home. So
I'm really doing on-the-job training. . . . Some things I've done, I wish I had

a father saying those things to me that I'm saying to him now. It would have helped me, given me guidance, and maybe I wouldn't have been such a follower of a crowd.

Murray prides himself on the time and energy he invests in raising his sons, noting that he has sacrificed some job opportunities in favor of family involvement:

> But coming up as a young man, without an image of father . . . never having a father to come [to athletic events] on father-son days . . . it [fathering] was just something that I put on the top of my life, to be there for my son. As a matter of fact, like my job, I could be promoted to another position, but I turned it down, because that promotion—it's not all about money—that promotion would have taken away from the priorities and the things I'm trying to instill in my son, so I told them I didn't need that, because my family comes first. My priorities are God, my family, and then my job. And by me not having a father around me, I put forth more. I watch him when he plays, I observe things that he does and what's going on around him. . . . All the things I wanted my dad to do with me as a young man are the things I strive to do with him.

Conclusions

Research on African American parents often focuses on low-income families and describes their parenting abilities as thwarted by either adverse social structural forces or public policies that are inimical to their well-being. Major theories of child development and child rearing stigmatize black parents by embodying a Eurocentric framework that implicitly depicts them as poorly equipped for the tasks of parenting. In this chapter, I have attempted to restore human agency to the scenario by using a social capital framework and focusing on parenting work. In addition, I have expanded existing research by providing some interracial comparisons for blacks and whites and some interclass comparisons for blacks. My findings show that black and white parents are quite similar in their overall prioritizing of their current values and future hopes for the children as well as in their views of the parenting role and their discipline strategies. These overall similarities in values and approaches to parenting, however, should not be allowed to mask important racial differences between the two groups of parents. For example, the majority of both black and white parents indicate that happiness and self-esteem is their most important current value for the child, but whites embrace this value significantly more often than do blacks. When the socioeconomic status of black parents is considered, however, we find that more affluent and educated parents rank self-esteem and happiness more highly than those in the lower class. Similarly, only a few white and black parents define themselves primarily as disciplinarians. Yet black parents as a group are significantly more likely to do so than are white parents, and poor black parents are more likely to do so than their more affluent counterparts. The picture that emerges is that important racial differences exist between white and black parents, and that controlling for social class among blacks diminishes but does not eliminate these differences.

In thinking about their children's futures, black parents are significantly more likely than white parents to say that having their children get a good education and a good job is their top priority. Less educated and low-income African American parents are even more likely than those in the middle class to embrace the value of a good education and a good job. Clearly, these are not things that African American parents take for granted; instead, they see them as important achievements for their children. Their concern may reflect the challenges they face in providing for their own children: Black parents (40%) were significantly more likely than white parents (26%) to say that being a good provider was their most important parenting role. Most view getting a good education as requisite to this responsibility: Black parents overwhelmingly want their children to attend college, and the interview data reveal a consistent pattern of instilling that expectation in children from a relatively early age.

Only a small percentage of black parents (10%) indicated that being a disciplinarian was their most important role and that spanking was their most frequently used disciplinary strategy (11%), yet black parents were significantly more likely than whites to give these responses. For the most part, these roles are emphasized more strongly among less educated and low-income blacks, yet none of the blacks interviewed completely rejected spanking as a method of discipline. It was clear from their responses, however, that they did not spank very often or rely on spanking more than other strategies. This was especially obvious when parents were asked how they differed from their own parents in their child-rearing work. A common theme was that they spanked less, relied more on communication, and gave their children more freedom.

The following chapter deals with a challenge uniquely affecting African American parents: What do you tell your children about being black in white America? And are racial socialization messages linked with self-esteem?

4

Racial Socialization

Black folks aren't born expecting segregation, prepared from day one to follow its confining rules. Nobody presents you with a handbook when you're teething and says, "Here's how you must behave as a second-class citizen." Instead, the humiliating expectations and traditions of segregation creep over you, slowly stealing a teaspoonful of your self-esteem each day. . . . By the time I was four years old, I was asking questions neither my mother nor grandmother cared to answer: "Why do white people write 'Colored' on all the ugly drinking fountains, the dingy restrooms, and the back of the buses?"

Melba Patillo Beals, *Warriors Don't Cry* (1994, p. 136)

One of the most pernicious outcomes of slavery has been an almost intractable denigration of blackness in American society. Although slavery evolved because of the need for a stable, cheap, controllable labor force, its ideological linchpin was the alleged innate inferiority of Africans. Kitano (1991) argues that slavery has been the single most important factor defining the status of African Americans because it classified black people as subhuman in ways that continue to shape race relations. Despite numerous success stories and role models, and a great deal of socioeconomic progress, African Americans as a group are still stigmatized as less intelligent, less attractive, and less capable than white people. This makes child socialization doubly challenging for black parents who, as Billingsley (1968/1988) has pointed out, have always had to teach their children not only how to be human but also how to be black in a white society. That children must be taught the meaning of being black speaks to the socially constructed nature of the meaning of race.

Racial socialization has been defined as parents' "attempt to prepare their children for the realities of being Black in America" (Taylor et al., 1990, p. 994). These realities are socially defined by parents based on their own personal experiences and their education, income, religious beliefs, and expectations for their children. Most see black-white relations as contentious and white hostility as widespread; for example, nearly 25% believe that most white Americans accept the racial views of the Ku Klux Klan, and nearly half do not believe that blacks will ever achieve social and economic equality with whites (Sigelman & Welch, 1991). As many as two-thirds of blacks feel that they simply do not, as a group, have the same opportunities as whites, and most believe that whites do not want to see them get ahead (Billingsley, 1992, p. 228). These attitudes, and their own personal experiences, underlie the need for racial socialization.

Many of the parents in this study grew up during the civil rights era of the 1960s and 1970s and vividly recall the difficulties they faced with racial integration. Melba Brown, a 35-year-old social worker and mother of two, was among a few blacks selected to be bussed to a predominantly white school in the 1970s, and this experience shapes her constructions of the realities of being black. Her strong religious orientation leads her to teach her children to be tolerant and forgiving of racism. Yet, as was the case with many black parents, her message also conveys a strong underlying racial sentiment: She tells her children that if they are not tolerant, they will "be as bad as some white people are." She draws on her own experiences to show her children that race is an important issue:

> I want them to be aware that they are black in a white world where there are people who may possibly treat you badly just because of that. But when people have a problem, you're not to hold that against them—so we've had those little lectures—to keep their minds open, and not be as bad as some white people are. . . . My racial experiences were real negative. I was one of the first few [blacks] bussed [to a white school] back in the 1970s, and I had some real negative experiences behind it. . . . I was the black girl in the class and then had the audacity to have a brain in my head and how dare me—and I mean I was really treated badly. Some of the stuff that happened to me was life-changing. . . . I had several teachers cheat, lie, lose my work . . . like I said, this is life-changing.

Although many parents like Melba have had negative racial experiences, there are very few who teach children messages of racial hatred. Michael Beard, a 35-year-old sales representative, tries to temper what he describes as the "black militancy" he felt in his earlier years with a more moderate position based on his current Christian orientation:

> Quite naturally, just being the era I grew up in and the stance that I believe—I'm quite pro-Afro American, but when you become a Christian you try to overlook that . . . a friend used to say that I hate white people, but it's not that I hate white people: I dislike people who dislike me. . . . I can understand how Marcus Garvey felt when he said, Let's just go back to Africa,

because . . . I guess my frame of mind is, Why can't we have our own stuff? But I think if you use being black as a crutch, it becomes a crutch. I'm more than the media say that I am. . . . I think if I can instill in my son some of the values I have, then race really won't make any difference.

Like most parents, Michael sees racism as something that is real but understands that it can also be used as a "crutch" to explain failure. Racial socialization can be a difficult task as parents walk a fine line between telling their children that racial discrimination and hatred do exist and may well affect the opportunities that are available to them, while assuring them that they can overcome these racial barriers with the right attitude and hard work. By engaging in racial socialization, parents are challenging the dominant society's depictions and assessments of black people; as Michael has pointed out, they want to teach their children that they are "more than the media" say they are.

In this chapter, I examine the racial attitudes of parents that underlie their efforts to racially socialize their children, specifically whether they think their children have already been victimized by racial discrimination and how they think race will affect their children's futures. As we will see, the attitudes of black and white parents are more divergent on racial issues than on any other aspect of child rearing. Second, I examine the issue of self-esteem among black children, specifically the common assumption that racism, negative stereotypes, and poverty result in low self-esteem among blacks. Although my findings are based solely on parental assessments of their children's self-esteem, they do not support the view of diminished self-esteem among black children. Finally, included in this chapter is an examination of the racial socialization messages parents give their children. While the majority of parents see racial-ethnic socialization as important, most adopt a rather reactive stance in discussing race with their children: They respond to the issue of race after their children become aware of its significance and start to ask questions. Parents strive to create a balance between acknowledging the importance of race and allowing their children to racialize every negative encounter with whites.

Parental Perceptions of Racial Barriers

I asked parents if they felt being a racial minority makes it more difficult to get a good education and a good job: 45% of black parents felt that being a racial minority makes it more difficult compared with about 29% of white parents (Table 4.1). Asked whether they felt their child had ever experienced unfair treatment because of his or her race, white parents

Table 4.1 Racial Attitudes of Parents by Race

	Parents by Race		Black Parents by Income Level		Black Parents by Education Level	
	Black	White	Low	High	Less	More
Questions/Issues	(N = 525)	(N = 204)	(N = 201)	(N = 117)	(N = 220)	(N = 300)
1. Being a racial minority makes it more difficult to get a good education and a good job.						
Agree	45.3	28.9***	36.3	36.8	42.3	47.3
Disagree	50.1	67.6**	51.2	43.6*	51.8	49.0
No response	4.6	3.5	2.5	5.1	5.9	3.7
2. Children are better off being taught by teachers who are of the same race as the child.						
Agree	22.7	10.8***	17.9	30.8***	19.5	24.7**
Disagree	73.0	87.7**	79.1	63.2**	75.5	71.3
No response	4.3	1.5	3.0	6.0	5.0	4.0
3. Has your child experienced unfair treatment because of his or her race?						
Yes	18.6	23.5*	10.1	25.4*	13.1	21.6**
No	79.6	56.4	89.1	71.2	85.4	75.8*
No response	2.2	2.5	.8	3.4	1.5	2.6
4. How will your child's race affect his or her future?						
Will have no impact	52.3	60.8*	61.2	42.2**	58.5	48.4**
Make it more difficult	40.9	6.9***	27.9	55.9***	31.5	46.8**
Make it easier	4.0	13.2***	7.0	1.7	4.6	3.7
No response	2.8	.1	3.9	.2	5.4	1.1

*p < .10; **p < .05; ***p < .01.
NOTE: Questions/issues 1, 2, and 4 are based on responses from the entire sample. Question/issue 3 is based on responses from a subsample of 323 blacks and 166 whites (N = 489).

(29%) were significantly more likely than black parents (19%) to report unfair treatment based on race. The higher percentage of white parents reporting racial unfairness no doubt stems from the fact that those in this study were attending predominantly black schools and perceived the exclusion that comes from being a racial minority. Among black parents, both income and education were positively related to having children who experienced unfair racial treatment. Parents earning more than $30,000 per year were more than twice as likely as low-income parents to say their child had experienced racism. High-income parents, because they have more education, are often more sensitive to racism and more confrontational in addressing racial insults.

Asked how they felt race would affect their child's future, 41% of blacks indicated that they thought their child's race would make things more difficult, compared with only 9% of whites. The sex of the focus child shaped parental beliefs about the impact of race on their children's future: The parents of sons (47%) were more likely than the parents of daughters (36%) to say that race would adversely affect their children's future (this information is not shown in the tables). Here again, we find that high-income parents are more aware of the barriers imposed by race than are low-income parents. Low-income parents attribute their status primarily to their own failure to get a better education, and they believe that education will allow their children to succeed despite racism. I asked 22-year-old Shawn Branson, whose 6-year-old daughter is currently in a special education class for slow learners, whether she thought being black would affect her daughter's success:

> No, not really. You just have to be determined, have a goal in life. If you have a goal in life or what you want to do and what you want to become, you can do it. She shouldn't have any problem, especially if she does well in school—that's the most important thing. You have to do well in school, and get a scholarship, or whatever.

More educated and affluent parents doubt that it's quite that simple. They have often experienced career mobility and often hold jobs in racially integrated settings, yet they find that race shapes their acceptance and progress. Their expectation of overcoming racial inequality through success and hard work has not always been realized; in fact, their occupational positions and education heighten their awareness of the gap between striving and achieving, and place them in social environments where they are even more likely to experience rejection or exclusion. They expect their children will also be achievers but feel that race will still make it more difficult.

Education and Racial Integration

Because African American parents believe strongly in the importance of education, the racial integration of schools was once held by many civil rights activists to be the key to economic mobility, social inclusion, and the end of racial stereotypes. Efforts to integrate schools, however, have never been completely successful: In 1988, nearly two-thirds of blacks attended schools where the majority of the students were nonwhite (Armor, 1992). Moreover, while the majority of blacks still firmly support racial integration, a significant minority have reconsidered the value of a racially integrated society, especially in terms of education. After three decades of efforts toward racial integration, which have included notable victories and failures, blacks are beginning to assess what they have lost in their efforts to become a part of mainstream society. In terms of education, it is common to hear blacks express the belief that white teachers and schools care very little about the education and well-being of their children, and that the lack of a common cultural background impedes the ability of teachers to understand or teach children. In a recent study, Wilkinson (1996) suggested that racial integration has been harmful for many black children. She argues that although the U.S. Supreme Court was correct to argue in 1954 that separate racial facilities are inherently unequal, forced integration and bussing have been psychologically and culturally destructive for African American children.

One result of this disenchantment has been the growth of independent black schools in urban areas, which differ from traditional schools in that African American culture and history are the bases of the curriculum. In her study of the impact of an Afrocentric transformation on the choice of a black school, Shujaa (1992) quotes one mother as saying:

> I want my son to have a very positive self-concept about himself and about Black people in general and what they can do. And I think to give him that positive self-image for him to be around Black professionals, to be around Black students and see that achievement is, indeed, possible. So, because I believe that, I live in a Black community, I work with community organizations . . . I shop in a Black community. I don't go across town because I believe that by supporting our community we make it strong and I want that positive self-image to also be fostered in my son. So, I chose a Black school. In fact, I never considered going to a White school. (p. 155)

In my study, I asked parents whether they thought children were better off being taught by a teacher who was the same race as the child: 23% of black parents felt that their children would be better off with a black teacher, with low-income parents less likely to support this view than high-income parents (see Table 4.1). Afrocentric schools are now becoming an option in the school districts of the parents in this study, yet only one mother indicated that her child had attended such a school. Asked about the racial socialization of her child, Candy Corbin, a low-income single mother of a 6-year-old, said,

> Well, he goes to an African-centered school . . . so Black pride and African pride is one of the things that they teach there, but we don't blow it all out of proportion. [Why did you choose this school?] Well, it was chosen for me. It wasn't the first thing on my list . . . but when I found out what kind of

school it was, I thought it might be interesting. I went to one of the programs, and was interested to see that they pray before their programs. They sing songs of worship. . . . They have a good principal, and you can see she's very cultural. And she teaches them to be proud of being Black. I want him to be proud, but I don't want him to be overwhelmed with that every day . . . just be a good boy.

Despite the concerns of a significant minority of parents, most blacks are still in favor of an integrated education (Billingsley, 1992). Toni Cason, for example, rejects the idea of a racially segregated school for her 13-year-old daughter, Taylor. Because we live in a racially integrated society, she thinks it's important to learn to deal with other races throughout one's education. She teaches her daughter about race by telling her

to respect herself but not to exclude [segregate] herself from other races. That's one of the reasons she's going to the school she goes to—there are a lot of different races who go there. I want her to know who she is, and her history, but I want her to also be able to deal with people of other races. She went to a predominantly black junior high . . . and I didn't care for that too much. Because what happens when you grow up in a black neighborhood, and go to a black grade school, junior high school, high school, college—then you hit the workforce, and you really don't know how to deal with them [whites], and they don't know how to deal with you.

Self-Esteem

The historical denigration of blackness in American society and the conviction among parents that their children will encounter racial discrimination, hostility, and rejection links the emphasis on racial socialization to the issue of self-esteem. Most parents agree that it is extremely important for their children to develop a positive self-concept, and it has conventionally been held that racism, negative stereotypes, segregation, and poverty all have a corrosive effect on the self-esteem of black children. Early researchers uniformly reported that these factors had damaged the self-concepts of black children, diminishing their sense of value and worth and even leading to self-hatred.

In 1940, Davis and Dollard examined the impact of race and racism on the personality development of southern black adolescents. They found stereotypes of black people as lazy, childlike, criminal, sexually promiscuous, and unfit for most employment firmly intact nearly a century after slavery had ended. Low self-esteem and self-hatred were common among the children they studied. A similar study by Kardiner and Ovesey (1951)

self-hatred assumption

also argued that the self-concept was shaped by the social conditions of one's life. They concluded that slavery, the destruction of the African culture and the black family, along with the idealization of whiteness, had taken a devastating toll on the self-esteem of children.

Much of the evidence for the self-hatred hypothesis rested on the assumption that black people had actually internalized the dominant value system to the extent that they preferred whiteness to blackness. Black parents were described as greatly concerned about the skin color and hair texture of their children. Davis and Dollard found that special advantages and status were often conferred on children with light skin and relatively straight hair. Such children were more likely to have their basic material needs of food, clothing, and shelter met—especially when having light skin was the result of having a white father. Although these fathers rarely openly acknowledged their black offspring, they did often provide them with some privileges and resources, especially when they had an ongoing relationship with their mothers. Light skin also meant higher social status and a greater opportunity for mobility through class barriers (Kardiner & Ovesey, 1951, p. 2).

Clark & Clark doll study

The best known early research on racial identity among young black children was conducted by Kenneth and Mamie Clark (1939, 1947) in the late 1930s and 1940s. They presented 253 black children between the ages of 3 and 7 with a white doll and a colored doll, and asked the children a series of questions about the dolls. Most of the children could identify their own race and the race of each doll, but having to identify themselves as black elicited extreme negative emotions in some children who, according to the Clarks, sometimes left the testing room in tears. The majority of black children preferred to play with the white doll and, perhaps even more distressing, explained their preference by saying that the white doll was prettier and nicer. These studies were used to document the detrimental impact of racial segregation on the self-identity and self-esteem of black children, and they seemed to be supported in the writings and experiences of blacks who grew up during the pre-civil rights era. Studies supporting the devastating impact of segregation on the self-esteem of blacks were crucial in abolishing de jure racial segregation in schools in the *Brown v. Board of Education of Topeka* decision of 1954. Of interest, however, the Clarks also discovered a regional difference in the responses of children: Those from southern racially segregated schools were less likely than those from the northern region to show a preference for the white doll.

THEORIZING ABOUT SELF-ESTEEM

According to social theorists, the self-concept develops as children learn to distinguish themselves from others with whom they interact and incorporate the values, attitudes, and expectations of others into their person-alities. Self-esteem, the more evaluative component of the self-concept, is based on feelings of competence, worth, and self-approval. It consists of either a positive or a negative attitude toward the self, with a negative self-attitude implying self-rejection and self-dissatisfaction (Rosenberg, 1965). Charles Horton Cooley's (1902/1964) concept of the looking-glass self captures both the interpretive and the evaluative aspects of self-concept formation. He explains that the self is socially constructed based on one's imagination of his or her appearance to others and of the evaluations others are making about that appearance. Self-esteem, one's estimation of one's value and worth, derives from the role-taking process in which others are used as mirrors and their appraisals are internalized. As a result, young children are typically capable of describing themselves as attractive, popu-lar, academically talented, or well loved.

Social psychologists view the self-concept primarily as a product of early socialization within the family. Given that the self is created at an early age, special significance is placed on the evaluations of significant others, such as family members and reference group members, who interact intensively with children during the early years. Thus, the impact of families and other primary groups is implicitly seen as more important than larger social struc-tural factors that come into play later. As Meltzer, Petras, and Reynolds (1975) explain,

> Social experiences, as mediated through the early social groups, the primary groups, begin to shape the child into a moral entity and give a particular direction to the development of the self-concept. While there are certain overriding expectations, patterns of behaviors, values, etc. which are dictated by the society at large, their influence upon the individual is, for the most part, tempered by the early social and primary groups. (p. 13)

Parents and other family members do play a vital role in the development of a child's self-concept. Being reared in a loving, nurturing family where one receives attention and emotional support is important for developing a positive self-concept. Studies of school age children have found that those with high esteem had more verbal communication with parents than oth-ers, and perceived that communication to be positive (Enger, Howerton, & Cobbs, 1994). Joseph (1994) emphasizes the value of spending quality time with children, as attentive listening and personal interest are effective ways to say to children that they are important and valuable. Positive self-esteem is related to accepting responsibility for what happens in life rather than feeling that events happen by chance (Enger et al., 1994). Parenting styles that foster success in other areas of life also enhance the self-esteem of children. Steinberg (1992) has pointed out that regardless of race, age, or social class, parental warmth, strict supervision, and allowing psycho-logical autonomy tend to foster confidence and success.

Although most black parents rank their children's happiness and self-es-teem as their number one value (see Chapter 3), they vary in their ability to instill a positive self-concept in their children. The majority of black children grow up in families where they are loved and the center of a great deal of attention from their parents and extended family. A significant mi-nority, however, live with poor parents who are socially isolated, depressed, and often unable to attend to the emotional needs of their children. Young teenage parents often lack parenting skills and do not understand the im-portance of talking and interacting with their children; rather, they invest their meager resources in material things in an effort to please their children.

Children's self-perceptions are also influenced by the larger social envi-ronment as children eventually learn to see and evaluate themselves from the perspectives and standards of the "generalized other," or the commu-nity. Thus, we judge and compare ourselves with others in the broader society, and it is in that society that we expect to receive affirmation. Coopersmith (1967, p. 37) concurs that although self-esteem is shaped primarily by the respect and acceptance we receive from significant others, it is secondarily affected by our status, position, and success in the world. Recent research has found that self-esteem is diminished among those who physically do not fit society's cultural ideal (Brenner & Hinsdale, 1978; Hendry & Gullies, 1978) and those who live in environments where they are different (e.g., in terms of race or class) from the majority group. Low self-esteem has also been found to lessen academic success and achievement (Harter, 1987) and may be related to crime, drug abuse, and adolescent pregnancy (Berns, 1993).

There are at least three reasons to assume that racial minority children will have lower self-esteem than majority children, according to Rosenberg and Kaplan (1982, p. 212). One is the idea of reflected appraisals, the tendency to see ourselves from others' point of view. While parents labor to instill in their children ethnic pride, their children also see that African Americans occupy the low-status position in virtually every arena of the larger society. They also note that blacks are often not adequately repre-sented in the media, schools, or other nonfamily institutions and are often negatively stereotyped. Second is the social comparison principle, in which we compare ourselves with others. Black children not only have much higher rates of poverty than white children, they are more likely to live in families that are stigmatized as dysfunctional and in communities with high rates of crime and drug dependency. These factors contradict parental mes-sages that they are "just as good as anybody else." Finally, Rosenberg and Kaplan discuss the self-attribution principle, which holds that we evaluate ourselves on the basis of behavioral outcomes. Black children often see themselves as not performing as well as whites in certain arenas, such as school.

Challenging Definitions of Blackness

Theories of how the self is socially constructed, the second-class citizenship of blacks in the United States, and the plight of many low-income African Americans make the notion of diminished self-esteem among black children seem plausible. Yet there is a great deal of evidence that black people have consistently rejected messages of racial inferiority. Racial socialization dates as far back as slavery when black parents, according to Blassingame (1972), tried to "cushion the shock of bondage" for their children and "give them a referent for self-esteem other than their master" (p. 79). Early research by Davis and Dollard found that the behavior of black people refuted the dogma of black docility and acceptance of racist norms; rather, blacks often defended themselves against the indignities of second-class citizenship, even when the penalty for doing so was high.

Black Americans have historically struggled to define and defend themselves, to validate their cultural heritage and family experiences, and to instill pride and positive self-esteem in their children. Historical research shows that although families could not always prevent verbal and physical assaults on their children, they could provide them with the inner resources needed to fight against racism. Gordon Parks (1992), a well-known writer, movie director, and photographer, described his experiences as a young teenager growing up in Kansas in the early 1900s:

> Our parents had filled us with love and a staunch Methodist religion. We were poor, though I did not know it at the time; the rich soil surrounding our clapboard house had yielded the food for the family. And the love of this family had eased the burden of being black. But there were segregated schools and warnings to avoid white neighborhoods after dark. I always had to sit in the peanut gallery (the Negro section) at the movies. We weren't allowed to drink soda in the drugstore in town. I was stoned and beaten and called "nigger," "black boy," "darky," "shine." These indignities came so often I began to accept them as normal. *Yet I always fought back.* (p. 26, italics added)

Fighting back has been a common response of blacks since the institutionalization of slavery. By the early twentieth century, this resistance was taking the form of northward migration and black nationalism. Marcus Garvey organized the largest black nationalist movement in history, with an emphasis on taking blacks back to Africa. According to Pinkney (1993),

Garvey also emphasized "pride in blackness, racial solidarity, and respect for the African heritage of black people" (p. 217). The ideology of black nationalism was also emphasized again during the 1960s by Malcolm X, the Black Muslims, and the Black Panthers. More mainstream efforts to challenge the negative portrayals of African Americans came from civil rights leaders and the black popular culture, such as leading black crowds to chant, "I am somebody." The widespread cultural endorsement of the value of black people, a growing emphasis on black pride, and the initiation of black studies programs no doubt elevated the self-esteem of many African Americans. The civil rights movement and racial integration expanded opportunities available to black people and helped parents talk with their children more openly and positively about issues of race.

This emphasis on racial-ethnic pride in the broader culture during the 1960s coincided with a greater emphasis on racial socialization in families. Racial socialization, defined as giving children positive messages about being black and coping with racism, is more common today than in the past: About two-thirds of black parents racially socialize their children but only about 50% of parents say they were racially socialized by their own parents (Billingsley, 1992). Educated and middle-class black parents, perhaps because they live and work in settings that require more racially integrated social interactions, and expect that their children will do the same, are more likely than other parents to focus on racial socialization (Taylor et al., 1990). Marshall (1995) found that nearly 90% of middle-income parents felt that ethnicity was important in raising their children.

Racial Socialization Messages

Studies of racial socialization messages have identified several major themes, which often vary based on parents' own socialization experiences, socioeconomic status, and integration into the mainstream society (Demo & Hughes, 1990). Parents usually teach their children about racism—that they should expect it and learn to cope with it—and they try to instill in their children messages of self-acceptance, racial pride, and racial solidarity. Racial socialization also includes the growing emphasis among African Americans on teaching children about their heritage and history (Billingsley, 1992; Thornton et al., 1990). Bowman and Howard (1985) found that parents emphasized ethnic pride, self-development, awareness of racial barriers, or egalitarianism. Some parents involve their children in distinctively African American cultural events, such as Kwanza, an African American Christmas tradition, or the Juneteenth celebration, which commemorates the end of slavery. Billingsley (1992) found that racial socialization is often expressed in terms of teaching children African languages and supporting black businesses. Racial socialization themes often resonate with the dominant societal ideology of success, although the underlying message is one of overcoming racism. For example, Thornton and associates (1990) found that hard work and a good education were the most common messages. More broadly, the ideology of success is combined with ideals of morality: Marshall (1995) cites studies showing that parental emphasis on education, hard work, humanism, religiosity, and equality are all part of their racial socialization messages. Bowman and Howard (1985) pointed out that the sex of the child may influence racial socialization messages: Parents are more likely to emphasize racial barriers with their sons but to emphasize racial pride and commitment with daughters.

My study concurs with earlier research in finding that the majority of parents believe race is important and say that they discuss it with their children. Yet parents do not focus inordinately on it; few, for example, select in advance a specific racial script to share with their children or a particular appropriate age frame. Rather, they tend to wait until their children become aware of racial issues and then they provide age-appropriate information. In the meantime, they simply make sure that their children are exposed to environments that emphasize the importance of black people, especially successful role models. Considering his previous self-professed "militancy" on the issue of race, I asked Michael Beard what he was teaching his 11-year-old son about race:

> I really don't come out and teach him anything about race . . . he's seen movies like *Malcolm X,* he knows about Martin Luther King and some of his stances, so I try not to preprogram him at this juncture. The thing that I found is that you have to deal with each person as an individual. So if I instill anything in him, it would be to evaluate each person based on their receptivity to you.

Similarly, Mary Haney emphasizes creating and participating in environments where the achievements and diversity of blacks are highlighted:

> When it's time to get books, I try to get books about blacks. And if they're not about blacks, they have pictures of blacks in them, okay. At church we do black history month programs, and at the day care center—that's when he really started—they just go through the whole thing, "Black Americans are thinkers, Black Americans are nonthinkers." That's why I really loved the day care . . . and we always kept him out of school for Martin Luther King's birthday. We explained who King was, a famous black American, and that

this is a holiday for us, and so he could stay home and celebrate his birthday with us.

Parents believe that children learn about racial differences in school, and they then try to address the questions their children bring home. Yadira Bright, mother of three children, said,

> I think race is taught to kids because it never became a factor until they went to school. The only time I talk to them about it is if they have a problem. I try not to make it a big deal—I want them to be proud of who they are—that's why I have black pictures in my house—I want them to be proud. I don't want them to feel that because they're black, they're bad. . . . But it's not something that's discussed often.

As mothers address the concerns their children have about race, many of which stem from contact with white students, it becomes apparent that children are learning about the preference given to whites in American society. Another mother said,

> We talk often about race, ever since he started school. He would come home and describe children by their color—everybody was brown or pink or white. He didn't know it was a different race at that time, but soon he started focusing on white and black. He'd ask why all the kids in a commercial were white, and they show only one black. He'd say they ought to show more blacks. He asks a lot of questions about why things are the way they are. . . . He's gotten now when he colors pictures, he makes all the faces brown, even Raggedy Ann and Andy. And he asked why Jesus was [white] and if you colored him brown, would that be wrong, and I told him it wasn't wrong. If it made him feel okay, do it.

As parents acknowledge to their children that racism and racial barriers exist, they face the risk of having their children explain their own problems and failures in terms of race. Thus, parents often challenge their children's tendency to racialize every event. Practically speaking, they teach their children to accept responsibility for their own behaviors rather than using racism as a ready excuse:

> [My son] had a problem at school, and the first thing he said was that they [the teachers] only agreed with the girl because she's white and he's black. But I had to talk to him and make him understand that sometimes that's easy to say but sometimes it's a cop-out, that not everything is black and white. If you're wrong, you're wrong; if she's wrong, she's wrong. They have black and white friends. I'm not real radical about black power, or whatever, but I want them to have pride in who they are.

Carrie Gaines, mother of 13-year-old Tiera, said,

> She's quick to do a thing, and then say that the other person doesn't like her because she's black. So I have to get the whole story to know if she's telling the truth or if she's just using race to get out of trouble for mouthing off.

At the same time, parents teach their children that in a predominantly white society, it is likely that they are going to have to learn to accept white authority. One black mother, teaching her daughter how to survive in the "real world," suggested that blacks are and will always be in a subordinate position:

> I tell her that she has to learn . . . that white people are going to be here, wherever she goes, and they're *always* going to tell her what to do. No matter what, there is always going to be some white person telling you what to do, and 9 times out of 10 you're going to have to do it, and do it with the right attitude.

Racial socialization for many black parents, as indicated earlier, means working hard and getting a good education. Although parents understand the importance of race and want their children to learn about their own history and heritage, they primarily want their children to prepare themselves for success by getting a good education. Paula Jackson, mother of 12-year-old Manual, pointed out,

> I like for children to know their culture, as far as their roots, our history, but I don't want them to dwell on that. . . . I know prejudice is out there, and I told the children that prejudice is out there, but don't use prejudice as an excuse. I try to teach my kids how to react, and to react, you need to be prepared, to have some kind of ammunition. And that's where their education comes in, to have something to go forward with. If you get your proper education, and you get real good at what you want to do, and pray—I really do believe they should have a good spiritual base—the doors will open for them. So don't use prejudice as an excuse.

Many parents feel faith in God can help overcome racial barriers. They want their children to know they can succeed if they combine hard work and faith in God:

> I'm trying to teach him work ethics, how he can mesh being a God-fearing child, a Christian, with some of these other things he wants to be. . . . So I'm trying to instill in him that if he puts God first, he can be whatever he wants to be. That not everything is going to come easy, that there are some things

you have to work hard for. And things that come easier often really aren't worth anything. So those things that you work hard for, those are the things that you appreciate more.

Redefining Physical Attractiveness

Recent years have witnessed a resurgence in the issue of skin color as the basis of self-esteem. Reddy (1994) has argued that colorism, an aspect of racism, is still powerful among both blacks and whites in American culture, where light skin, straight hair, and European features are the standards for beauty. This colorism dates back to slavery, when light-skinned blacks were often given greater privileges than dark-skinned blacks. Creating divisions among people of color is a common strategy for domination and social control; in fact, due to widespread colonialization by Europeans, light skin is almost universally accepted as superior to dark skin. Black Americans have often internalized these European standards of beauty and tried to imitate white Americans. In 1965, Clark argued that hair straighteners and skin bleaches were evidence that blacks had come to accept their own inferiority; in fact, he argued that "few if any Negroes ever fully lose that sense of shame and self-hatred" (p. 65). A recent study by Robinson and Ward (1995) of African American adolescents found that a relationship existed between satisfaction with skin color and self-esteem. They concluded that students described as either "lighter" or "darker" in skin color were less satisfied that those who were in between. bell hooks (1992) speaks of being "painfully reminded" of the skin color/hair texture issue while visiting friends on a once colonized black island:

> Their little girl is just reaching that stage of preadolescent life where we become obsessed with our image, with how we look and how others see us. Her skin is dark. Her hair is chemically straightened. Not only is she fundamentally convinced that straightened hair is more beautiful than curly, kinky, natural hair, she believes that lighter skin makes one more worthy, more valuable in the eyes of others. (p. 3)

Racial socialization includes black parents' effort to help children redefine beauty, or at least question why they consider the characteristics of Europeans to be more physically attractive than those of blacks. Darrick Donaldson, father of 7-year-old Eric, said,

> He's just beginning to notice racial differences. We try to focus on the positive, point out black role models, blacks who are achieving. We did the

test where you have two dolls, one black and one white, and ask the child which is the prettiest. He chose the white one, so we talked about that.

Given the common designations of races by skin color, children often have some difficulty identifying themselves as black, as few people are literally black or white, and the skin tones of blacks are especially varied. Blacks co-opted the once-derogatory label of "black" and imbued it with pride, yet young children do not so easily embrace the label. Asked what she told her 13-year-old daughter, Jazmine, about race, Sharon Booker said,

I don't make it [talking about race] a regular thing; just occasionally. She used to not like being black, or at least she always thought she was white. I had to go to great lengths to convince her that she was not white. [Why did she think she was white?] I think because when she started school she had white instructors, and there were only a few black kids, but for some reason she decided she was white. I had to convince her that she was a black kid, just light-complexioned.

Hair texture is another concern among African American children. Sherry Davis talked about her 7-year-old son's sudden interest in having hair that was like that of the white children, although he was going to a predominantly black school:

He started with his hair—he wanted his hair to be curly . . . in big curls, and I told him we could go get a kit for him to make it curly. So I told him if that makes him feel better about himself, I'm all for it. But I told him I wanted to let him know that however his hair looked, I still loved him and he was still beautiful. But he said it would make him feel good, so he wanted his hair to grow so it could be curled.

Laura Raymond's 13-year-old son also worries a lot about his overall appearance—a situation not uncommon among adolescents—but he is especially preoccupied with his hair:

His cousin has this humongous wave thing in his head [hair], and so my son begged me to get [the same thing]. . . . I told him his hair wasn't horrible. I said, " . . . Your hair is beautiful; you have Black hair. There's nothing wrong with your hair that a haircut won't cure." But he kept begging me and begging me, so I finally put it [a hair straightener] in there. . . . But I try to make him realize that whatever features he has, he's black. And I'm black, his daddy's black, his sister's black, his family's black, and to be proud of that.

Self-Esteem Revisited

The common contention that black children have poor self-esteem was challenged during the 1960s. Despite racism, discrimination, and the fact that African Americans as a group occupy low positions in most institutions, it is quite difficult to determine whether race diminishes the self-esteem of black children. In their 1982 overview of self-concept research, Porter and Washington describe the theories of the 1950s and early 1960s as the "mark of oppression" approach, where blacks were "assumed to internalize nega-tive racial images of themselves with a devastating effect on comprehensive self-esteem" (p. 225). They noted, however, that actual research findings on self-esteem are quite mixed.

Some argue that black children's self-esteem has never been adequately measured, and that the self-esteem of black children is as high or higher than that of white children (Crain, 1996; Cross, 1985; McAdoo, 1983; Staples & Johnson, 1993; Whaley, 1993). Cross (1985) has been especially influential in analyzing the black self-hatred hypothesis generated by the doll studies conducted by the Clarks. According to Cross, these studies were not direct measures of self-worth, as racial group preference is not a proxy for self-identity. Black children are more likely than whites to grow up in a multicultural society, to be exposed to both white and black dolls, and to be more accepting of both. In a review of more than 100 studies conducted between 1939 and 1977, Cross noted that most (72%) reported black self-esteem to be equal to or higher than white self-esteem. McAdoo (1985) also rejected the notion involved in the self-hatred hypothesis among young black children:

> These children felt that they were competent and valued individuals and believed that they were perceived positively by their mothers. They felt that they were as highly regarded by their teachers. These findings of positive feelings of self-worth . . . cause one to question the commonly held view of a lower value that minority children place upon themselves because of the negative messages communicated to them in the environment. (pp. 238-239)

The interviews conducted for this study also found little evidence of children with low self-esteem, at least based on the views of their parents. Parents overwhelmingly felt their children had high levels of self-esteem, although they worried about certain aspects of their self-esteem, such as satisfaction with their personal appearance or shyness. They did, however, link positive self-esteem with their children's accomplishments. I asked Sherry Davis how her 7-year-old son Harry felt about himself:

I think he feels pretty good about himself. He says that he's smart, and he asks about getting good grades—[asking] does he have to get all As. But he likes school, he thinks he's a good person. I asked him if he knows I love him, and he said, "Yes," so he knows everybody loves him. I don't think he has any problem with self-esteem. His school performance is excellent.

Speaking of his 9-year-old son, Deitrich, Norman Rodney notes that he does very well in school and was one of a few students chosen to participate in an expanded class including fourth through sixth graders:

He's very creative and inquisitive—he likes to know what's going on and why did things happen. He's a pretty intelligent young man. He thinks very highly of himself when he accomplishes things. He likes to show off what he does. He has good self-esteem, very high.

Similarly, Kim Cole described her 11-year-old son, Van, as

creative and competitive; he has a quick temper, cooperates most of the time, and performs well in school. He seems to have a high level of self-esteem, I guess you would call a big ego—I forgot to mention too he has a very sharp sense of humor; he's very witty. . . . He's very artistic, too, and he can take things he's never seen and figure out how to use them or do something interesting with them.

The relationship between race and self-esteem continues to be contro-versial. Although some researchers have rejected the view of low self-esteem among black children, others continue to see this as an important issue. For example, the belief that black children have high levels of self-esteem is contradicted by psychologists Powell-Hopson and Hopson (1990) in their replication of the self-esteem research done by the Clarks in the 1940s. These researchers found that, nearly 40 years later, 65% of black children chose a white doll instead of a black one (compared with 67% in the Clark study), with 76% saying that the black dolls "looked bad" to them. Black children continue to live in a world where blackness is disparaged in the toy and game market (Wilkinson, 1974) as well as the media. Powell-Hopson and Hopson suggest that the words parents' offer to build positive self-esteem in their children may be inadequate to over-come dominant cultural messages. Their research raises the question of whether teaching children to verbally affirm pride in their race translates into high self-esteem, as noted by Arthur Dozier:

Authority, beauty, goodness, and power most often have a white face. Most of the heros, from He-man to Rambo, are white. In the '60s we were naive,

too, in thinking that saying "Black is Beautiful" was enough. The change has
to permeate society. (Powell-Hopson & Hopson, 1990, p. xx)

Many studies of self-esteem are, in fact, seriously flawed. For example,
age, gender, and social class are rarely considered to be important factors
in the development of black children's self-esteem. As is the case in studying
other aspects of African American life, black children are viewed as a monolithic, undifferentiated group. Many studies focus on young children and
assess whether they feel good about themselves and loved by others. Yet
research shows that young children often lack a distinctive view of themselves (Whaley, 1993), and that they tend to make finer distinctions in how
they view themselves as they grow older (Pallas, Entwisle, Alexander, &
Weinstein, 1990). Research by Branch and Newcombe (1986) found that
older children were significantly more pro-black and anti-white in the multiple choice doll test.

Gender norms also shape children's appraisals of their self-esteem. Because of a cultural emphasis on gender-appropriate behavior, boys and girls
tend to evaluate themselves on the basis of different criteria as they grow
older: Boys tend to emphasize their athletic abilities, and girls, their appearance (Pallas et al., 1990). In assessing the self-esteem of black children
from northern and southern regions of the country, McAdoo (1985) found
that boys initially had higher levels of self-esteem than girls, although boys
in the South lost this advantage over time.

Research rarely examines intragroup variability or the impact of social
context. For example, social class affects self-concept: McAdoo (1983) reported that upper-middle-income children felt more positive about themselves than did low-income children, while Crain (1996) suggested that
social class is an even more powerful predictor of self- concept than is race.
Pallas and associates (1990) found that advantaged children gave themselves higher evaluations in terms of academics and character than did less
advantaged children.

Finally, it appears that a host of psychological and behavioral characteristics are indicative of having positive self-esteem. Yet self-esteem is
rarely measured in terms of black children's sense of mastery, competence,
self-control, or aspirations, and the studies that exist are contradictory. For
example, blacks often appear to have high self-esteem but rank low on
feelings of self-efficacy and adequacy, control over their environment, and
satisfaction with life (Porter & Washington, 1982), all of which are important components of esteem and of feeling like a worthwhile and productive
person. Crain (1996) pointed out that black students tend to have higher
global self-concepts than other racial groups, but significant dimensions of
the self-concept are often not measured. A study by Walter Allen (1981),
comparing black and white male adolescents between the ages of 14 and

18, also raises doubts about the connection between self-esteem and more tangible attitudinal and behavioral characteristics. He found that while black sons had higher educational expectations than did white sons, they had lower self-esteem, a lower academic self-concept, and significantly lower occupational expectations. Expressing pride in being black and embracing the African-oriented cultural styles do not necessarily translate into a sense of self-confidence, mastery, or achievement.

Despite the recent research on racial socialization, few studies have assessed the impact of changing racial beliefs and racial socialization on children. The assumption is that racial socialization benefits children by fostering a positive ethnic identity and teaching them to cope with the stress of racism and rejection. In fact, examining the consequences of racial socialization in itself is extremely difficult, especially given the diversity of racial socialization messages and differences in the extent to which parents emphasize race. Demo and Hughes (1990) found that blacks who said they were racially socialized during childhood, compared with those who were not, had stronger feelings of closeness to other blacks, more concern over black issues, and a stronger commitment to black separatism.

Bowman and Howard (1985) examined the effects of racial socialization on adolescents and young adults in three-generation families. They found that making children aware of racial barriers led to a greater sense of personal efficacy, better academic performance, and higher levels of motivation. Racial socialization may make children less reactive to racial insults and derogatory remarks: Phinney and Chavira (1995) found that the children of parents who had discussed racial discrimination were more likely than other children to ignore incidents of prejudice and less likely to use verbal retorts. In a study of ethnic socialization among middle-income African American parents with children who attended predominantly white schools, Marshall (1995) found that ethnic socialization was actually predictive of lower classroom grades, although the issue of directionality is unclear. Overall, there is much work to be done in assessing self-esteem among black children, delineating the multiple variables that affect it, and determining the role played by racial socialization in the construction of the self.

Conclusions

In this chapter, I have expanded on current research on two important issues: racial socialization and self-esteem. I argue that although the concept of racial socialization is relatively new, black parents have always racially socialized their children. In the past, those messages included teach-

ing the customs and racial dissimulation required of blacks for survival in
a racial caste system, but today racial socialization more commonly refers
to teaching pride and self-acceptance. Although quantitative studies typically report that about two-thirds of black parents engage in racial socialization (Billingsley, 1992), I would argue that racial socialization is nearly
universal among black parents, who can scarcely escape talking about
racism and racial pride and who engage in myriad subtle strategies to challenge the denigration of blackness. At the same time, I point out that black
parent-child relations are not consumed with the issue of race, and that
black parents rarely make precise plans about when and what they will tell
their children about race. I describe how the racial socialization messages
grow out of parents' own experiences and the broader cultural images of
black-white relations, and how they support black pride, the dominant
society's ideology of success, and themes of morality. I also relate racial
socialization to changing self-concepts, a seemingly obvious but rarely explored connection. Much research work still needs to be done to understand the complex nature of self-esteem among black children, especially
how it varies based on age, race, and social class. My personal observations
and research lead me to conclude that black children do typically have a
positive global self-esteem; indeed, black children are often explicitly
taught to accept blackness and *say* that they are proud of their race and of
themselves. A much deeper and enduring sense of esteem, however, must
be linked to real achievements. In this study, blacks who were most confident of their children's positive self-esteem were quick to enumerate their
success experiences. In the next chapter, I explore how gender affects child
rearing.

5

Gender Socialization

"You acting womanish," i.e., like a woman. Usually referring to outrageous, audacious, and willful behavior. Wanting to know more and in greater depth than is considered "good" for one ... Responsible. In charge. Serious ... Committed to the survival and wholeness of entire people, male and female ... Loves the Moon. *Loves the Spirit. Loves love and food and roundness. Loves struggle.* Loves the folks ... *Loves herself. Regardless.*

Alice Walker, *African American Womanist,*
Poet, and Writer (quoted in Arisika Razak, 1990, p. 167)

Girls growing up in African American families rarely escape the accusation, most often made by their mothers, that they are "acting womanish." Depending on the context, the charge can either be a serious condemnation of behavior that is entirely inappropriate for one's age or a playful and even flattering assessment of a daughter's ability to manage, manipulate, or take control of situations. In either case, Alice Walker's elaboration of this African American folk expression makes it clear that definitions of womanhood are socially constructed and culturally variant. Her articulation of the womanish concept implies that women are strong, active, responsible, imbued with a sense of their own worth, and heartily embrace life, love, sexuality, and community. Her womanist perspective resonates with black feminist scholarship, which asserts that the gender ideologies of middle-class, white Americans have never been fully institutionalized among black people (Collins, 1990; King, 1988). This scholarship also has effectively challenged the earlier research that pathologized the organization of gender in black families as matriarchal and dysfunctional (Frazier, 1939/1949; Moynihan, 1965), and has coincided well with the white feminist critique of patriarchy. Very little research, however, has actually examined gender processes in African American families, especially the gender socialization of children.

This chapter focuses on gender role socialization, the notion that "individuals observe, imitate, and eventually internalize the specific attitudes and behaviors that the culture defines as gender appropriate by using other males and females as role models" (Ickes, 1993, p. 79). Although gender ideologies are constructed on the basis of social environmental factors, the family is the most important setting in which gender roles are learned and perpetuated (Crouter, McHale, & Bartko, 1993; West & Zimmerman, 1987). Culturally defined notions of the appropriate attitudes and behaviors for males and females shape parents' expectations for their children and may even affect their perception of the parenting role. For example, a summary of sex role socialization studies conducted by Block (1983) found that parents expect their sons to be "independent, self-reliant, highly- educated, ambitious, hard-working, career-oriented intelligent, and strong-willed" and their daughters to be "kind, unselfish, attractive, loving, well-mannered, and to have a good marriage and to be a good parent" (p. 1341). Also, research has found that mothers typically view sons as more difficult to raise than daughters, and mothers of sons are more likely to believe that they should not work outside of the home (Downey, Jackson, & Powell, 1994). The attitudes of parents are conveyed to children in a variety of ways and, as Bem (1983) has pointed out, children learn to prefer the behaviors and activities deemed appropriate for their sex by the age of 4 or 5.

Modern feminism has challenged the legitimacy of traditional sex role socialization based on the argument that it victimizes and disadvantages women by relegating them to the domestic arena. This critique of traditional gender roles coincided with changes in the economy, especially the growth of "female-typed" work, which was drawing more women into the workforce. Thus, while most black women have always worked outside of the home, by the 1980s more than half of all white women were employed. And, despite the fact that women still lag behind men in earnings and occupational prestige, they have made considerable gains during the past 20 years.

This progress by women may have led many people to believe that gender is no longer a significant barrier to the success of women: Fewer than 30% of the parents in this study agreed with the statement that being a woman makes it more difficult to get a good education and a good job, with white parents significantly more likely to agree than black parents. This racial gap suggests less emphasis on gender, especially as a barrier for women, among black respondents. Overall, there was a high level of support for gender equality among black and white parents in this study. More than 90% of all parents agreed on the equal importance of a college education for girls and boys, and agreed that husbands and wives should share equally in child care and domestic work. However, while they strongly supported the *belief* that husbands and wives should share equally in house-

Table 5.1 Gender Attitudes: Percentage of Parents Agreeing With Each Statement

Statement	All (N = 729)	*Black Parents (N = 525)	White Parents (N = 204)
Husbands and wives should share equally in doing housework and taking care of the children.	91.8	90.1	96.1*
If possible, mothers of young children should be full-time homemakers and fathers should be responsible for the economic support.	47.5	47.6	47.8
It is just as important for girls to attend college as it is for boys to do so.	93.4	91.6	98.0***
+Being a woman makes it more difficult to get a good education and a good job.	24.0	21.7	29.3**
+My child's sex (e.g., being male or female) will make his or her future more difficult.	11.2	13.0	7.2
+Both parents share equally in caring for this child.	25.0	20.6	33.3**

*p < .10; **p < .05; ***p < 01.
NOTE: + = Based on the responses of a subsample of 488 (322 black and 166 white) parents.

work and child care, most indicated that the mother *actually* did most of the child-rearing work.

In this chapter, I briefly examine theories on the social construction of gender ideologies and then apply those theories to the experiences of white and African American women. In this analysis, I concur with scholarship showing that their unique historical experiences have led black women to embrace multiple roles, and that these roles have belied images of them as submissive and dependent on men and produced greater gender equality in families. Yet this falls far short of an adequate analysis of the complexity of gender relations among blacks. First of all, practically all of the work on gender among African Americans has focused on women, ignoring how or whether the African culture or American experience has restructured the roles of men. As Hunter and Davis (1994) have observed, black women denied the prerogatives of femininity are described as drawing on African traditions and forging strong work, family, and community roles, while black men are seen as essentially stripped of their masculinity and marginalized. In this study, only a few parents felt that their child's sex would make his or her future more difficult (Table 5.1), but among blacks, parents of sons were more likely than parents of daughters to feel that way (this information is not shown in the tables). Indeed, by the 1980s, an alarming epidemic of academic failure, crime, substance abuse, and unemployment among young black males led some to dub them a "vanishing species."

Second, despite scholarly support for the legitimacy and viability of a distinctive African American culture, the gender roles of black people have been widely criticized and pathologized. African Americans are immune neither from the impact of those criticisms nor from the pressure to conform to the dominant society's gender norms. In her account of growing up with a brother in a two-parent, patriarchal family, bell hooks (1992) makes it clear that black children are often expected to assume the same gender roles as white children:

> As young children, we were brother and sister, comrades, in it together. As adolescents, he was forced to become a boy and I was forced to become a girl. In our southern black Baptist patriarchal home, being a boy meant learning to be tough, to mask one's feelings, to stand one's ground and fight—being a girl meant learning to obey, to be quiet, to clean, to recognize that you had no ground to stand on. I was tough, he was not. I was strong willed, he was easygoing. We were both a disappointment. (p. 87)

hooks touches on two forces that may push some black families toward embracing more traditional gender roles: religion and social class. African Americans typically describe religion as very important in their lives (see Chapter 6), and traditional gender ideologies are ingrained in Christianity. As we shall see in this chapter, many blacks, especially those who are first-generation middle class, see traditional gender roles as evidence of their respectability, heterosexuality, and success. Additional evidence that blacks often do not easily wear their nontraditional gender roles is seen in the tradition of "love and trouble" (Collins, 1990) between black women and men, a situation that includes mutual criticism for failing to conform to traditional notions of masculinity and femininity. Thus, I examine three ways in which gender roles and ideologies may be transmitted to children. First, as parents were asked to indicate either a son or a daughter as the "focus child," I examine how gender affects the current value priorities and future hopes of parents, their view of the parenting role, and their discipline strategies. In interviews, I directly ask parents to describe how gender affects their child rearing. Then I look at the organization of gender in the family, such as the extent to which parents convey the importance of gender equality by sharing in the home. I conclude by examining the gender dilemma among blacks, a sometimes contentious social context that directly shapes how blacks view being a male or a female.

Theorizing About Gender

Gender ideologies of male superiority/domination and female inferiority/ subordination are ancient in origin, almost universal, and, despite a few exceptions, have been institutionalized cross-culturally by assigning different roles to each sex. Because some degree of sex stratification can be found in every culture, it was traditionally assumed that sex roles reflected the innate, biological, God-given abilities and talents of males and females. Feminists, however, have thoroughly refuted the assumption that sex roles are rooted in biological differences; rather, they have demonstrated that biological sex has been used as the basis to socially define and construct gender roles, and that the social construction of gender varies in different social environments and cultures. For example, although she found no societies where women dominated men, Chafetz's (1988) research revealed that the degree of sex stratification varies across cultures, based mostly on the nature and organization of work, the kinship structure, and ideologies about sex inequality. Sex equality was greater in societies where the labor of women was integral to the survival of the group, where labor was not divided on the basis of sex, and where married women lived with or near their families of origin. Sanday (1981) also found the level of sex stratification to be linked to the social environment. After studying more than 150 societies, she argued that male dominance and aggression, and the exclusion and subordination of women, were more likely in environments that were dangerous or where resources were uncertain or in scarce supply.

The social construction of gender in American society lends credence to the connection between sociocultural and economic forces and sex stratification. Although the ideology of female inferiority was rooted in the Judeo-Christian heritage, the characteristics used to describe women and their work roles were shaped by economic forces. Women legally had a lower status than men in colonial American society, yet they were valued because of their important work roles in the family-based economy and because immigration patterns and maternal mortality made women scarce. By the 1800s, however, their roles were being redefined by the forces of industrialization, which negated the need for female labor force participation. The exclusion of women from paid labor roles gave rise to the doctrine of two spheres: the view that men belonged in the public arena and women in the private arena. Moreover, men were increasingly described as having characteristics (i.e., rational, aggressive) that were seen as valuable in the public arena, while women were seen as having characteristics compatible with their domestic roles (i.e., submissiveness, nurturance). This new gender ideology assumed the primacy of marriage and childbearing in women's lives and made the home the appropriate domain for women. This gender arrangement was much more available to affluent white families than working-class or racial-ethnic minority families (Dill, 1988), and women in these groups continued to participate in the labor force. This definition of gender roles was challenged by early feminism during the nineteenth century and more thoroughly by a second wave of feminism in the 1960s.

Black women also have historically challenged the denial of equal rights to women. Due to race and class barriers, however, they were largely absent from the early feminist movement (Hymowitz & Weissman, 1978), although they eventually formed their own organizations devoted to improving life conditions for all black people. Although difficulties and strains continue to exist, contemporary feminism has been more successful in forging an alliance between women of diverse races and social classes. In recent years, many black women have embraced gender as a major dimension of social inequality and have broadened feminist theory by showing that race and class influence the construction of gender and the exploitation of women (Dill, 1979; hooks, 1981). Black feminists have observed that the concept of femininity used to describe and control white women has rarely been applied to black women, and that race has been a crucial factor in how capitalism and patriarchy appropriate female labor. For example, while white women have been excluded from productive labor and relegated to unpaid, devalued reproductive roles in the family, black women were exploited for their productive labor, first as slaves and later by their concentration in menial, low-paying, labor market positions (Hall & Sprague, 1997). Black feminists have argued that gender norms are constructed quite differently among black people and have suggested that they do not play a central role in the socialization of African American children.

The Social Construction of Gender
Among Blacks

As the contemporary women's rights movement dovetailed the civil rights movement, the saliency of race in defining the experiences of African Americans initially made it difficult for some black women to focus on the issue of gender. Although black women have always seen gender equality as important, to some extent the explicit focus on gender emerged almost inadvertently during the early 1970s, as black family scholars challenged Moynihan's (1965) thesis of extensive family pathology among blacks. Much of this so-called pathology, according to Moynihan, was rooted in the gender roles found in black families. Following Frazier's lead (1939/1949), Moynihan saw black families as matriarchal and argued that the economic roles of men had been usurped by single women who had illegitimate children and ran families, thus undermining the male family role and helping to create and perpetuate racial inequality. His view reflected the dominant theoretical perspective of the 1950s, which saw the only viable family model as a breadwinner-homemaker unit. This notion, however, was increasingly being contested by both feminists and black family scholars, both of whom saw gender equality as a possibility. While agreeing that gender is socially constructed by sociocultural and economic forces, black scholars contended that the gender roles and ideologies of middle-class white society had never been fully accepted among black people. They argued that single women, especially those supported by their larger kinship groups, were quite capable of heading families, and that married black couples shared the responsibility for economic and domestic work and had relatively egalitarian marital roles. The overall view was that African American families were culturally unique rather than pathological, and that their gender ideologies arose from their African cultural heritage and American experience.

The cultural perspective emphasizes that black families in the United States were never allowed to conform to white American gender roles or social definitions of masculinity and femininity because blacks were brought to the United States primarily as workers. In her 1984 book on the history of the African American female experience, *When and Where I Enter* (1984), Paula Giddings points out that "racial necessity has made Black women redefine the notion of womanhood to integrate the concepts of work, achievement, and independence into their role as women" (p. 356). Similarly, Dill (1988) explained that, because of slavery and racial exclusion, black people have always been forced to subordinate their family roles to their work roles. She found that even after slavery had ended and millions of blacks had moved into the sharecropping system, they were criticized for trying to emulate the breadwinner-homemaker family system that was prescribed for whites because it excluded women from productive labor. Although this labor was a necessity for black women in the United States, Burgess (1994) has argued that it reinforced West African cultural values in which women were expected to be economically productive and had some power and authority in sociopolitical matters. The family, economic, and political roles of black women have led them to define womanhood differently from their white counterparts—to view it in terms of strength and activism.

Arguably, the black cultural tradition has fostered at least a degree of gender equality in black families; the question here is whether the sex of the child affects parents' behaviors, values, or socialization strategies. The gender socialization of black children has rarely been the topic of systematic study, yet most research assumes that gender equality is the norm in black child-rearing practices (Lewis, 1975; Peters, 1988; Reid & Trotter, 1993; Scott, 1993). An early study by Lewis (1975) argued that "the black child, to be sure, distinguishes between males and females, but unlike the white child he is not inculcated with standards which polarize behavioral expectations according to sex" (p. 228). According to Lewis, all black children are taught to "mother" and are instilled with similar traits of assertiveness, willfulness, and independence. More recently, Scott (1993) has argued that parents emphasize the development of similar traits in their sons and daughters. Explaining the difficulty of raising black daughters, he pointed out that they

> are socialized to be at once independent and assertive as well as familistic and nurturant . . . to be sexually assertive . . . to be as authoritative, individualistic and confident as African American sons are, and as economically self-sufficient and personally autonomous as sons are. (p. 73)

Peters (1988) supports the gender neutrality hypothesis by arguing that age and competency are more likely than sex to be the basis for defining children's roles in black families. Similarly, Reid and Trotter (1993) actually observed the interactions of children between the ages of 8 and 10, and reported that black children exhibited less gender-stereotypical behavior than did white children. Thus, the hypothesis of gender neutrality in black child rearing is widely supported in previous studies but for the most part is not grounded in empirical research.

Current Priorities and Future Hopes

The findings in this study suggest that neither black nor white parents today make very many gender distinctions in their child-rearing work. For example, as indicated in Table 5.1, the overall ordering of value priorities are the same for black and white parents, regardless of the sex of the child. The single largest category of black and white parents emphasize self-esteem as the most important value and, while both are slightly more likely to emphasize this for daughters than for sons, the differences are not statistically significant. This greater emphasis on the self-esteem of daughters may reflect the common finding that the self-esteem of girls tends to decrease as they reach puberty. When black parents are compared based on their income and educational levels, we see that the gender gap in concern over self-esteem is more prevalent among parents with less income and education than among more affluent parents. All parents see respect and obedience as their second most important priority, with white parents of

Table 5.2 Current Values by Sex of Child: Percentage of Parents Ranking Each Item as Their Top Priority

| | Comparison of values by race of parent and sex of the focus child: | | | |
| | Blacks Parents of | | White Parents of | |
	Sons (N = 262)	Daughters (N = 257)	Sons (N = 93)	Daughters (N = 109)
Happiness and self-esteem	51.4	57.8	60.2	71.4
Respect and obedience	37.4	37.6	29.5	16.5***
Doing well in school	31.7	25.6	17.0	17.1

| | Comparison of values of black parents by income and sex of the focus child: | | | |
| | Low-Income Parents of | | High-Income Parents of | |
	Sons (N = 91)	Daughters (N = 107)	Sons (N = 68)	Daughters (N = 47)
Happiness and self-esteem	49.4	56.7	60.6	59.6
Respect and obedience	38.8	38.8	33.3	24.4
Doing well in school	41.2	34.1	14.8	17.8

| | Comparison of values of black parents by education and sex of the focus child: | | | |
| | Less Educated Parents of | | More Educated Parents of | |
	Sons (N = 108)	Daughters (N = 111)	Sons (N = 151)	Daughters (N = 144)
Happiness and self-esteem	46.2	56.2	57.7	59.7
Respect and obedience	43.8	44.2	35.5	32.6
Doing well in school	43.9	39.6	23.9	18.4

*$p < .10$; **$p < .05$; ***$p < .01$.
NOTE: Tables do not necessarily equal 100% because a few parents chose more than one value as their top priority. *Low income* equals $15,000 per year or less, and *high income* equals more than $30,000 per year. *Less educated* means having a high school diploma or less, and *more educated* means having at least some college through postgraduate work. Six black and two white parents did not indicate the sex of the focus child.

sons significantly more likely to emphasize this than parents of daughters. There is no statistically significant difference among black parents in their support for this value, although those with high incomes are similar to white parents in emphasizing this more for sons than daughters. Overall, black parents place a higher priority on doing well in school than white parents, but there are no significant differences in the importance of this value based on the sex of the child.

The parents in this study make very few gender distinctions in terms of the future hopes they have for their children (Table 5.3). As a group, black parents of sons and daughters are equally likely to emphasize getting a good education and a good job but, although the differences do not reach statistical significance, black parents with more income and education emphasize this more for sons than for daughters. Thus, it appears that social class may be positively related to embracing the traditional gender norms of white society. Less affluent and educated black parents make virtually no gender distinction in their support for this value. Having a strong, loving family ranks second as the future hope of black and white parents, regardless of the sex of the child. Here again, there is a slight tendency for parents of daughters to emphasize the value of family more than parents of sons. Finally, simply wanting their children to grow up being nice and compassionate human beings received the lowest priority ranking of parents, with virtually no gender distinction in support for this future hope. Overall, then, the picture that emerges from these two sets of variables—current priorities and future hopes—is that neither black nor white parents make very many statistically significant gender distinctions. But there is a tendency for less affluent and less educated black parents to emphasize the importance of happiness and self-esteem more for daughters than for sons, and for white and affluent black parents to emphasize respect and obedience more for sons. Compared with the parents of sons, we also see a greater percentage of parents with daughters emphasizing the importance of having a strong and loving family, which can be seen as support for traditional gender norms.

Parenting Roles and Discipline

Parents were also asked to prioritize three parenting roles in terms of their importance and to indicate which discipline strategy they used most often. The single largest category of parents ranked being a teacher and guide as their top priority, followed by being a good provider, and, least important, being a disciplinarian (see Table 5.4). The only statistically significant gender distinction was found among white parents, who were much more likely to emphasize being a teacher and guide for sons than for daughters. Although not to the same extent, almost all parents placed a greater value on teaching and guiding sons. This is an important gender distinction in that being a teacher and guide suggests training a child for autonomy and independence, and thus reflects a traditional gender role distinction. Similarly, parents of daughters more heavily emphasized their role as a good provider, suggesting that girls more than boys need to be

Table 5.3 Future Hopes by Sex of Child: Percentage of Parents Ranking Each Item as Their Top Priority

	Comparison of values by race of parent and sex of the focus child:			
	Blacks Parents of		*White Parents of*	
	Sons (N = 262)	*Daughters* (N = 257)	*Sons* (N = 93)	*Daughters* (N = 109)
A good education and job	63.3	60.3	52.2	49.0
A strong/loving family	30.7	39.7	28.4	35.6
Being nice and compassionate	16.4	15.0	25.6	21.4

	Comparison of values of black parents by income and sex of the focus child:			
	Low-Income Parents of		*High-Income Parents of*	
	Sons (N = 61)	*Daughters* (N = 66)	*Sons* (N = 68)	*Daughters* (N = 47)
A good education and job	71.6	69.0	50.8	44.7
A strong/loving family	27.2	33.7	37.5	37.2
Being nice and compassionate	18.8	16.7	21.3	23.3

	Comparison of values of black parents by education and sex of the focus child:			
	Less Educated Parents of		*More Educated Parents of*	
	Sons (N = 108)	*Daughters* (N = 111)	*Sons* (N = 151)	*Daughters* (N = 144)
A good education and job	70.9	72.8	54.5	48.6
A strong/loving family	31.1	38.4	32.6	40.7
Being nice and compassionate	21.6	19.3	21.3	20.3

$*p < .10; **p < .05; ***p < .01.$
NOTE: Tables do not necessarily equal 100% because a few parents chose more than one value as their top priority. *Low income* equals $15,000 per year or less, and *high income* equals more than $30,000 per year. *Less educated* means having a high school diploma or less, and *more educated* means having at least some college through postgraduate work.

taken care of. Although it is unclear how this role is actually played out in families, this suggests some tacit support for the idea of girls as more dependent than boys. Few parents saw their primary role as that of disciplinarian, but parents of daughters were much more likely to do so than parents of sons. Here again, this supports traditional gender role training by suggesting that girls require more control and discipline. These subtle gender distinctions were more evident among high-income and educated black parents than among their less affluent, less educated counterparts.

Table 5.4 Parent Role by Sex of Child: Percentage of Parents Ranking Each
Item as Their Most Important Parenting Role

| | Comparison of values by race of parent and sex of the focus child: | | | |
| | Blacks Parents of | | White Parents of | |
	Sons (N = 262)	Daughters (N = 257)	Sons (N = 93)	Daughters (N = 109)
Being a teacher and guide	63.4	58.2	77.8	71.4*
Being a good provider	37.2	44.4	23.9	27.6
Being a disciplinarian	8.5	9.9	1.2	5.9

| | Comparison of values of black parents by income and sex of the focus child: | | | |
| | Low-Income Parents of | | High-Income Parents of | |
	Sons (N = 91)	Daughters (N = 107)	Sons (N = 68)	Daughters (N = 47)
Being a teacher and guide	62.1	54.8	77.3	67.4
Being a good provider	44.6	47.3	21.5	27.3
Being a disciplinarian	11.4	17.7	6.2	9.3

| | Comparison of values of black parents by education and sex of the focus child: | | | |
| | Less Educated Parents of | | More Educated Parents of | |
	Sons (N = 108)	Daughters (N = 111)	Sons (N = 151)	Daughters (N = 144)
Being a teacher and guide	59.6	64.6	71.2	59.7
Being a good provider	45.4	46.0	30.1	37.7
Being a disciplinarian	17.6	15.8	6.4	11.4

*$p < .10$; **$p < .05$; ***$p < .01$.
NOTE: For explanations of *low* and *high income* and *less* and *more educated,* see the note to Table 5.3.

This may mean that gender-appropriate behavior becomes more important among blacks as social class increases.

Finally, parents were asked to indicate which discipline strategy they used most: reason and logic, loss of privileges, and spanking. Unlike white parents, black parents of daughters were significantly more likely to emphasize reason and logic, suggesting perhaps that the discipline of sons required stronger, more tangible measures. All black parents emphasized loss of privileges more for sons than for daughters, with parents who are more affluent and educated much more likely to make this gender distinction. This may reflect the fact that black parents who are better educated

Table 5.5 Discipline Strategy by Sex of Child: Percentage of Parents Ranking Each Item as Their Most Frequently Used Discipline Strategy

	Comparison of values by race of parent and sex of the focus child:			
	Blacks Parents of		White Parents of	
	Sons (N = 262)	Daughters (N = 257)	Sons (N = 93)	Daughters (N = 109)
Reason and logic	44.4	57.8**	56.2	56.2
Loss of privileges	53.0	45.2	46.2	44.3
Spankings	12.1	10.2	1.2	5.0
	Comparison of values of black parents by income and sex of the focus child:			
	Low-Income Parents of		High-Income Parents of	
	Sons (N = 91)	Daughters (N = 107)	Sons (N = 68)	Daughters (N = 47)
Reason and logic	50.0	54.7	45.2	60.5
Loss of privileges	55.4	51.2	54.4	30.4
Spankings	8.9	8.4	8.3	6.7
	Comparison of values of black parents by education and sex of the focus child:			
	Less Educated Parents of		More Educated Parents of	
	Sons (N = 108)	Daughters (N = 111)	Sons (N = 151)	Daughters (N = 144)
Reason and logic	48.3	59.6	48.6	59.5
Loss of privileges	52.5	47.8	51.7	38.2
Spankings	17.9	10.8	7.2	9.3

$*p < .10; **p < .05; ***p < .01.$
NOTE: For explanations of *low* and *high income* and *less* and *more educated,* see the note to Table 5.3.

and more affluent include a broader array of discipline strategies, or that the children in this social class have more privileges that can be withdrawn. Very few parents say they rely on spanking as their most frequent discipline strategy, and there are few gender differences in the use of spanking.

The Role of Gender in Child Rearing

As indicated in the foregoing analysis, there were few statistically significant differences in the socialization values, views, and strategies of black and white parents, but there was some evidence that traditional gender norms are still at work (see Table 5.5). Conducting interviews allowed me to ask parents directly about the importance of gender socialization in rearing their children, and thus to understand some of the complexities in their gender ideologies. Although the survey data above suggest slightly more gender distinctions among affluent and educated black parents, interview data show that these parents were least likely to explicitly endorse traditional gender role socialization. One explanation for this seeming contradiction may lie in the different types of questions asked in surveys and the interviews. It may also, however, reflect less awareness among parents of subtle gender distinctions or the tendency of parents, when asked directly, to give a more socially desirable response. In any event, parents, especially those in the middle class, tended to reject the notion that gender influenced various aspects of their child rearing, such as assigning household tasks or supporting their children's interests. As Sherry Davis, a college-educated, married mother of two young sons, said,

> No gender roles for me—my husband says I traumatize the kids by talking so much about what they're going to do when they get older . . . we treat all able bodies the same: work is work, and anybody can do it. I plan to have him help with anything that needs to be done. I wouldn't care if he did feminine things, like take dancing. He wanted to take dancing lessons a long time ago, and he loves to brush and fix hair, but lately he's turned toward male stuff, playing ball. But I tell him I'll love him regardless of what he does; be happy with his life, [and] I won't have a problem with it.

Another married, employed mother, Paula Jackson, has two daughters and one son. She believes that gender plays very little role in her child rearing, and emphasizes the importance of teaching both girls and boys independence. Asked about how gender shaped her expectations for 12-year-old Manuel, she said,

> I have the same expectations of him as I do from my daughters. . . . I tell my daughters that they should be able to take care of themselves, and he should be able to take care of himself, whether he's married or not. He should know how to wash his clothes, keep his house, take care of his books—he should be able to be independent, just like the girls should . . . we talk about this all the time, and when I forget, my girls remind me!

Vickie Mellon, the single mother of one young son, emphasized the importance of teaching her son egalitarian marital roles and participation in domestic work:

I will definitely teach my son that men and women are equal; he is not the head of anybody. His wife will always have input and say-so in whatever is going on in their lives. And he needs to know that . . . when we were growing up, boys washed dishes, boys cooked; girls washed dishes, girls cooked. My mother taught us pretty equally to do everything, just in case you were on your own you wouldn't have to depend on somebody.

Parents clearly expect both their sons and their daughters to participate in housework, and they emphasize the value of the children knowing how to take care of themselves. Similarly, the career expectations of parents are not notably shaped by the child's gender. Timothy Shannon, a 42-year-old schoolteacher and father of three children, said,

I'm teaching my daughter to have a career. If she then chooses to go back in the home, a decision between her and her future spouse, then that's fine . . . my daughter wanted to be a doctor, but she talks about being a nurse now, and it kind of ticked me off, because some lady at church told her that because she was a girl she couldn't be a doctor. . . . I was really upset about that [because] if my daughter wants to be a doctor, we're going to find the money to pay for it.

Children, however, learn gender norms from socialization agents other than their parents. Melba Brown, legally separated from her husband since her children were quite young, said that as a single mother she does not make gender distinctions in rearing her son and daughter. She contended that children just naturally learn them from the broader culture:

I don't try to treat her differently [but] she knows she's a girl, and she demands it. She is always saying, "I'm a girl," and her role as a female and my son's as a male are so pronounced . . . it's like, you take out the trash, I butter the bread; you shovel the snow, I fix the hot chocolate . . . I don't know, I guess it's learned behavior. I'll take blame for it, but I don't know where it came from because I'm a single parent here: I'm fixing the hot chocolate, shoveling the snow; I'm cutting the grass, and I'm preparing the dinner . . . and I wasn't complaining.

More educated and affluent parents say that they do not adhere to gendered patterns of child rearing in assigning domestic work to their children or in supporting their children's career ambitions. There is emphasis among some parents, especially those who are less educated, newly middle class, or both, that "girls should behave like girls and boys should behave like boys." Two sentiments underlie these beliefs: respectability and heterosexuality. Black families have been highly stigmatized and denigrated as dysfunctional, based largely on the view that males and females have not assumed their "proper" roles. Thus, parents from lower-class backgrounds often see the ability to adhere to middle-class norms as a sign of respectability. Elisha Martin said that she tells her 11-year-old daughter that she is a "warrior" and must "carry on the struggle by fighting every day of her life for the respect of black people," and for her own personal respect. This could be viewed as a very strong depiction of womanhood, yet Elisha also expects her daughter to be "ladylike":

> I tell her that she has to carry herself well, and she can't go around being loud and screaming and yelling because that is one thing she likes to do. I tell her she has to sit properly and is expected to act like a lady by carrying herself well—when you go somewhere, you have to sit properly . . . so I speak to that a lot, that she's a girl and these are the kinds of things girls should do, like being ladylike.

Being ladylike is a way to earn respect, according to Elisha. Asked whether she would teach her daughter that men and women should have equal rights and equal responsibilities, Elisha also holds contradictory views:

> I will in one sense, but not in another. In terms of the family, I'm teaching her that a man is supposed to take care of her. When she gets in the real world and finds out that's not the case, that's another story. But in the workplace, I'm teaching her that they are equal.

Timothy Shannon emphasized that he wants his son to learn what it means to be a *man,* "not a *black* man," and for him that means having respect for women:

> We teach him that you treat yourself and you treat your girlfriend or your wife with a tremendous amount of respect, that you don't just look at her like an object. How do you do that? I show respect to my wife, my mother-in-law, all other women, and by doing that it teaches him how to respect women. Because he's not going to do what I say. Kids absorb things from the people who mean a lot to them. If I didn't mean a whole lot to him, he would find someone else to get his moral values from.

A second factor affecting parents' feelings about gender-neutral child rearing is sexuality or, more explicitly, the fear that not emphasizing sex-typed behaviors could somehow foster homosexuality in their sons. McCreary (1994) pointed out that males are much more likely to avoid feminine behaviors than females are to avoid masculine behaviors, and that the gender role transgressions of males are more harshly punished by parents. His research revealed that this was due less to social status (i.e., female behaviors are less valued) than to views about sexual orientation: Males who do not display gender-congruent behaviors are seen as homosexual. Homophobic attitudes are strong in black communities, as is the belief that homosexuality is learned rather than inborn, and this is especially true for persons with a strong Christian orientation. Some parents interviewed for this study, when asked questions about gender roles, responded by talking about sexual orientation. Asked if she thought there should be differences in the way girls and boys are reared, Yadira said,

> You know, I watch my kids . . . they say how kids are born homosexuals? I find that hard to believe, you know . . . but I've watched my kids, and my boys are boys and my girl is a girl. But when [my son] liked to play with dolls, I've caught myself saying, "No, you don't need to play with that!" . . . so I don't really encourage [boys playing with dolls]. But he only did that for a little while; he's not really into that now . . . it's not that he acts prissy or anything . . . it's just the fact that he had that doll that bothered me a little bit.

Similarly, although Murray Haney does nearly all of the family cooking, he refused to buy his son a toy stove. They explained,

> [Mary] Our son wanted a stove and refrigerator for Christmas once and I was going to get it, but he [the father] wouldn't let me, even though he's a cook. [Murray] Well, today I know which way he's going, so I would. [You mean his sexuality?] Yeah. But if he wants to play with girl things now, it's okay, because I know which way he's going.

The Organization of Gender in the Family

Children learn gender roles not only through the explicit child-rearing philosophies of their parents but, often more powerfully, through the organization of gender in their own families. As indicated earlier, the parents in this study are highly supportive of gender equality in sharing child care and housework, although they admit they have not met this ideal. As was the case in this study, other researchers also have found that black women are primarily responsible for both housework and child care (Wilson, Tolson, Hinton, & Kiernan, 1990).

The interview data reveal that the gender division of labor is based mostly on whether the wives are employed: Full-time homemakers, predictably, do most of the child care and housework, and dual-earner couples share. Yadira Bright, a stay-at-home mother with three children, takes on most of the responsibility for the home because of her husband's efforts to earn a living and try to start his own business. Asked who had most of the responsibility for parenting, she said,

> I think I do, because I'm here, and because right now he's working a full-time job and trying to start a business. And when he's done with that job he usually goes to the office . . . but I'm trying to get him to where he'll have some input in what they do. He does help with their homework, but usually I have to say, "Get the kids," or "Don't you hear that?" But I tell him when they do things, like misbehave, that he needs to talk to them, but it's usually me telling him to do something. He wants to do more of the fun things—play basketball, take them places like to the movies, but I'm the disciplinarian.

Sonya Davis, a 40-year-old mother who is a full-time housewife, was asked who was most responsible for caring for her daughter:

> Me. *[What percentage of the work do you do?]* Ninety percent. *[What does her father do?]* She has to have medicine rubbed on her every night; he always does that. He always turns the shower on for her. He always puts her to bed, and makes sure she says her prayers.

Both Yadira and Sonya had quit their jobs in recent years, thus opting to stay at home and devote more time to their children. Although they would have appreciated a little more support from their husbands in parenting, they voluntarily entered the role of full-time homemaker and have few overall complaints about this gender arrangement. They define domestic work and child care as primarily their responsibility.

There is clearly much more sharing in dual-income families, in which sharing child care does not seem to much of an issue at all. Although she is employed, Barbara Jackson enjoys taking care of her children so much that she sometimes finds it difficult to share child care work with her husband:

> I am learning—I mean I love to take care of my children—but I'm learning in just the last few years to share it. But I just really enjoy doing it. I am one of 12 kids: My mother had eight boys and four girls. My mother had to work in order for us to eat . . . [and] I did a lot of taking care of children. My mother just kind of dumped that on me. So I still do it today. My husband is incredible . . . he's just a great help. He loves to help the kids with their homework, and as they get older he takes more responsibility. And he loves to plan our vacations and go on field trips with the kids at school.

In fact, dual-earner couples were best at sharing family work. In the interview with Norman and Phyllis Rodney, Phyllis pointed out that primarily, Norman does about everything. He has always cooked—he's a better cook than I am. . . . I think men and women should share equally in the responsibility of the home, but it depends on what the strengths and weaknesses of the two people are. Like if a person cannot cook, I don't want them cooking for me. But I think there should be an equal sharing—child care, definitely.

Black fathers in dual-income families, perhaps because many grew up in fatherless homes or feel that most black men do not help with child care, take special pride in their participation in the domestic arena. Murray and Mary Haney almost vie to determine who does the most in caring for their two sons:

[Murray] As far as rearing the children—total rearing? That even includes cooking? [Mary] I would have to take a bigger rank in it, simply because I take them to school and pick them up . . . but, nevertheless, he is responsible for dressing them. I do most of the cooking, but he does all the bathing. So it's probably . . . well, I do the laundry and I do the clothes. I think that's where I'm going to get the upper hand. [Murray] Give me that question again? I would say 50/50. [Mary] Do you think so? [Murray] I would say so, because I think we're pretty even. [Mary] Well, 51/49, because I do the laundry. But really, it's pretty even. [Murray] Well, I used to do the laundry, but I got fired. [Mary] And he used to take them to day care and to school . . . okay, it's probably 50/50.

A notable feature of my interviews was how easily and proudly fathers participated in the care of children and family life in general. In each case, this participation in family life was made possible by a stable economic position. Fathers who are unable to legitimate their family roles because they lack such economic positions often play marginal roles in the family and may find that they are widely criticized and denigrated. Mothers struggling to raise children alone often feel abandoned and express hostility toward absent fathers, thus creating a social environment of contentious gender relations. As most socialization is subtle and indirect, I maintain that this environment can have an important impact on how girls and boys come to define their gender roles.

The Gender Dilemma of African Americans

In a study examining the meaning of motherhood in the black culture, Collins (1987) described the socialization of girls by saying,

Black daughters are raised to expect to work, to strive for an education so they can support themselves, and to anticipate carrying heavy responsibilities in their families and communities because their skills are essential for their own survival as well as for the survival of those for whom they will eventually be responsible. (p. 7)

If black daughters are essentially taught to "do it all," what are black sons taught? Are they taught the same values? The theme of black women challenging narrow definitions of their roles is common, but less has been said about whether black men have challenged Eurocentric notions of masculinity or redefined manhood in ways that include characteristics or roles sex-typed by the dominant culture as female. African American males face pervasive discrimination and disadvantages in the larger social environment; indeed, Gibbs (1988) has argued that every American institution has failed to respond to the needs and problems of black males, who have been "miseducated by the educational system, mishandled by the criminal justice system, mislabeled by the mental health system, and mistreated by the social welfare system" (pp. 1-2). But do family socialization patterns also disadvantage males? Although few studies have examined how families socialize black male children, some have suggested that parents support competence and self-reliance more in their daughters than in their sons (McAdoo, 1988; Staples & Johnson, 1993).

In a 1984 research article, Staples also pointed out that black mothers are less likely to discipline their sons or to teach them independence and responsibility. He posited three possible explanations for this: (a) that mothers have accepted the ideology of whites and see their sons as worthless and irresponsible, (b) that black women are morally and intellectually superior to males and simply expect less of them, and (c) that mothers protect and coddle their sons out of fear for their sons' safety (p. 78). Given the high risks of physical harm that black boys face, whether from the racist acts of public officials or the violence in their own communities, Staples concluded that mothers' differential treatment of sons was motivated mostly by concern over their safety. Yet it is also the case that child-rearing strategies are based on parental perceptions of the opportunities and barriers their children will face in becoming successful. It may well be that mothers invest in their daughters because they see them as having a greater opportunity to succeed in mainstream society.

In any event, if nontraditional gender norms are the rule in black families, it could be that girls benefit more from socialization practices that allow them to develop "male" characteristics than do boys for embracing female-typed behaviors. Carr and Mednick (1988), for example, examined the impact of sex role socialization practices on the achievement motivation of black preschool children. They found that having a nontraditional sex role orientation heightened girls' achievement motivation but lessened that of boys. The failure of men to attain success, as it is defined by the traditional gender role norms of the dominant society, has also led to the pervasive denigration of males in black families and communities (Ladner, 1971; Stack, 1974; Wilson, 1996). Although they may be socialized into accepting strong, self-reliant roles, ethnographic research has found that the majority of African American females want to marry a man who can help support them and a family (Anderson, 1989; Jarrett, 1994), and they blame black men for their inability or unwillingness to contribute to successful marriages. As Ladner (1971) observed more than 25 years ago, black adolescent females form poor opinions of men early in life:

> The idea that men are weak or impulsive was formed very early . . . it was found that some young girls had firmly established the idea that men are "no good" by the time they were eight years old. These young girls had observed interpersonal conflicts between adult males and females in their homes and in the families of other relatives and friends, and had based their conclusions on the same. (p. 188)

Many children are exposed to what many see as almost uniformly bad relations between African American males and females. This gender dilemma between black men and women stems primarily from their inability to conform to the gender roles prescribed in the dominant society. From slavery through the current postindustrial economic transition, significant numbers of black men have been unable to fulfill the family provider role, and women have had to compensate by combining family work with employment. And because patriarchal privileges and power rest as much on economics as tradition, black men have been unable to establish themselves as heads of their families or to obtain the respect that comes from that position. In fact, numerous studies have shown that black male participation in the family correlates directly with their ability to provide economically for their families.

Most research has failed to examine the gender consequences of this issue; rather, it has argued that there is simply a greater degree of gender equality in black families; that poor, single-mother families are viable; and that children in father-absent families have other male role models. These themes gained even greater credence with the resurgence of feminism and its critique of the middle-class, nuclear family. Feminism helped idealize the work, family, and community roles of black women and contributed to what Dyson (1993) has called "the womanist tradition in African-American culture," with an "articulation of powerful visions of black female identity and liberation" (p. 185). The irony, Dyson noted, is that during this same period of time, the black male predicament was reaching its nadir, as seen in the escalating rates of violence, homicide, and suicide among black men.

The declining status of African American males during the past 20 years has become a major social issue. Black male adolescents in urban areas are especially likely to perform poorly in school, enter society unprepared for either marriage or labor market participation, and, unable to achieve masculinity through the traditional route of economic success and power, resort to crime, violence, and sexual prowess as evidence of their manhood. Concern over their high rates of drug use, incarceration, and death during the 1980s led to the widespread sentiment that black men were a "vanishing species." Blake and Darling (1994) have pointed out that the mortality rate of African American males between the ages of 15 and 30 is three times higher than that of their white counterparts, and that black females start to outnumber black males after the age of 14. They believe the inability of black males to conform to Eurocentric conceptions of manhood is the key problem. The rate of interpersonal violence between black males and females is extraordinarily high; Straus, Gelles, and Steinmetz (1980) found wife abuse to be 400% higher in black than in white families. Ucko (1994) suggested that this may be the result of a conflict between African cultural expectations of strong, independent females and the American norm of male control over women.

The failure to conform to traditional gender roles takes a high toll on women and men. While men may resort to violence as a coping strategy, women often rely on childbearing as a way to achieve status and meaning in their lives. Not only are rates of depression high among single mothers (McLoyd, 1990), but a recent study, comparing black and white males and females, reported that black women experienced the highest levels of discontent and dissatisfaction (Austin & Dodge, 1992). The gender dilemma has created an environment where black males and females routinely criticize and blame each other for their presumed shortcomings: Black women are sometimes accused by their male counterparts of not being submissive, supportive, or appropriately "feminine." Women, on the other hand, assert that men should simply be secure enough to handle a woman's strength. Maggie Terrance, explaining what she saw as being responsible for the high rates of divorce among blacks, said,

> Well, if a person cannot handle your strength, that means [he's] insecure. And it's sad to say, but we do have a lot of insecure black males. I don't want my daughter to limit herself so that this man will be nice to her. There's more to life than that. And I don't want my son to go and treat a woman badly because she's sure of herself, instead of checking out himself to see what he's all about. And that's what I try to teach my children. I think black female strength could be a reason why there's such a problem, but it's because of [men's] insecurities.

Black women often blame black men for their inability to take care of their families, and some believe that black men simply are not taught responsibility. Asked how she would explain the high rate of nonmarital pregnancy and childbirth among African Americans, 30-year-old Kelly Coleman said,

> Since most women don't mind being married, it must be the men. I would imagine that men, black men and white men, are taught differently. The white men are taught to take responsibility for the family, that it is his responsibility, whereas the black man has seen, too much of the time, women being so responsible that he doesn't even feel responsible, nor is he taught that he's responsible. So he doesn't marry that woman and take responsibility for the family. Not just the teaching, but just seeing so many black women take responsibility, what's to encourage him to take on that role? Unless you deliberately teach it to him, that's not what life is going to teach him.

That black women are often more successful than black men in obtaining an education and getting a job adds to the gender dilemma. Based on the argument that black men are more threatening in a white environment than black women, who also have the special advantage of being a "double minority," some argue that black women simply have an easier time than men. Only a few parents thought that this might be the case for their own children, but none agreed that it had been true in their own experience. Terry Carter, a 36-year-old divorced mother of two children, saw opportunities for women expanding and thought this would make it easier for her daughter. She was also one of the few who adhered to the belief that things are easier for women:

> I think she will have a better career than she would have in the past, because there are so many black females entering the labor force in every area . . . pioneering the way for our children. She'll have it better; I'm more concerned about my son than I am my daughter. Society has a tendency to lift up a black woman before they'll lift up a black man—it's easier for the black woman now to accelerate in the workforce. Because our companies and corporations are still being headed by the white male, and in his mind the black male coming up means surpassing him in life rather than just on the job. And they have a tendency to keep their foot on the black man. Now the woman, that's another story. . . .

Vickie Mellon, however, the mother of a son, did not believe that being a black male would make it more difficult:

> No, I don't think my son will have it harder than if he were a girl, because a lot of the groundwork is being laid for him right now. I believe each

generation should try to improve what happened to them. My mother improved what happened; each generation should push the next one a little bit higher. So for that reason I don't think he'll have it that much more difficult.

None of the few men interviewed in this study said that they thought women had it easier, and women were quite vociferous in their rejection of the notion that they personally had found success more easily because of their gender. Laura Raymond, a married mother of two children, has been fairly successful in her career in the insurance industry. Yet, asked if black women have it easier, she said,

> I hear that black women are able to do more, move better through the workforce and things like that, I *hear* that, but I don't *see* that, you know? I don't see it; I'm not a witness to it. My opinion is you got it hard either way. . . . I feel the sentiment is, "If you're black, get back," and it almost doesn't matter if you're a woman or a man. That's just my opinion. People say black women have it easier, but I look at the company I've been with and I see some of the other women who have about the same experience and education as me—I think in some areas I even have a little bit more knowledge and a little more education—but for some reason they've reached certain levels that I haven't reached, and it's not that I haven't been trying, because I have. . . . So I think either way, black people just have it rough, period. Okay, I'm going to be biased here: Women might have it a little bit rougher because a lot of times we have the mother role, and we can't step out of that, and men can.

Other respondents also noted the dual responsibility among black women for handling home and career, and definitely did not see the woman's role as easier. Jackie Brady, single mother of 7-year-old Johnny, said,

> I don't think black women have it easier than black men—*No*, I don't!! Do you? I think black men use that as an excuse. Hell no, I don't have it easier; I work every day, hard! Nobody ever comes to me and says, "Jackie, why don't you let me take care of Johnny for a little while" or "Johnny's such a cute little boy, how about me buying his clothes for the year?" Nobody does that for me. And as far as men? . . . his daddy's gone. Who's it easier for, me or him? He's out kicking and married and I have this responsibility. . . . I feel men use it as an excuse, to excuse themselves from responsibilities, to excuse themselves from self-success, for self-motivation.

Finally, Shirley Becker, a widow who works for the federal government and operates her own business during the evenings and on weekends, succinctly stated,

I don't think women have it easier over black men. I think women are just more go-getters than black men are—I can't think of the right word—but she'd be more of a driving force to succeed in what she wants to do, because black women overall are like that compared to black men.

Conclusions

African American women have a long tradition of fighting for both gender and racial equality; still, the recent emphasis on gender entered black family studies through the back door, primarily in response to the Moynihan report of pervasive gender role confusion in black families. Since then, a great deal of excellent scholarship has managed to reject the black matriarchy thesis and reconceptualize the organization of gender among blacks as a valid cultural alternative. The burgeoning literature on gender among African Americans has largely focused on how women have managed to broaden the concept of womanhood to include images of strength and independence as well as the ability of women to simultaneously participate in a variety of roles. Feminism has helped propel interest in the study of the womanist tradition among African Americans, and the work of black feminists has expanded gender studies to include the impact of race and class on women. Most researchers have contended that gender neutrality is the norm in the socialization of black children, and have argued that blacks in general are less likely to embrace rigid gender roles. The black parents in this study were considerably more likely to say that race would make their child's future success more difficult than to say that gender would.

The findings of this study reveal that there are some gender differences in the expectations parents have for their children, their perceptions of the parenting role, and their approaches to discipline. Most of these gender differences are relatively minor but tend to increase when social class is considered. Overall, compared with the parents of sons, parents of daughters are more likely to be concerned about their children's happiness and self-esteem, more likely to see having a strong, loving family as their most important future hope for the child, and more likely to emphasize the importance of being a good provider and a disciplinarian. Parents of sons, on the other hand, were slightly more likely than those with daughters to emphasize respect and obedience as a current value, getting a good education and a good job as a future hope, and being a teacher and guide as a parenting role. Gender distinctions appear to increase with social class. In the interviews, the majority of parents did not see gender as affecting most aspects of their parenting, such as participation in housework or career interests. Reluctance about gender equality in child rearing was most evident among those who equate traditional gender roles with respectability or have fear that female-typed interests in sons are related to homosexuality. In dual-income families, gender equality was also evident in the division of housework between spouses. I conclude with a discussion of the gender dilemma, or the strains experienced by African Americans who do not conform to the traditional gender norms of the dominant culture.

6

Beyond the Nuclear Family

*"In the old days you would know everybody. You would have
been inside everybody's apartment . . . On our block you would
get chastised by any old lady. 'Boy, what are you doing over
here? Does your mother know you are over here?' She'd get you
on your toes by the ear and she'd drag you home . . . Oh yeah.
You had about twelve mothers, seventeen fathers. Everybody
knew what you did."*

Mitchell Duneier, *Slim's Table* (1992, p. 207)

These comments from working-class black men at *Slim's Table*, captured
in Duneier's ethnographic study, express sentiments that are common
among people who grew up in racially segregated neighborhoods of the
pre-civil rights era. Coming of age in the late 1950s and early 1960s, I
experienced participation in the extended family, community, and church
as part of the interwoven unity of my life. Our three-bedroom home housed
my two parents, five siblings, paternal grandmother, and, more temporar-
ily, a steady stream of relatives who, like my father, had eagerly abandoned
the rapidly fading sharecropping system of Arkansas in favor of industrial
and domestic jobs in the North. Most of my extended family members
eventually found their own homes, most often in the same area, and this
close proximity strengthened family and community relations. Schools and
housing were racially segregated and, because public accommodations acts
had not been passed, we had limited access to restaurants, parks, theaters,
or other facilities located outside of our neighborhood. Yet our neighborhood was anything but the "institutionalized pathology" Clark (1965) described as the "dark ghetto."

Rather, it was composed of remarkably diverse families who felt a
strong sense of community. My parents had one of the few breadwinner-
homemaker marriages in the area; more common were dual-income families, single employed mothers, and grandparents who were raising their
grandchildren. We knew and interacted frequently with our neighbors,
extended kin, and members of the church family. Overall, adults exerted a

formidable amount of social control over children, so that very little unacceptable behavior went unnoticed or unaddressed. Many of the family and community resources of African Americans, however, have now diminished, as have the availability of public resources. In looking beyond the nuclear family, I discuss the impact of the community, extended families, religion, and public policy on child rearing in African American families.

The Community

African Americans who grew up before the civil rights movement, many of whom have achieved a great deal of educational and occupational success, commonly lament the loss of the strong sense of community that they once had. I spent the first 15 years of my life living in the same house, surrounded by people I knew well and cared about. Kinship ties, geographic stability, and lasting friendships with neighbors created a cohesive community setting for children. A unified effort between parents, teachers, friends, and church members to supervise and support children just seemed to naturally evolve in this setting. Yet our community was shaped as much by structural as cultural forces; for example, racial segregation fostered similarities in social class and life opportunities, and in a sense undergirded the unity and consciousness of kind we experienced.

The structural forces that would forever alter our way of life, however, were already in the making, namely, school desegregation and urban renewal. We lived amidst constant rumors that our neighborhood school would be closed with racial integration, and that urban renewal efforts—namely, the creation of a freeway—would result in the loss of our homes. Both events eventually unfolded: First, school desegregation dispersed the children in my neighborhood to two different "white" schools, where we were sternly admonished not to engage in some of the play activities typical of our own culture. Despite these efforts, school desegregation turned out to mean nothing more than a longer walk to school and access to better supplies and facilities, as white flight quickly transformed the school into a predominantly black school.

Urban renewal came more slowly, but the homes in our neighborhood were eventually purchased at "market value"—a sum far too meager to allow most homeowners to invest in better quality homes—and we were forced to move. So we dispersed into different sections of the city, causing a pattern of desegregation and resegregation, and forever diminishing the sense of community we once had. Wilson (1978) attributed part of the decline in black communities to loss of the "vertical integration" among African Americans of all social classes that existed prior to the 1960s. Since then, he argued, the more affluent blacks have abandoned inner-city areas, thus intensifying the concentration and consequences of poverty among people still living there. While those in poor neighborhoods often have a high level of social integration, it is primarily in middle-class neighborhoods, according to Wilson (1996), that parents have control over their children.

The assertion that inner-city black neighborhoods are suffering from the loss of middle-class residents is challenged by Massey (1990), who argues that it is actually racial segregation, not integration, that has produced the urban underclass and its persistent poverty. According to his analysis, the inability of many African Americans to acquire housing in racially integrated areas has led to concentrations of unemployment and poverty in selected urban areas and the creation of an underclass characterized by high rates of family disruption, welfare dependence, school failure, and crime (p. 350). Indeed, racial segregation continues to be the norm in most neighborhoods. More than 60% of the 10 million black households in the United States are in predominantly black areas, and 30% are in areas that are 90% black (Leigh, 1996). Leigh (1996) notes that nearly half of all blacks in metropolitan areas live in high-poverty neighborhoods. In addition, African Americans (42%) are less likely than white Americans (68%) to own their own homes, and the mean value of homes owned by blacks ($55,500) is less than the mean value of homes owned by whites ($91,700). Thus, black children are quite likely to grow up in high-risk, racially segregated areas where the quality of housing is poor.

Duneier's (1992) research rejects a second implication in Wilson's thesis—that the loss of the middle-class means the loss of morality and respectability in black communities. His ethnographic research highlights the availability of working-class role models in the black community—men who value caring, respectability, hard work, and family. The presumed reliance of lower- and working-class blacks on their middle-class counterparts, Duneier argues, has been overdrawn by sociologists who "fail to acknowledge the historical strength of the black working and lower working classes, creating the impression that without middle-class and even upper working class respectability, the black community is devoid of its moral base" (p. 130). Anderson (1991) concurs, noting that there are two lifestyles in inner-city neighborhoods, described by residents as "decent" and "street." The culture of decency, characterized by strong families, hard work, and efforts to get ahead, is highly regarded by neighborhood residents. Yet young people are often lured into the street culture of drugs, violence, and sex, as it appears to offer more certain and immediate gratifications.

McLanahan and Sandefur (1994) examine the consequences of race, social class, and family structure on the quality of community life available to children by comparing dual- and single-parent families. They found that white children are more likely to live in affluent communities than are black children, regardless of family structure. Overall, black children are much more likely to live in neighborhoods with high levels of poverty, female-headed families, AFDC recipients, jobless fathers, vacant buildings, and high school dropouts (p. 118).

Black children are also more likely to attend schools that are racially segregated and to have friends with behavior problems who do not value education. McLanahan and Sandefur also found that children who live in single-parent families experience more residential moves, further diminishing the strength of community ties. Single-parent families move twice as often as two-parent families, and moving for the latter group is much more likely to entail acquiring better homes and jobs. School quality and geographic mobility, according to McLanahan and Sandefur, account for about 10% of the disadvantage associated with living in a single-parent family. They also note that neighborhoods characterized by two-parent families provide more organized sports, after-school programs, libraries, and other activities. The 1992 Carnegie Council on Adolescent Development noted the importance of out-of-school activities for children, especially as a buffer for those in high-risk neighborhoods:

> In their study of the nonschool hours of youth, they found that unscheduled, unstructured, and unsupervised time spelled trouble for young people. The report recommended that communities build networks of youth organizations that incorporated the interests, energies, and ideas of young people, and that they be given roles of responsibility within these organizations— teaching others, caring for facilities, and planning activities, finances, and governance of the youth groups. (Heath & McLaughlin, 1993, p. 4)

Despite numerous problems in many neighborhoods, community participation and self-help efforts are still very common among black people; in fact, there is a proliferation of such efforts in many areas. In some cases, community residents have taken on the responsibility for stopping crime, closing drug houses, and improving environmental aesthetics. There are also efforts to prevent teenage pregnancy and protect children. A 1981 survey found that two out of five black adults contribute money to community self-help groups, and about 25% participate in the efforts of these groups (Hill et al., 1993, p. 92). Still, community self-help today is more contrived, formalized, and directed at specific social issues than in the past. Older African Americans, often seeing their younger counterparts as lazy, unmotivated, and immersed in a culture that embraces drug use, violence, and misogyny, lament the loss of community they once found in inner-city areas.

Extended Families

Often cited among black Americans is the African proverb, "It takes an entire community to raise a child," and autobiographical and scholarly works all attest to the presence and value of extended families in the socialization of children. Extended families are a proud tradition among blacks, as they have been a primary resource for survival and child rearing. In the family research of the 1950s, an extended family was defined as having more than two generations residing in the same household. Billingsley (1968/1988) used this definition when he described extended families as households in which at least one related child or adult lives with a nuclear family. Black children (31%) are more likely than children of other races (20%) to live in extended families based on coresidence (Tolson & Wilson, 1990), and this is especially the case for children of single mothers. Stack (1974) described black children as born into an extended kin network, where they are cared for by multiple relatives. This female-based kin network provided valuable aid to teenage mothers, most of whom were neither emotionally nor financially prepared to rear children alone. Extended families provide single mothers with a greater opportunity to get an education, work, and maintain social contacts (Wilson, 1989). Some studies show that single mothers in extended families, compared with those living alone with their children, have lower levels of psychological distress and higher levels of self-esteem and personal efficacy (Taylor et al., 1990).

Extended families often have been seen as compensating for absent or minimally involved fathers. Ruggles's (1994, p. 145) historical research supports this view by showing that from 1880 through 1960, single-parent and parentless households were much more likely to be extended than were other households. Tolson and Wilson (1990) studied 64 families and found that the addition of a second adult, whether father or grandparent, brought significant resources to the family: a stronger religious orientation, additional caregivers, and more social support for mothers. Pearson, Hunter, Ensminger, and Kellam (1990) reported that 10% of black grandmothers live with their first-grade grandchildren, and they were significantly involved in parenting. Their role was secondary to the mothers, however, and even more circumscribed when fathers were in the home.

When defined by the coresidence of more than two generations, the prevalence of extended families among blacks has decreased sharply since the 1980s (Ruggles, 1994). This reflects a growing preference for the nuclear family among blacks but also public assistance policies that restrict aid to mothers who live alone with their children. Most current research on extended families among blacks focuses less on coresidence than systems of mutual aid and support, and it generally argues that extended family ties continue to be strong. Based on a survey of more than 2,000 African Americans, Taylor (1986) concluded that close extended family relationships, characterized by frequent interaction and mutual aid, are extremely important to blacks. More than 35% of his respondents interacted with an extended family member nearly every day and 90% felt very or fairly close to their extended family.

In a similar study, nearly 85% of African Americans reported having a relative or friend they could call on during a serious emergency, and family members were found to be the most important source of support due to the "permanence of relationships and the operation of explicit normative expectations for affection and mutual assistance" (Taylor, Chatters, & Mays, 1988, p. 301). McAdoo (1983) pointed out that black children often spend considerable time visiting with grandparents and other relatives during holidays and vacations or when mothers were busy working, and that the majority expect their own parents to take care of their children if they are unable to do so. The availability of social support may help dissipate some of the stress caused by undesirable life events, according to Ulbrich, Warheit, and Zimmerman (1989). Their research noted that blacks experience more adverse life events than whites, but they were less vulnerable to the stress of such events because of the extended family system and attributed many events to social inequality rather than personal failures.

Are extended family ties among blacks rooted in cultural traditions or economic factors? Afrocentric theorist Nobles (1985) traced the importance of the extended family to black Americans' African heritage, in which the family is seen as being composed of several households with "lines of authority and decision-making transcending any one house unit" (p. 86). Similarly, it has been pointed out that

> the deep sense of kinship has historically been one of the strongest forces in traditional African life. Kinship is the mechanism which regulates social relationships between people in a given community; almost all of the concepts pertaining to and connected with human relationships can be understood and interpreted through the kinship system. (Harvey, quoted in Hill et al., 1993, p. 106)

Caldwell's (1996) study of the West African family system reiterates this theme and describes its origin. He explains that the

> essence of lineage is the reverence for ancestry and descent, for the West African concept of the lineage is a continuing line stretching infinitely backward into the past and forward into the future, with those now alive having responsibility for its continuation. The force that made the concept meaningful was a belief in the survival, for at least some generations, of male ancestral spirits with the abilities to interfere in this world. This belief lingers

and it is a powerful element in giving the old, especially old men, such respect and power. This also means that higher fertility is far more rewarding than anywhere else on earth, for the young materially assist their parents at every stage of their lives, and failures to do so can lead the old to curse the young, often significantly with infertility, thus effectively denying them continuing lineage. (p. 335)

Although the traditional African concept of family has influenced the creation of extended family, some studies have found that economic factors shape their continuation. Wilson (1989) has argued that the long tradition of extended families owes its persistence to a "high incidence of poverty, unemployment, extramarital births, and marital dissolutions" (p. 383), and most empirical study supports this assertion. Scheirer's (1984) research found that multigenerational households in particular are the product of economic necessity, as the majority of parents, married or single, would prefer to have their own homes. Mutran (1985) reported a combination of cultural and economic forces that supported extended family ties among blacks, with age influencing the importance of each factor. Her study found that black elderly parents both give and receive more help than do white elderly parents. She suggested, however, that while cultural ideology might explain the mutual aid offered by older African Americans, economic factors appear more likely to explain the assistance given by the young. Moreover, she concluded that controlling for social class eliminates much of the racial difference in mutual aid. The argument for the economic explanation is persuasive, especially when one defines the extended family in terms of coresidence. Extended family ties based on mutual support and assistance, however, persist among blacks in the middle class (McAdoo, 1981).

The research data that were collected for this study found that African Americans continue to value and participate in extended families. Based on an analysis of survey data, black parents were significantly more likely than their white counterparts to report that their extended family was very involved in helping rear the child (Table 6.1); still, nearly half of all blacks did not report such involvement. Among black parents, a low income significantly increased the likelihood of having the extended family very involved in helping raise the children, suggesting that such participation is greater among the poor and may be based on economic factors. The interview data provide an interesting perspective on the qualitative nature of extended family involvement; they show that extended family ties are often stronger and more satisfying among the affluent. For middle-class parents, extended families are based more on free choice than on a sense of obligation and involve the provision of emotional-psychological rather than material support. Laura Raymond, a middle-income married mother of two children, is proud of her strong, supportive family ties, especially as they

Table 6.1 Extended Family: Percentage of Parents Ranking Extended Family as
"Very Involved" in Helping Raise the Focus Child

	My extended family is "very involved" in helping to raise this child:
All Parents	47.7
black parents	55.3
white parents	33.1***
Black parents	
low income	60.9
high income	45.8**

$*p < .10; **p < .05; ***p < .01.$

relate to child rearing. She describes the support she receives from her
mother and siblings this way:

> My family is very important—everybody raises him [her son]; it's like
> everybody's involved. I have used this . . . like if one of his teachers calls and
> says he's acting up in school? I tell his aunt, both of his aunts, his grand-
> mother, his grandfather—besides me and his dad—his paternal grandmother,
> so it's like everybody knew. And so even though they love him and they care
> about him, they make it a point to let him know—"What's this I hear about
> you talking out in school? You don't do that. I expect better from you."

Grandmothers often make special investments not only by spending time
with children but also by sharing a religious orientation with them. Deron
Donaldson describes his 7-year-old son's relationship with his grandmother
this way:

> He has a very strong relationship with his grandmother. He spends every
> Saturday evening with her—they cook, play games, watch TV, talk—and she
> takes him to church on Sunday. He always sits with her in church. He sits
> with her in church every Sunday instead of with us.

Extended family ties may be weaker and less satisfying among those who
need them the most—poor, single mothers. Although they are more likely
than their affluent counterparts to reside in extended family settings, the
support they receive from grandparents is more obligatory, more material
in nature, and less likely to produce satisfying relationships based on reci-
procity. In some poor families, the resources of grandparents are meager
and simply stretched too far. Some grandparents have too many grandchil-

dren to invest very much time and energy in each one; they are affectionate caregivers for their grandchildren but often do not develop close, personal relationships with each child, nor can they remember all the birthdays or attend special events. Shawn Branson, a 21-year-old mother of four, said that her own parents were young and already had numerous grandchildren. Asked how involved her parents were in helping her raise her 6-year-old daughter, Shawn hesitatingly said,

> Well, she don't see her father. Well, my parents, they . . . well, she does go over there every weekend, so they're really fond of her. They help me a lot with her. They're just average grandparents really, not really making any difference.

Another single mother, Jackie Brady, also feels alone when it comes to rearing her son.

> Nobody helps me—I'm serious, and I have a lot of siblings. And that's one of my gripes—remember I told it was just me and [my son]? Well, it is, basically. No, they haven't been helpful. That's why I have no regrets about moving. My sisters, they come through when they feel like I'm leaving or doing something without them. . . . I think they mean well, but as far as helping, no, nobody helps me with him, financially or any other way, and I just have to face that. That's just the way it is.

Shirley Becker, a widowed mother, also feels alone in rearing her two children. She has never had much family on her own, and, when he was alive, her husband always objected to such support:

> No, I haven't had much—no, I haven't had *any* assistance. It was just me and my husband. My immediate family doesn't live here, but I have some relatives here. But never have they done anything, and my husband was one of those who didn't want to lean on family. He didn't believe in it. So we survived it. We did it ourselves.

As previously noted, extended families traditionally meant the coresidence of more than two generations in a single household. Based on this definition, it was easy to say that extended families were more common among blacks than whites. When extended family ties are based on mutual assistance and support, however, it is difficult to make this argument, as most families do provide some assistance to their members.

The bulk of research has fallen far short of providing a clear definition of or measure for extended family ties and, given that it rarely includes diverse races, it does not compare the strength of family ties in various racial groups. A recent study by Roschelle (1997), however, explored supportive networks by interviewing a broad sample of respondents from a national survey of households. Moreover, her study compared four racial groups: blacks, Chicanos, Puerto Ricans, and non-Hispanic whites. She concluded that extended families do not represent a cultural norm for racial minority families; in fact, whites received more child care help and household assistance than any other group (p. 181). Of interest, the economic explanation did not hold much sway either. Although some have argued that poverty was responsible for the maintenance of extended family ties, it now appears that the escalation of poverty since the 1980s has reduced participation in extended kin networks. There is clearly a need to reconceptualize the meaning and nature of extended families.

Do Children Benefit From Extended Family Participation?

Extended families have been an important tradition and survival mechanism for African Americans; thus, researchers have rarely examined their negative consequences or their demise in modern America. For the most part, extended families have been viewed favorably, as evidence of our African roots, ability to share and adapt, and sense of caring and collective responsibility. And it seems clear that children usually benefit from extended family arrangements, especially in cases where they expand the number of loving adults involved in their care and provide resources that were otherwise unavailable. In some cases, however, the traditions involved in extended families, such as sharing resources, child keeping, and informal adoption, can also cause significant problems and conflicts. For example, when participation in the extended family means coresidence, more often between single mothers and their own parent(s), it may strain the economic resources of parents, lead to overcrowding in households, and create conflicts over the division of child care and household duties. Mothers and grandmothers do not always agree on child-rearing issues, and conflicts often leave mothers feeling that their authority is being undermined and grandmothers feeling unappreciated. It is difficult for any two adults to negotiate issues such as these, and even more so when the adults involved have a temporary and sometimes obligatory relationship that arises from poverty.

When extended family households are based on poverty, there is also often a great deal of geographic mobility involved because most single mothers prefer to have their own homes. Efforts to establish this independence often means several moves, with children changing neighborhoods and schools each time. And, as Wilson has pointed out, children in extended families are "exposed to a significant level of fluidity in the formation of families," which may include continuous changes in household composition. Few studies have examined how these factors affect black children, but child development research overall suggests that children benefit from stable environments and consistent emotional bonding with parents.

In her study of child keeping among low-income blacks, Stack (1974) noted that children were often "transferred back and forth, 'borrowed' or 'loaned,' " (p. 66) for a variety of reasons: having mothers who were too young or too poor to care for them, for the convenience of starting a new relationship with a man, or simply as a way of fostering kinship ties. Stack suggested that children simply accept the reality of these arrangements, but she provided little speculation about how it affects their emotional well-being. She did, however, point out that such arrangements are not always consensual; for example, mothers may not agree with their kin network's appraisal of their ability to raise their own children. Mothers, in fact, may feel that their rights are being compromised by such arrangements, and even those who willingly allow others to raise their children for a period of time sometimes have difficulty regaining custody (Hill, 1994). A study of extended family relationships among blacks in a small southern community also pointed to their advantages and disadvantages. Dressler (1985) found that "young women perceive the highest level of extended kin support and yet report the greatest number of depressive symptoms" (p. 45) as they saw extended kin ties limiting their autonomy and independence. Of interest, he noted that the buffering effect of extended kin support on life events was only evident among males.

Extended family ties mean that black children are subjected to the authority of a wide variety of adults, relatives and nonrelatives, who claim parenting prerogatives although many are not vested in the child on an intensive, long-term basis. Children are often expected to respect all adults and to obey them, which can lead to the imposition of inconsistent externally imposed rules that make little sense to the children involved. Such rules provoke rebellion in children and, in many cases, efforts to manipulate the rules to their own advantage. It may also mean informal adoption by grandparents or other relatives, which can lead to feelings of rejection (Hammons-Bryner, 1995). One mother in my research reports having been steadily shifted from home to home and believes she was deeply traumatized as a result:

> My godmother had most of the responsibility for taking care of me; that's as far back as I can remember. I can't remember when I started living with her; I was too young. But I remember leaving for a long time. . . . Mama got married and they came and got my sister and I and moved us with them.

Then we moved with my aunt; then we moved back [to] where grandpa was.
. . . Then Moma married again and then we moved to [another city] and lived
there. She stayed with him a couple of years or something, then she divorced
him and we moved to Kansas City. . . . I was always back and forth, back and
forth.

The Demise of the Grandmother's Role

Grandmothers, called by Frazier (1939/1949) the "guardians of generations" because of their aid in caring for children and keeping families together, have traditionally been the backbone of the extended family. Grandmothers continue to provide care for their grandchildren, sometimes in the
absence of parental care. More than 1 million black children live with their
grandparents, and in 38% of those cases, both parents are absent (Billingsley,
1992). In recent years, extended family resources have waned with the
growth of poverty and early age initiation into parenthood and grandparenthood. Among low-income blacks, grandmothers are often in their thir-
ties and are less willing than grandmothers in the traditional black family
to assume primary responsibility for rearing their grandchildren. Based on
a study of 30 low-income teenage mothers, Ladner and Gourdine (1984)
reported that

> grandmothers complain about unmet emotional and social needs. They
> appear to feel powerless in coping with the demands made by their children.
> They comment frequently that their children show them no respect, do not
> listen to their advice, and place little value on their roles as parents. (p. 23)

Burton and Bengston (1985) also found modern grandmothers more
disappointed and less accepting and supportive than traditionally depicted
in family studies. Two important factors affected the attitudes of grandmothers in their studies: the fact that being a grandmother is associated
with old age and that the role came when they were overcommitted. One
grandmother in their study pointed out, "You may think I'm a terrible
person for feeling this way but I can't help it. I am just too young to be a
grandmother. That's something for old folks, not for me."

Another pointed out, "I'm 39, footloose, and fancy-free. I love my
grandbaby, but I don't have time for knitting booties and babysitting. I've
done my part. Now it's my turn and I could care less who doesn't like it."
Black women may be becoming more acculturated into the mainstream's
society's notions about the appropriate age to become a grandmother, and
may feel especially burdened if they still have their own children at home.

Overall, African Americans accept but do not welcome early grandparenthood. Many warn their children that if they have babies early in life, they are going to have to assume care for them alone, although this rarely happens. One mother in my study, asked to explain the sex education she had given her 14-year-old daughter, said, "The bottom line: Don't do it, and if you do I'm not taking care of any babies!" Parents have high educational expectations for their children and, realistically, see early childbearing as a major obstacle to fulfilling those expectations. Many black women also feel that they have been tied to child rearing their entire lives, first helping rear their siblings and then their own children, often with very little help. By their midthirties, they are facing the prospect of freedom from child-rearing responsibilities for the first time in their adult lives, and they want to pursue other interests and activities.

Not only are grandmothers less willing to accept child care responsibilities, but the notion that grandmothers improve the quality of parenting provided by mothers, especially those who are young and poor, has also been challenged in recent years. Chase-Lansdale, Brooks-Gunn, and Zamsky (1994) examined parenting practices in 99 young, low-income, African American multigenerational families. They concluded that, overall, coresidence with grandmothers had negative consequences on the quality of parenting for mothers' and grandmothers' parenting, although there was some variability based on the ages of the mothers.

Despite these challenges and changes, blacks often cling to the earlier era of strong extended families and the wisdom of grandmothers as the solution to current problems. Melba Brown, legally separated from her husband and rearing two children as a single mother, is a social worker with broad experience in dealing with African American families. For her, the main problem is that black parents have lost extended family resources yet have not learned to obtain help from other sources:

> I work in social work, and I have a lot of black kids in foster care—the system has a lot of black kids. And why are these kids coming into care? Why can't they make it at home? . . . I think black people traditionally don't seek help; we don't admit we have a problem that we cannot handle. And we won't seek help, so it mushrooms and explodes and we end up with authorities stepping in and telling us how to raise our kids and how to live our lives . . . a lot of problems in the black family could be helped, not by professionals, but by asking your grandmother! We didn't have these problems 50 years ago, and why not? Because we were making use of our own support systems. Grandma was right there, auntie was down the street. We were taking care of our own family; we didn't have a foster care system raising our kids, but we weren't being prideful either.

Religious Resources

Deeply rooted in the African American experience is a sense of spiritually that typically takes the form of church membership. Using recent survey data, Brashears and Roberts (1996) concluded that black Americans may well be the most religious group in the world. They noted that in 1991, nearly 81% of black people were church members, and 93% felt religion would become even more important to them during the next few years. The National Urban League Black Pulse Survey found that two-thirds of blacks attend church either weekly or several times a month and that 70% regularly send their children to Sunday School (Hill et al., 1993). During the 1960s, some research predicted rising disaffection among blacks with the traditional church, which emphasized emotionality, otherworldliness, anti-intellectualism (e.g., the uselessness of formal education), and authoritarian relationships between leaders and followers. In fact, a sizable number of blacks have joined nontraditional churches or become apostates (Ellison & Sherkat, 1990), yet the majority of blacks consider religion to be a crucial aspect of their lives. Religion continues to be a vital resource for black parents in rearing their children. The church provides many services and programs aimed at children and youth, including day care, preschool programs, remedial education, drug abuse and pregnancy prevention, tutoring, and recreational activities (Hill et al., 1993, p. 87). In recent years, the mentoring of black males has become a special mission in many black churches.

African American interest in religion stems from its importance in West African society. Ohuche and Otaala (1981) have pointed out that in the traditional worldview of Africans, time moves cyclically, with people tied to an endless cycle of death and reincarnation in a world alive with both evil and ancestral spirits (pp. 14-15). Much of the African religious system revolved around getting assistance or protection from these spirits. Black Americans, of course, have embraced Christianity but have Africanized its style of worship based on their own ethnic heritage. Yinger (1994) notes that there is a close and natural affinity between religion and ethnicity: "Almost nowhere . . . can an ethnic order be described and analyzed without reference to a religious factor" (p. 255), and he pointed out that the connection is nowhere more apparent than among African Americans. Slavery and racial segregation have no doubt enhanced the importance of religion among blacks. As Yinger points out, the fundamental facts of religion are that evil, pain, bewilderment, and injustice exist, and that one "can ultimately be saved from those facts" (p. 256).

The church has played a significant role in the lives of African Americans, from the efforts of the underground railroad to the civil rights move-

Table 6.2 Religion: Percentage of Parents Ranking Religion as "Very Important" and Indicating That the Focus Child Was "Very Involved" in Religion

	All	Black Parents	White Parents
Religion is very important in my life	62.1	71.2	38.9***
Child is very involved in religious training	33.5	39.8	21.3***

*$p < .10$; **$p < .05$; ***$p < .01$.

ment of the 1960s. Black churches are also central in the community, as noted by Ellison and Sherkat (1990). They have served as centers for the discussion of community issues, as sources of material, emotional, and social support, and as places for political leaders. The church is often described as one of the few institutions built, financed, and controlled by blacks (Rogers-Dulan & Blacher, 1995). In 1965, Clark described the black church as compensation for "the daily subservience and emotional restraints" imposed on blacks due to their inferior status as well as an important "social and recreational club and a haven of comfort for the masses of Negroes" (pp. 174-175). Through the church, blacks gain authority, political power, the opportunity to make financial decisions, and the freedom to display and develop a broad array of artistic talents. Studies show that participation in organized religion exerts a significant positive impact on the health and life satisfaction of African Americans, and that religious involvement promotes continuity in personal and family relationships and systems of social support (Levin, Chatters, & Taylor, 1995).

The vast majority of black parents (71%) in this study ranked religion as very important in their lives, and they were significantly more likely than whites to do so (Table 6.2). Neither income nor education had much of an impact on blacks' ranking of religion. Black parents were also nearly twice as likely as white parents to say that their child was very involved in religious worship or training. Still, although more than 70% of black parents ranked religion as very important, only about 40% of black children were very involved in religious training, leaving a gap between professed ideology and behavior. One parent named her son's Sunday School teacher as the only other person who has had a big impact on her son's life:

[My son] just loves her! And I think whatever she teaches in Sunday School just sticks to his mind. And we try to teach them at home, but he's always saying, "[My Sunday School teacher] said if you do this or that, this will happen." So I think she has been a real good influence on him as far as church. He's crazy about her. Other than that, I can't really think of anybody who really helps rear him.

Most of the values parents teach their children reflect Christianity, as noted by Sonya Daniels in talking about her daughter:

> I think we've taught her excellent values. We have always told her to love people and to treat them just as you want to be treated. We tell her over and over not to do things to people that she doesn't want done to her. Don't laugh at people, don't call people ugly, don't make people feel bad about themselves. We tell her that over and over again. We've taught her to be sensitive. . . . And we have told her she doesn't take property that doesn't belong to her. And another thing I harp on is that she needs to keep herself for marriage, that you don't sleep around with everybody and anybody.

Similarly, Melba Brown emphasizes the importance of family and religion:

> I'm highly religious, and all my values stem straight out of the scriptures—a love for God, a concern for your fellow man. Family is a strong value I try to instill, and family loyalty and ties with each other. . . . Because when all is said and done, all you have is family—friends will walk off and leave you. So I try to teach them some closeness and the importance of it. I spend a lot of time with my parents and my sisters and their children, and that is something that they [my children] have seen.

According to the Haneys:

> Our religious values are top priority, that God is first in your life and don't think that just because someone's not watching you, that God isn't. And the love of family, and to treat people equally, to be nice to people. And to always do what he knows is right, regardless of what other people want him to do. To do the thing he knows is right, to always tell the truth.

Clearly, blacks see the solution to their problems more in terms of returning to the earlier days of community, family, and religion.

Public Policy

Public policy is an important aspect of the social context in which families operate, as it helps shape the ecological opportunities and risks parents and their children face (Garbarino & Kostelny, 1995). In the United States, public policy often has been developed around the central cultural ideologies of individualism and familism, both of which fail to acknowledge the changing nature of the economy and of families. A central credo of American capitalism and democracy has been the belief that there is ample opportunity for economic success and mobility among individuals who value education and hard work. Similarly, families have been idealized as economically sufficient, breadwinner-homemaker units, capable of providing care for their members. Thus, despite many economic fluctuations and a few challenges from socialists, it was not until the Great Depression of the 1930s that the United States, like most major industrialized capitalist nations, became a welfare state. The collapse of the American economy challenged the notion that economic solvency was available to all those who were willing to work, and helped the country face the fact that economic declines are endemic in a capitalist economy. Prior to the depression, only a small percentage of relief for the poor came from public funds. In 1935, however, Congress passed the Social Security Act, which established social insurance and public assistance programs, creating a government-funded and public-administered welfare system.

This resulted in the development of a two-track welfare system (Fraser & Gordon, 1994). Persons in the first track of the welfare system receive social insurance benefits (e.g., workman's compensation, Social Security), which are higher and not stigmatized, as recipients are thought of as entitled to the benefits. According to Abramovitz (1996), social insurance programs now cover 95% of all wage earners but are rarely seen as part of the welfare system. In the second track of the welfare system are public assistance programs (e.g., Aid to Families With Dependent Children [AFDC], food stamps), where the benefits are poorer and, because they are tied to neither a work history nor a disability, are much more controversial. Much of the concern during the 1930s over creating public assistance programs was that they would lead to a "belligerent dependence" among the poor; thus, such programs were subject to "means-testing, morals-testing, moral and household supervision, home visits, and extremely low stipends" (Fraser & Gordon, 1994, p. 322).

Although entry into World War II ended the Great Depression and created a new era of unprecedented economic prosperity for the majority of America, poverty continued to be an enduring feature of life for millions of other Americans. During the economic renewal of the 1950s, social scientists like Michael Harrington (1962) were calling attention to the fact that many people, especially those living in rural and inner-city areas, were still victimized by poverty and its consequences. During the 1960s, a proliferation of federal and federal-state programs were implemented in President Johnson's War on Poverty. The Great Society Programs included food stamps, Medicare, Medicaid, Head Start, Job Corps, legal services, and many other programs. At the same time, the number of people receiving AFDC, or welfare, grew tremendously during the 1960s and 1970s and stabilized during the 1980s with about 3 to 4 million families (or 10-11 million people) receiving welfare benefits (Abramovitz, 1996). Much of the increase was among African American women, many of whom had previously been excluded from receiving AFDC benefits prior to the 1960s (Fraser & Gordon, 1994). Concern over government spending for domestic programs was evident by the 1970s, and policy makers began to evaluate many Great Society programs as ineffective and to curtail their budgets. Welfare programs were especially targeted for spending cuts.

The Omnibus Budget Reconciliation Act (OBRA) of 1981 was the first major effort to cut the cost of public assistance by limiting eligibility for welfare grants and attempting to provide only for the truly needy. According to Harris (1997), the OBRA supported work requirements rather than work incentives; thus it eliminated previous policy that allowed welfare recipients to keep a portion of their earnings without having them deducted from their grants. Therefore the OBRA changed welfare from a system that encouraged simultaneous receipt of income from a job and welfare to a system providing cash assistance only for those unable to secure jobs. "These changes . . . pushed thousands of women into low-paid jobs, dangerous welfare hotels, drug-plagued streets, and unsafe relationships," according to Abramovitz, while "they also shrunk the public sector workforce, no doubt forcing some of the women who had lost jobs to apply for AFDC" (pp. 23-24). The Family Support Act of 1988 also sought to curtail the government's responsibility for poor families by implementing broader state powers to collect child support from noncustodial parents and, more significantly, to make welfare recipients work for their grants. The notion of requiring welfare recipients to work originated in 1967 with the Work Incentives Program, but this program received relatively low funding and low priority. Workfare programs proliferated during the 1980s, under a variety of different names. Katz (1989) points out that most workfare either provides minimum wage jobs with no benefits, thus leaving the family in poverty, or requires welfare recipients simply to work for their grants.

Welfare reform has continued to be an important political issue in the 1990s, with the Clinton administration vowing to "end welfare as we know it." The Personality Responsibility and Work Opportunity Act signed into law in August 1996 assumes that families can and should sustain themselves through employment: It requires able-bodied recipients to work after two years or lose benefits, and limits the time one can collect welfare benefits over a lifetime to five years. The emphasis on forcing welfare mothers, even those with young children, to enter the labor force assumes that most welfare mothers do not want to work—a notion refuted by Harris's (1993) study of work among welfare mothers. It also creates a contradictory ideology that values the importance of full-time motherhood for middle-income married women but not for poor, single women. The Urban Institute in Washington estimates that this welfare reform bill will cause 2.6 million people, including 1.1 million children, to fall below the poverty line (Page, 1996). Although welfare reform is popular among both liberals and conservatives, many believe the current welfare act will have serious negative consequences for poor women and their children. Senator Daniel Moynihan, a longtime welfare scholar, has been quoted as saying, "The premise of this legislation is that the behavior of certain adults can be changed by making the lives of their children as wretched as possible. This is a fearsome assumption" (Page, 1996, p. C9). This welfare reform bill stands to have especially severe consequences for black children, as it represents yet another way in which the resources available to them are diminishing. Although most welfare recipients are not African Americans, nearly half of them are, and they stand to be disproportionately affected by these cuts. Only in time will the impact of this welfare reform initiative become clear.

Conclusions

Although clinging tenaciously to their traditions and strengths, African American families clearly have been changed as a result of the civil rights movement of the 1960s. Few would argue that these changes have had a negative impact on most African Americans; to the contrary, they have meant greater opportunities for educational and economic success. As a result, black children today are much more likely to live in middle-income families than in the past. Yet those who are left behind, growing up in poor inner-city families, often have even fewer resources at their disposal. In this chapter, I have discussed some changes in traditional resources available to black Americans—the community, extended families, religion, and public assistance. For the most part, there has been a diminution of resources available beyond the nuclear family, and this is especially apt to affect the children who need them the most. Many grow up in communities where adults exert little control over children, and drugs, violence, nonmarital sex, and school failure are the norms. Extended families and religion continue to offer some resources for black children, but these resources are often stronger and less strained among the more affluent than among those who truly need them. It is within this context that African Americans often look back at the world they once knew—a world of close-knit families and communities.

7

Continuity and Change

I have written to you because a world into which I was born, a world that nurtured and sustained me, has mysteriously disappeared.

Louis Gates, Jr., *Colored People* (1995, p. 237)

Henry Louis Gates's beautifully written autobiographical account of growing up during the 1950s is dedicated to his two daughters, whom he fears may never experience the world he grew up in. That world is viewed by many black people, at least retrospectively, as one in which the majority of African Americans were unified by a "consciousness of kind" that inspired racial solidarity immersed in the distinctive humor, music, religion, and linguistic styles of their own culture, and were unified in their conviction that most of their troubles (e.g., poor education, poverty) stemmed from external forces, namely, racism and segregation. Although their vision of the past is no doubt romanticized, nostalgia for what has been lost runs deep among many black people. Gates captures the sentiments of those who take pride in the victories of the civil rights movement in abolishing the American racial caste system, yet understand that the price has been a significant loss of black culture and cohesiveness. Indeed, it seemed that African Americans had scarcely begun to discover, articulate, and validate their cultural values and traditions when things began to change.

The past 25 years have witnessed a proliferation of black family studies, uncovering much about our African heritage and our lives under slavery and racial segregation. The myth of black families destroyed by slavery has been thoroughly refuted and, since the civil rights era of the 1960s, many revisionist scholars have reconceptualized contemporary African American families as culturally unique and viable, rather than pathological. Their work illustrated how the African and American experiences had converged, producing families characterized by extended family ties, spirituality, a strong work ethic, a high valuation of children, and greater gender equality (Billingsley, 1968/1988; Hill, 1972; Stack, 1974). These themes continue to inform our understanding of black families, yet the evidence supporting

149

them has diminished in the post-civil rights era. The strength of extended families has waned, the prospects of employment for millions of young adults has been undercut by the postindustrial economy, marriage rates have plummeted, nonmarital childbearing among teenagers has increased, and the rates of crime and violence have reached epidemic proportions in some neighborhoods. Although the end of de jure racial segregation has substantially reduced visible barriers to opportunity, it clearly has fallen far short of producing racial equality. In fact, many of the educational and economic gains made during the late 1960s had begun to wane barely a decade later.

Much of the problem lies in the economic decline and polarization of Americans since the 1980s: The wealthy have become wealthier and the poor more impoverished. A similar, albeit less pronounced, trend has occurred among African Americans: While there has been an overall decrease in black household income in the mid-1980s, both the percentage of blacks earning under $15,000 and the percentage earning more than $75,000 increased between 1974 and 1994 (Hurst, 1998). Many blacks have moved into the middle class, while the economic position of those in the working and lower classes has declined, often due to job loss, underemployment, and cuts in welfare benefits. Among blacks, two-parent and/or dual-income families have the highest income and single mothers have the lowest, making family structure a good predictor of economic standing. In my research sample, fewer than 18% of married parents had family incomes of less than $15,000, compared with 62% of single parents. Regardless of family structure, however, African American families continue to earn less than white families, and these racial gaps in income are substantially exceeded by the racial gap in wealth (Oliver & Shapiro, 1995).

It is within the context of these important sociocultural and economic changes that I have examined child-rearing work in African American families. I began by noting that, despite uniform agreement on the importance of children in black families, very few scholars have researched the work that parents do in rearing their children. Contributing to that sparse body of literature has been the goal and challenge of this study. To accomplish this, I collected and analyzed data from black and white parents, and situated these new data within the context of existing research. A central assumption of the study has been that the historically divergent experiences of black and white Americans have produced important differences in the work and challenges of parenthood. Both slavery and the racial caste system that existed during most of U.S. history have played a pivotal role in the development of African American families. Race was made the basis for segregation and exploitation, severely restricting economic opportunities and access to the resources needed for assimilation into mainstream society. Moreover, racist policies were justified by elaborate and pervasive ideologies of black inferiority. While recognizing these social structural barriers, I have embraced a social constructionist view, showing the interactive nature between cultural and structural forces. Black parents have never been merely passive responders/adapters to social structural forces but are active creators and definers of reality.

One important contribution of the present study is its examination of the impact of social class on the child-rearing work and values of African American parents. Social class is arguably the single most important factor influencing parents' child-rearing values and the behaviors of parents (Kohn, 1977), as well as childhood outcomes (Zinn & Eitzen, 1987). Poverty substantially reduces the chances that children will receive the resources they need for optimal development, such as health care, a good education, and safe neighborhoods; it can also have a corrosive effect on parenting skills. A strong correlation exists between poverty and single motherhood, especially among teenagers, yet the causal direction of the link is debated. Single parents, poor parents, or both, because they often do not have the economic or social resources they need, may encounter more difficulties in child rearing than other parents; indeed, the evidence is clear that poverty has elevated levels of substance abuse and child neglect among many. The struggle among poor parents to meet the basic material needs of their children may supplant concern over the emotional and psychological well-being of children and result in more severe disciplinary measures. But the tendency to equate poverty with single-parenthood and stereotype all poor parents as being alike is misleading. As I have noted, single parents are not all poor, and poor families are not uniformly overwhelmed with the demands of parenthood. Although nearly one half of black children live in poverty, the majority of poor and nonpoor black children grow up in families where they are loved and where adult family members invest as best they can in their development and success.

Including a sample of white parents has also added to the strength of these findings. The white parents in this study were in many ways (e.g., age, education, social class) similar to their black counterparts. Their children attended predominantly black schools, and the majority of them lived in mostly black neighborhoods (see Appendix A for further discussion). Sociological research on child rearing using a racially diverse sample is scant; thus, questions about the relative impacts of race and class on parenting are left unanswered. This study has found substantial similarities in the survey responses of black and white parents but has also discovered some differences that highlight the roles that class and culture continue to play in shaping black priorities.

This study has raised some questions that rarely have been asked, such as whether racial socialization can enhance children's self-esteem, and has empirically examined some commonly held ideas, such as the contention that gender neutrality prevails in the socializing of black children. It also has focused on the actual work that parents do in rearing their children, viewing that work within the social capital framework (Coleman, 1988) of parental investments in their children. I began this book with an exploration of the history of African American parenthood and concluded with a look at how families have changed since the civil rights era. My objective has been to provide a somewhat comprehensive overview of the developmental history of black families and examine contemporary parenting priorities and strategies. In this final chapter, I briefly summarize the major findings of the study and highlight some areas for future research.

Black Parenthood in Historical Perspective

Childbearing and child rearing are viewed cross-culturally and cross-nationally as important activities as they are essential for the continuation of all societies. In colonial American society, having an adequate supply of children was undermined by high rates of childhood mortality from infectious diseases—a situation that slavery made much more severe among blacks than whites. In a sense, both black and white children were valued for their economic utility, yet the meaning of parenthood was severely circumscribed for blacks, as their children were the property of and ultimately controlled by white slave masters. Black women gave birth to numerous children, often under brutal, dehumanizing circumstances, where personal volition was absent and paternity was not officially acknowledged. Their parenting prerogatives were severely curtailed by slavery. They could exert little control over the lives of their children and were powerless to protect them from the indignities of slavery, including abuse or sale by white slave masters. Research on childhood and parenting among slaves is relatively scarce but overall suggests that the African traditions of childbearing, motherhood, and extended families continued to be important. These traditions, however, essentially were used to enhance the quantity and productivity of slaves, and thus the economic standing of slave owners. Families provided one of the few gratifications available to slaves and, as best they could, parents loved their children and tried to protect and socialize them.

Modern medicine, better sanitation, and improved standards of living dramatically reduced rates of infant and maternal mortality for most Americans during the nineteenth century. The rise of an industrial economy and advances in productive technologies helped reorganize families by reducing the demand for female and child labor and creating the breadwinner-homemaker family model as the new ideal. In industrial America, the emphasis on childbearing was replaced with an emphasis on child rearing; thus, overall fertility rates declined while concern over the welfare of children grew. The emphasis on having fewer children coincided with the ideology that married, full-time, homemaker-mothers were best suited to meet the needs of children. By the early 1900s, a Children's Bureau had been created in the Department of Labor to allow mothers, even those who were poor, to stay at home and care for their children. The gender and age divisions of labor being advocated in the new industrial order by the early 1800s, however, were largely irrelevant to black people, as most were still enslaved workers in the southern agricultural economy. The labor demands imposed on black men, women, and children alike continued to emphasize the importance of work roles over family roles (Berry, 1993; Dill, 1988). Although gender structured the family roles of slaves to some extent, the development of a patriarchal family or a breadwinner-homemaker division of labor was a moot issue for most black people.

After the abolition of slavery, many black people tried to reunite their families and legalize their marriages. Parents sometimes had to fight for the right either to get or to keep custody of their children, as laws were passed in some states allowing the children of poor or unmarried parents to be indentured. The majority of black people continued to live in the South, many involved in a sharecropping system that relied on the labor of all family members, and parents continued in the preindustrial tradition of seeing children as workers. The formation of breadwinner-homemaker families confining men to economic roles and women to domestic roles continued to elude blacks, most of whom were still struggling to survive economically. Parents saw the value of education, but black schools were poorly equipped and often organized around the needs of the agricultural economy. In addition, the abolition of slavery was followed by the legalization of racial segregation, which restricted the ability of black Americans to acquire property, secure employment, get an education, vote, or use public facilities. In the South, racial segregation was buttressed by jim crow regulations governing race relations to ensure the attitudinal and behavioral subordination of blacks to whites. In such a setting, racial socialization no doubt took the form of teaching children to conform to the racial codes necessary for their survival.

Family research during the early twentieth century understood the black family as being shaped by slavery and racial oppression, both of which were blamed as giving rise to dysfunctional black family patterns. The studies conducted between 1930 and the 1960s focused mostly on low-income blacks, and the concepts of class and culture were often conflated or used interchangeably. These studies highlighted the existence of aberrant family patterns (e.g., violence, juvenile delinquency, illegitimacy, father absence) and provided a fairly dismal view of black families. Overwhelmed by racism and poverty, and having internalized the racial hatred directed at them by whites, most black Americans were described as incapable of creating strong, stable, loving families. As parents, fathers were seen as weak, ineffectual, economically impotent, and absent, while mothers were unnaturally independent and domineering. For the most part, they were portrayed as inadequate child rearers—as violent, capricious, and indifferent toward their own children and unable to exert proper social control over their children's behavior. Middle-class black parents, on the other hand, were described as more effective than their lower-class counterparts: They tried to instill mainstream cultural values in their children, but racism and segregation limited their ability to fully embrace the white family system. Although primarily the work of liberal social scientists who understood the structural constraints placed on black people and supported an end to the racial caste system, this research resulted in the social deficit model of the black family.

The revisionist scholarship of the late 1960s and 1970s challenged the social deficit model of black families by emphasizing their strength and resiliency. This work reconceptualized African American families as being strong, adaptable, and functional although organizationally and culturally different from white families (Billingsley, 1968/1988). Slavery and persistent racism were still seen as important forces, but it was emphasized that these forces led to the creation of a vibrant African American culture that enhanced the survival of families. Some characteristics of these families included flexible gender roles, extended families, an absence of the concept of illegitimacy, a strong religious orientation, and a work ethic (Hill, 1972). African American scholars especially reclaimed the importance of African cultural values in shaping black families—cultural traditions that were seen as having helped blacks to evade some of the classist and sexist ideologies of mainstream American society. These cultural patterns included an emphasis on sharing, cooperation, survival of the group, and, in many cases, the importance of kin relationships over relationships based on marriage (Billingsley, 1992). The cultural approach stressed the importance of children and parenting in black families, often challenging the myth of absent fathers and contending that women derive much of their status from motherhood (Collins, 1989). As Afrocentric theorist Nobles (1985) argued, among black people "the family's reason for being can be considered child-centeredness" (p. 83). This study explored that assertion.

Black Parenthood in Contemporary Perspective

One of the major tasks of child socialization for parents is teaching children values. Often the exact nature of the values parents are expected to teach, or the strategies for teaching them, are more assumed than articulated. There is a core set of values that virtually all parents try to teach their children, such as honesty, responsibility, and hard work, and, when these values are not evident in the lives of children, parents are typically seen as responsible for this. Despite the constancy of these core values, studies show that child-rearing values change over time, due largely to major social and economic transformations. Industrialization and modernization were central forces in a revolution of child-rearing norms and values during the early twentieth century. Essentially, the emphasis on values such as loyalty to the church, patriotism, obedience, conformity to external rules, and good manners decreased, while the emphasis on independence, curiosity, and social-mindedness increased (Alwin, 1988). Parents became less authoritarian in their discipline strategies and more authoritative and permissive. These new child-rearing values gradually were defined as "the right" way to parent, and those who did not embrace them were seen as disadvantaging their children. Yet the family arrangement and economic position of the middle classes most often resonated with this new value orientation. As Kohn (1977) insightfully observed, the child-rearing values of parents are shaped by structural characteristics of their jobs and parental perceptions of what it takes to succeed in the work world. Given the inheritability of social class standing, learning autonomy might coincide with the future careers of middle-class children, while obedience/conformity could lead to employment success among working-class children.

This study has examined how race and social class influence the value priorities of African American and white parents. Overall, I found widespread agreement among black and white parents in their value orientations: Both groups rank their children's happiness and self-esteem as their top priority, followed by respect and obedience, and, last, doing well in school. While the overall priority ranking of these three values is the same for black and white parents, there were some important racial differences in the percentages of parents ranking each value as a top priority. For example, although both groups gave happiness/self-esteem their highest ranking, white parents were significantly more likely than blacks to do so. Despite their overall economic similarities, white parents in this study were slightly less likely than black parents to earn under $30,000 per year and were much more likely to be among the small number in the sample earning more than $50,000 a year. I believe that their greater emphasis on the psychological well-being of their children reflects their class and race standings, which, together, give them more assurance about their ability to meet their children's material needs. Blacks parents, on the other hand, are significantly more likely than white parents to emphasize their role as provider, indicating that their ability to be a provider is not simply taken for granted.

African American parents were also nearly twice as likely as white parents to rank obedience and respect in their children as their top priority.

Blacks with lower incomes and levels of education ranked respect/ obedience even more highly than their more educated, middle-income peers. Having children obey and be respectful is an important cultural value among blacks, where respect for the elderly is emphasized and is reinforced by traditional religious ideologies that teach the subordination of children and advocate the use of physical punishment. Poor parents, who live in unsafe neighborhoods and often feel they are losing control over their children, have even more incentive to emphasize this value, as their children's physical well-being may depend on it. The emphasis on obedience and respect ties in with the greater tendency among blacks than whites to view being a disciplinarian as their most important role: Although emphasized by only a minority of parents, blacks were three times more likely than whites to describe this as their most important parenting role.

Similarly, blacks were more than five times more likely than whites to be among the few parents who said spanking was their most frequently used discipline strategy. While the emphasis on respect, obedience, and discipline among black parents often has been used as evidence of poor parenting and even a propensity toward child abuse, it is important to understand these values in cultural context. Although child abuse and neglect do adversely affect children, strict discipline does not and can be socially defined as loving and protective.

Doing well in school ranked least in importance among the three values included in the study; however, parents who were interviewed often pointed out that self-esteem was given a higher priority because it is a prerequisite to academic success. The findings of this study concur with most previous research that has found black parents to have very high educational aspirations for their children. In this study, black parents were quite determined to have their children attend college; nearly 90% said they expected their children to attend college and more than 70% ranked attending college as "very important." Social class did not affect black parents' educational aspirations for their children. They saw a college education as vital to their children's success and, contrary to the notion that blacks do not equip their children for academic success, most of those interviewed often had already begun to instill in their children that college was a necessity. Yet indications of obstacles to that goal were already evident. For example, parents who are themselves poorly educated often are less capable of effectively advocating for their children's education, and some children were already in classes for slow learners. In this study, black parents as a group (37%) were significantly less likely than white parents (46%) to say that their child was doing above-average work in school. A special challenge for black parents of sons is luring them away from the ambition of being a professional athlete, as the most visibly successful black males are in sports.

In their everyday parenting work, the primary focus of black parents is responsibility. When I asked parents to describe the most important things they do in socializing their children, they talked about having their children participate in family work, care for themselves, and take care of material possessions. Consistent with earlier studies, I found that lower-class parents interpret responsibility in terms of accelerated development and self-care in their children; children are often expected at an early age to be somewhat independent. Middle-class black parents, however, have a broader definition of responsibility, one that includes autonomy in carrying out personal hygiene, household duties, homework assignments, and other activities. They often had clear-cut rules and expectations for their children, devised strategies to punishment and reward children, and were consistent in explaining their expectations and supervising their children's behaviors.

Concern over the prevalence and causes of nonmarital pregnancy among black teenagers has led to abundant research on teen sexuality and its many correlates, such as poverty and single-parenthood. Although most studies focus on the social factors that help perpetuate early sexual involvement, the notion of rampant immorality and irresponsibility among blacks is common, as is the belief that African American parents condone teenage childbearing. Few studies have directly examined the sexual expectations black parents have for their children. This study did so and found that black parents of both sons and daughters overwhelmingly would like their children to marry before having sex (83%) and before having children (92%). The majority (85%) felt children should receive some sex education before age 12, said they had already discussed sex with their child (72%), and favored having schools teach children more about sex (66%).

My interviews gave me an opportunity to examine the survey response data on sexuality in more detail. In doing so, it became clear that parents face the usual difficulties in discussing sex with their children, that is, what to say, how much to say, and when to say it. They also tend to underestimate, I believe, their children's readiness to learn about sex. Some, for example, said they would wait for evidence of serious interest in the opposite sex or the onset of menstruation before discussing sexuality. Although most parents said they would allow the use of contraceptives if needed, most were very conflicted about it, as it contradicted their religious beliefs and seemed to give permission for sexuality. Moreover, many parents simply felt a sense of hopelessness, a concern that they simply did not have the power to effectively sway their children away from sex and nonmarital pregnancy, as such activities are not only prevalent among blacks but often are status-enhancing.

The racial socialization of African American children has received significant attention in previous studies, as race is a salient aspect of identity for blacks. Racial socialization is viewed as parents' efforts to teach their children about race, how to cope with racism and rejection, and how to challenge the dominant culture's negative depictions of African Americans. Previous studies have shown that most black parents racially socialize their children, that racial socialization may be more common today than in the past, and that parents seek to instill in their children a broad range of positive messages about being black.

This study expands on that literature by examining some of the racial attitudes and experiences of parents and their children, assessing the importance of racial socialization, and questioning its link with self-esteem. The notion of racial socialization assumes that black children will face some type of discrimination or unfair treatment based on race: In this study, 19% of black parents felt their children had already received unfair treatment on some occasion based on race, compared with 29% of white parents—statistics no doubt reflecting the fact the data were collected in predominantly black schools. More affluent black parents were more than twice as likely as their low-income peers to believe their child had experienced racism, perhaps because they had higher expectations of equality or were more aware of subtle racist behaviors. About 41% of black parents felt their child's race would make his or her future more difficult, compared with only 9% of white parents.

Although racial socialization is an important issue, I found that parents overall did not pay a great deal of attention to racial matters. Parents who were interviewed said that the issue of race did not come up very often, and they clearly did not appear to have a specific racial message to be conveyed at a certain age. Most parents assumed a somewhat reactive stance in discussing race, primarily addressing their children's racial issues as they arose. Their racial socialization messages were largely embedded in their lifestyles: They exposed their children to literature, movies, and art inclusive of blacks; participated in black cultural traditions (family reunions, Kwanza, and so on); and emphasized successful African American role models. Most parents did not want race to become or be used by their children as an explanation for lack of achievement, so their primary message was that racial barriers could be overcome with determination, hard work, and prayer. Given the historic denigration of the abilities, intellect, and attractiveness of blacks, racial socialization is sometimes seen as enhancing the self-esteem of children. I examine parental perceptions of their children's self-esteem and conclude that self-esteem may rest more on actual achievements than on messages of racial pride.

Gender neutrality in child socialization is sometimes viewed as the norm among African Americans, yet that hypothesis has rarely been subjected to empirical investigation. Both the African tradition of women combining work and family roles and the American experience of slavery militated against confining black women to domestic roles or viewing them as submissive, helpless, or dependent. Some have suggested that daughters growing up in black families are not taught to assume narrow, rigidly defined gender roles. I point out in this work, however, that less has been said about what black sons are taught; in fact, the hypothesis of gender neutrality among blacks rests almost exclusively on the work and community roles of women. And while feminist scholarship has applauded black women for escaping the narrow confines of femininity prescribed in mainstream society, black men are more commonly denigrated for their failure to conform to the masculine ideal of being the head of the family and the economic provider. Indeed, by the 1980s, many had declared a crisis among young black men who, lacking the ability to find work or to marry, too often relied on aggressiveness, hypersexuality, and a "cool pose" to gain masculine status.

I examine the issue of gender socialization in this research in several ways: by asking parents how they felt their child's gender would affect their future, assessing gender roles in the home, seeing if parental values and parenting styles were affected by gender, and looking at the broader context in which gender is discussed. Neither black nor white parents in this study appeared very concerned about the impact of gender on their children's lives. Overall, 24% of all parents in this study said that being a woman makes it more difficult to get a good education and a good job. Asked whether their own child's sex would make his or her future more difficult, only 11% of parents said that it would, showing that even parents who feel gender is generally a factor in success do not believe it will affect their own children. The sex of the child did not have an impact on parents' responses to these questions. At the same time, the majority of all parents (92%) expressed strong support for gender equality in the domestic arena, while only 25% said that the parents in their families equally shared in caring for the child. My interview data also revealed a gap between ideology and reality: Men and women talked about gender equality in the domestic arena but rarely actually achieved that goal.

Do parents of daughters have different value priorities and future hopes for their children than parents of sons? Does the gender of the child affect discipline and parenting roles? The results show that gender equality is pretty much the norm on these dimensions, especially for black parents as a group. However, when social class is considered, I found that African American parents with more education and higher incomes make more gender distinctions than their less educated, low-income counterparts. For example, educated black parents emphasized getting a good education and a good job more strongly for sons than for daughters, implicitly preparing them for the male breadwinner role. More affluent parents of sons are also more likely than those with daughters to emphasize being a teacher and

guide, a parenting role that can be seen as training children for more autonomy and independence. On the other hand, educated black parents of
daughters were more likely than those of sons to emphasize the parenting
roles of disciplinarian and provider, suggesting that girls require more social control and providing for than boys. The interviews revealed that black
parents, especially those who are newly middle class, equated aspects of
the traditional gender roles of white America with respectability. They
want their daughters to be "nice young ladies" and their sons to be
"gentlemanly."

Whatever specific gender ideologies may exist among blacks, there is
also an important and pervasive gender context that helps shape children's
thinking about the roles of men and women. African American children
frequently grow up in families headed by women who "do it all" and in
which males are absent or only marginally involved. Male denigration is
often pervasive in these settings: In some cases, women blame men for the
failure to provide for the family while men counter that it is simply easier
for women to succeed. Because most socialization is indirect, I argue that
the gender attitudes of children may be shaped by a context in which
women, often single-handedly, manage both family and employment roles
and males are marginalized. The parents in this study saw single-mother
and absent-father families as problematic and placed most of the blame on
individual lifestyles and decisions rather than social forces. They rejected
the idea that black women have an easier time than black men.

I conclude by looking at child socialization within the larger social context, specifically the impacts of community, extended families, religion, and
state policy. These contexts have changed dramatically since the 1970s;
communities are less cohesive and more dangerous, extended family resources have diminished, and religious heterogeneity among blacks has
grown. Recent studies are beginning to document these changes and their
adverse impact, yet the "strengths perspective" continues to be the dominant approach to understanding black families. Although validating the
way African American families have survived and overcome numerous obstacles, this perspective often ignores the growing concern among black
people about their families and communities, a concern that was evident
among the parents in this study. The strengths perspective views black families as resilient and well functioning despite massive economic changes, and
may promote the notion of blacks as capable of drawing on community
and extended kin resources to meet their needs.

I found broad support for traditional black cultural values among the
parents in this study. Black parents (71%) were significantly more likely
than white parents (39%) to say that religion was very important in their
lives. Similarly, 55% of blacks, compared with 33% of whites, indicated
that their families were very involved in helping them raise their children.

Yet the interview data reveal that these resources are strongest among those in middle-class families and often least available among those who need them the most, such as poor single mothers.

Public assistance to families has also decreased in recent years. Families clearly are seen as responsible for providing for the welfare of their children and, despite expansions in the welfare state during the 1930s and again in the 1960s, the largest welfare system in the United States is still the family (Aulette, 1994). Public assistance to single mothers, initially defined as vital to the well-being of families, has now been redefined as an obstacle to the creation of stable families. Single mothers in need of public assistance are commonly stigmatized as lazy, immoral, and irresponsible and now often are forced to accept employment to receive their benefits. The lack of day care and jobs paying living wages may further jeopardize the welfare of their children.

Future Directions

This study has synthesized, expanded, and updated the literature on child rearing in African American families. Much more work needs to be done, however. Feminist scholars, for example, have increasingly sought to broaden our understanding of the multiple social factors that influence our lives, especially the intersection of class, race, and gender. This may be an especially useful framework for studying child socialization, especially given the increased class diversity that exists among African Americans. The class-race-gender framework raises many important questions: Is growing up female the same in middle-income and poor black families? Are there ways in which middle-class black males have challenged the masculine ideal? How do social class and gender affect the racial socialization messages children receive? Is the impact of race on self-esteem independent of the influence of class and gender? Does social class influence black parents' views of what constitutes culture? Such questions will bring considerable clarity to the complexities of child rearing and help us address other theoretical questions, such as the extent to which structure and culture shape the family patterns of African Americans.

Studies including broader and more diverse samples are crucial to understanding the patterns of child socialization. Only a few studies, for example, have carefully examined the role of fathers in child rearing, although the evidence suggests that father involvement with children is increasing. Fathers and mothers may interact with children in gender-specific ways; for example, it has been suggested that fathers gender-socialize their children more than mothers do. In general, it has been noted that fathers have different child-rearing styles and values, and that they make their own distinctive contribution to the development of children. Studies have often been more determined to examine the consequences of father absence than father presence among blacks, thus producing little research on fatherhood. How involved are fathers—emotionally and physically—in caring for children? How is that involvement shaped by their own family experiences? The importance of fatherhood was reaffirmed in my interviews, both for those who grew up with their fathers and for those who did not. Most of the few fathers interviewed in this study were in the latter category, yet they took a special sense of pride in being involved with their own children and had a deep desire to be the kind of father they never had.

Finally, I think there is a need to rethink many of our previous assumptions about black childhood. The revisionist scholarship of the 1960s and 1970s was vital in dispelling stereotypes and myths about black families by emphasizing their strengths, but now it may be time to "revise the revisionists." Nearly 50% of black American children live in poverty, and rates of child abuse, academic failure, juvenile delinquency, drug dependency, and teen sexuality are high. Although researchers have addressed many of these issues, there is still a tendency in black family studies to view children as safely situated in a protective extended kin network. Neither black families nor the black cultural traditions are static forces but are continually in the processes of evolution and redefinition. For example, my study found that parents strongly endorsed religion as important, yet only 40% described their children as being very involved in religious training. Is there a gap between attitudinal support for religion and behavior? How has black participation in religion changed in the past few decades? How involved are black churches in meeting the needs of the children? How effective are they as agents of social control, self-help, or political activism? And, although African Americans continue to see the extended family as important, have kinship patterns changed over time? How widespread are traditions such as child keeping and informal adoption? Continuing poverty and economic success both have challenged the nature and the relationships of the traditional black family, and it is incumbent upon scholars to produce research that captures the contemporary realities of black families.

Appendix A
Research Methodology

This book on child socialization in African American families grew out of an interest in understanding how gender roles and ideologies are constructed in families and conveyed to children. As I began to explore this issue a few years ago, I found that two fairly distinct literatures existed, both primarily produced in the past 15 years. One burgeoning literature focused on black women and explained how their unique historical experiences led them to escape narrow conceptions of femininity and contributed to a legacy of strength, independence, and nontraditional roles among women. The other literature focused on black men and revolved around the "vanishing species" theme, suggesting that men, especially those who are young, were seriously impaired as a result of their failure to embrace the traditional gender roles accorded men, especially that of breadwinner. Very little research explained gender in the context of explicit child socialization, and reflective and autobiographical accounts abounded almost to the exclusion of systematic research.

In 1992 I acquired a small internal grant from my university to study gender socialization in black families. My initial plan was to rely solely on in-depth interviews with black parents as I not only have a great deal of experience conducting interviews but am convinced of their efficacy when examining relatively new issues. I did not want to limit my research to hypothesis testing or variable analysis but wanted to capture the nuances available in interview narratives. The use of qualitative data is also consistent with the long tradition of symbolic interactionism and the social constructionist perspective in sociology, which underlies this research study. This perspective sees social reality as socially created and defined, and sees actions as guided by reflective processes of the human mind (Blumer, 1969).

Social class and race are especially likely to shape the construction of reality, and racial-ethnic minorities often have different experiences and perceptions than do the majority group. In this study, I attempted to examine reality from the standpoint and lives of black parents. I see the interview process as allowing traditionally subordinated populations to share their experiences using their own voices and as a strategy for creating at least some symmetry between interviewer and respondent (Mishler, 1986). I believe that research should provide some benefits for the participants and that there are essentially two ways in which that happens. One is by allowing respondents to be a part of the research process. This means that they know what is being studied, why, and by whom, and that they have the opportunity to articulate their own experiences in a process that is often quite empowering. The second way is to conduct social research that has policy implications.

Early in the research process, it became clear to me that it would be difficult to study gender socialization without exploring the broader issue of general child socialization. Expanding the study was exciting to me, especially in light of the absence of research in this vital area. I spent several months reading, searching, and

analyzing existing literature on childhood socialization and assessing its implications for African American children. In doing so, ideas for my own study began to
crystallize, and I outlined an interview guide of the major questions I wanted to
explore with parents. I decided to solicit respondents for the research through the
Kansas City school districts (which span two states) and, based on my preparatory
research, to focus on children between the ages of 10 and 12, or fourth and fifth
graders. My plan was to mail letters directly to parents, explaining the study and
soliciting their participation in the research through volunteering to be interviewed.
I contacted the central office of one school district for permission to obtain a list
of parents' names and addresses. I explained the study to several administrators,
emphasizing the voluntary participation of parents and that the study had been
approved by the university's committee on human experimentation. The process
turned into a difficult one: There seemed to a consensus that the parents' names
and addresses were in the public domain, yet no one seemed able to determine
exactly who had to give permission to release the information. I finally decided that
I would simply contact the principals of various schools directly to solicit their
participation, and I did so by mail. I followed up with a phone call and found most
principals receptive to the idea. Of those who refused, the most common reason
was that they had already involved parents in too many studies or, similarly, that
they were in the process of doing their own research study. One principal declined
because the response rate of parents in her school to materials sent home was very
low, and she feared a poor response.

Once I gained permission to contact parents, I sent letters home with elementary
school children, explaining the study and asking those who were interested to
return the enclosed form with their names and telephone numbers. The response
rate from the first school was under 10% (130 letters sent, 12 returned), and some
of those who returned the letters gave their names but did not have a telephone,
making it impossible for me to contact them. Nonetheless, I interviewed those
parents who volunteered and solicited from them the names of other parents who
might be interested (see Appendix B). Most of the parents were interviewed in their
own homes; one was interviewed at the day care center she owned and operated.
Interviews generally lasted about 90 minutes or longer and were tape-recorded.
They were later transcribed verbatim. Most parents seemed to enjoy talking about
their children, although a few were concerned about having the "right" answers to
the questions. A few were especially enthusiastic, both about sharing their views
and about being a part of a book written about black families. Upon thanking one
mother for the interview, she promptly said, "Hey, if a black PhD is writing a book,
I want to be one of the people who helps her get it done!" Similarly, I enjoyed
talking to parents, being a good supportive listener, and validating their life
experiences.

The questions on my interview guide were quite broad, and I made some minor
revisions after almost every interview. I continued, however, to ask a core set of
questions that revolved around values, race, gender, and extended families. I eventually interviewed 35 parents, although more had volunteered to be interviewed.
In analyzing interview data, I spent considerable time listening to tapes, reading the

interviews, categorizing data, and identifying patterns and issues. I did some color coding of specific topics in the interview and made lots of margin notes and comments.

To reach a larger sample, I developed a survey to be sent home with children, completed by their parents, and returned to the school (see Appendix C). After collecting surveys from several schools, I revised the initial survey by adding more questions and creating a subsample (smaller group) of parents responding to some questions. At the end of the survey, parents were asked to give their names and telephone numbers if they were interested in doing an interview. I initially distributed surveys to parents of fourth and fifth graders but later sent them to all parents in the school. Parents were asked to complete only one survey and to focus on the oldest child who is age 12 or under and living with them. Some did and some did not, but the vast majority did chose a single child upon whom to focus. Parents were also invited to call me if they had any questions about the survey, and several of them did. Typically, they wanted to know more about who I was, whether I had children, and even how I felt about a specific question on the survey. One mother, for example, called to talk about the question on sexuality. In the process, she explained that she had been told little about sexuality growing up and had a baby at age 13. She was now the 29-year-old mother of a 16-year-old, wondering how parents really can teach their children abstinence. The response rate for surveys ranged between about 20% and 50%, with about 5% of those returning surveys agreeing to be interviewed. I collected nearly 800 surveys but did not use the ones from respondents who indicated that their race was Hispanic, Asian American, or Native American, as their numbers were too small. I entered what turned out to be 58 variables in an SPSS program and ran simple descriptive statistics, which I have tried to integrate with interview data to provide a broader picture of African American parenting attitudes. I used basic descriptive statistics (chi-square) in analyzing my findings.

These data were collected over a three-year period from 12 urban schools in two school districts in the greater Kansas City area. Although it is nearly impossible to determine the extent to which my nonrandom, sometimes snowball, sample matches the populations from which it was drawn, some information about each school district is useful. The two school districts are located in the two adjoining cities of Kansas City, Kansas, and Kansas City, Missouri. In each city, the black population is about 30%; however, the schools are predominantly black. The white residents living in these areas are often older and/or childless; they have fewer children and are more likely to send them to private schools.

Of the 13 school districts in the greater Kansas City area, the two included in this study have the largest enrollments. They also have the most black students, the highest rates of poverty, and the lowest median family incomes. There are nearly 29,000 school age children in the Kansas City, Kansas, area, and most attend school in the district. The median income for those living in Kansas City, Kansas, where School District 1 is located, is about $28,000, but the median family income for those with children attending school in that district is $22,000. School District 2 in this study had a 1995 enrollment of 37,151, which was 80% of all the school-age children in the district, according to the district's coordinator of research. Nearly 65% of the students participate in the subsidized lunch program, another indicator that children attending the public school in the area are poorer than people in the larger community. This reveals some general similarities between the sample included in this study and the overall populations in the area.

There are several important methodological issues to be kept in mind when examining the findings of this study. Central among them is that the parents in this study were not randomly selected and are not particularly representative of all African American parents. A major shortcoming is that they are from a limited geographic area. There is also some selection bias in operation, especially considering the fact that most parents did not return the surveys. The survey questions were drawn from the issues commonly discussed in research on black families, and some questions were formatted based on the child-rearing studies of Melvin Kohn. Still, errors were made in the construction of the survey. A call from a parent brought an obvious error to my attention. This black mother called to discuss the difficulties she was having raising her white stepdaughter—drawing my attention to the fact that I had only asked for the race of the parent and assumed that it was also the race of the child. This clearly was not always the case.

In some cases, parents either misunderstood or resisted answering questions on the survey. For example, instead of ranking items such as current values on a scale from 1 to 3, with 1 being the most important, a few parents either ranked only one value or indicated that all values ranked number one in priority. This was especially the case for both low-income and less educated parents, who may have been less likely to understand the survey. Given these difficulties, my confidence in the findings of this research reside not only in the responses of parents but also in my own experiential knowledge of the field and the work of numerous other African American family scholars.

Appendix B
Interview Guide

1. DESCRIPTION OF FOCUS CHILD: In this interview I want to focus on your oldest child who is age 12 or under. . . . Could you describe this child for me [self-concept, friendships, school progress]? How would you describe your relationship with this child?

2. CHILD-REARING STRATEGIES: What are the most important things that you do as a parent to socialize and train this child? Are there others who are involved in raising this child? If yes, describe their involvement.

3. VALUES: At this stage in your child's life, what are the most important values that you are trying to teach him or her? How do you teach these values?

4. RESPONSIBILITIES: What are some of the things you expect this child to do all by him- or herself?

5. DISCIPLINE: How do you discipline this child? How often does that happen? How effective is this discipline?

6. RACIAL SOCIALIZATION: What do you teach this child about being black? Has this child encountered unfair treatment based on his or her race? How racially aware is the child? About how often do you talk about race with this child? Are you satisfied with what this child's school is teaching about race, such as black history? How do you think being black will affect his or her future?

7. GENDER: People have different ideas on whether girls and boys should be treated differently and whether parents should have different expectations of sons and daughters. . . . What is your opinion on this issue? Explain.

8. SEXUALITY: Some people say that parents and children have much more liberal sexual views today than in the past. . . . What is your opinion on this issue? Explain. What is your view of sex before marriage? What is your view of having children before marriage?

9. FUTURE: How do you see your child's future? What are your most important hopes for his or her future?

10. INTERGENERATIONAL: How different are your parenting values from those of your own parents? Are different issues emphasized more?

Appendix C
Parenting Survey

1. How many children do you have?_____

2. What are the ages of your children?_____

3. What is the age, grade level, and sex of YOUR OLDEST CHILD WHO IS AGE 12 OR UNDER AND LIVING WITH YOU?

Age_____   Grade level_____   Girl____or Boy_____

4. Thinking about the child you have described above, which of the following words describe this child? Check **ALL** the words that do a GOOD JOB of describing this child.

____Aggressive   _____Emotionally mature   _____Helpful at home

____Caring/Sensitive   _____Athletic   _____Responsible

____Strong-willed   _____Hardworking   _____Obedient

5. How are you related to the child you have described above?

_____Mother   _____Father   _____Grandmother

_____Other (Describe how you are related)_____

Answer all questions focusing on your oldest child who is age 12 or under and living with you. PLEASE FEEL FREE TO MAKE ADDITIONAL COMMENTS ON THE SURVEY.

6. If you had to choose **JUST ONE** of the VALUES listed below as the most important thing you are trying to teach this child, which one would it be? Write a "1" beside the **ONE** most important value.

_____Doing well in school

_____Being happy and feeling good about him- or herself

_____Being obedient and respectful

Look back at the list above, and write a "2" beside the **VALUE above that is second most important.

7. Which **ONE** of the following would you most like to see this child have as she or he grows up? Write a "1" beside the **ONE** most important thing.

_____A strong, loving family

_____A good education and a good job

_____A kind and compassionate personality

Write a "2" beside the **FUTURE HOPE** above that is second most important.

8. Which **ONE** of the following PARENTAL ROLES is most important to you? Write a "1" beside the **ONE** most important parental role.

_____Being a teacher and guide

_____Being a disciplinarian

_____Being a good provider

Write a "2" beside the **PARENTING ROLE** that is second in importance.

9. Which **ONE** DISCIPLINE STRATEGY do you use most often with this child? Write a "1" beside the **ONE** strategy you use the most.

_____Loss of privileges

_____Spankings

_____Reason/logic

Write a "2" beside the **DISCIPLINE STRATEGY** that is the second most used.

10. In general, how satisfied are you with this child's **OVERALL DEVELOPMENT**—that is, his or her level of maturity, attitudes, and behaviors? (CHECK ONE)

_____Very satisfied

_____Somewhat satisfied

_____Not very satisfied

11. How well is this child doing in **SCHOOL**? (CHECK ONE)

_____Above average

_____Average

_____Below average

12. How involved is this child in **RELIGIOUS WORSHIP** or training? (CHECK ONE)

_____Very involved

_____Somewhat involved

_____Not very involved

13. How involved is this child's **EXTENDED FAMILY**, that is, his grandparents, uncles, aunts, and other relatives, in helping to raise him or her? (CHECK ONE)

_____Very involved

_____Somewhat involved

_____Not very involved

14. Who does **most** of the **WORK** involved in taking care of this child—like cooking meals, meeting with teachers, teaching and training, discipline? (CHECK ONE)

_____Father   _____Both parents equally

_____Mother   _____Other (please explain)

15. How do you think this child's **SEX** (being a girl or a boy) will affect his or her ability to get a good education and a good job? (CHECK ONE)

_____This child's sex will make it easier.

_____This child's sex will make it more difficult.

_____This child's sex will have no effect.

16. Has this child ever experienced unfair treatment from adults or other children because of his or her **RACE?**

_____Yes   _____No

17. How do you think this child's **RACE** will affect his or her ability to get a good education and a good job? (CHECK ONE)

_____This child's race will make it easier.

_____This child's race will make it more difficult.

_____This child's race will have little or no impact.

18. Do you expect this child to attend **COLLEGE?**

_____Yes   _____No

19. How important is it to you for this child to attend college? (CHECK ONE)

_____Very important

_____Somewhat important

_____Not very important

20. Have you discussed possible careers/jobs with this child?

_____Yes   _____No

21. Does this child have a specific job/career interest?

_____Yes   _____No

If yes, what?_____

22. Have you discussed sex/sexuality with this child?

_____Yes   _____No

23. At what age do you think parents should have a discussion with their children about sex?

_____5-8 years old   _____9-12 years old   _____13-17 years old

24. Are you teaching (or will you teach) this child that it is important to get married before having sex?

_____Yes   _____No

25. Are you teaching (or will you teach) this child that it is important to get married before having children?

_____Yes   _____No

26. Would you like for the school to teach this child more about sexuality?

_____Yes   _____No

Do you "Agree" or "Disagree" with the following statements? (CIRCLE ONE)

27. When possible, it is better for everyone if the man earns the main living and the woman takes care of home and family.

Agree   Disagree

28. If a husband and wife both work full-time, they should share equally in housework and taking care of the children.

Agree   Disagree

29. It is equally important for girls and boys to attend college.

Agree   Disagree

30. Being a woman makes it more difficult to get a good education and a good job.

Agree   Disagree

31. Being a racial minority makes it more difficult to get a good education and a good job.

Agree   Disagree

32. Generally speaking, children are better off being taught by teachers who are of the same race as the child.

Agree   Disagree

33. Which of the following do you believe is MOST responsible for the problems families are facing today—such as teenage pregnancy, single parenthood, divorce, and poverty? (CHECK ONE).

_____Discrimination and/or the lack of good opportunities

_____The personal decisions, choices, and lifestyles of individuals

Now, could you please give me some information about yourself?

34. What is your marital status?

_____Single, never married

_____Married

_____Divorced

_____Separated

_____Widowed

35. How old are you?_____

36. What is your race?

_____Black/African American

_____White/Caucasian

_____Hispanic

_____Asian

_____Other (Specify)

37. What is your employment status?

_____Employed

_____Unemployed

_____Retired

_____Other (Specify)

If employed, what is your occupation?_____

38. What is the highest level of education that you <u>completed</u>?

_____Grade school or less

_____Junior high school

_____High school

_____Some college

_____4-year college degree

_____More than a 4-year college degree

39. What is your family's yearly income?

_____Less than $15,000 per year

_____$15,001-$30,000 per year

_____$30,001-$50,000 per year

_____More than $50,000 per year

40. How important is religion in your life?

_____Very important

_____Somewhat important

_____Not very important at all

Please write additional comments below or on the back of this survey, or feel free to call me at home (375-1727) or school (913-864-4111) with your comments.

You may also contact me by mail:

> Shirley A. Hill, PhD
> University of Kansas
> 722 Fraser Hall
> Lawrence, Kansas 66045

Thanks so much for your help!

References

Abramovitz, M. (1996). *Under attack, fighting back: Women and welfare in the United States.* New York: Monthly Review Press.

Adams, B. W. (1980). *The family.* Chicago: Rand McNally.

Age at which young men initiate intercourse is tied to sex education and mother's presence in the home. (1994). *Family Planning Perspectives, 26*(3), 142-143.

Allen, W. R. (1978). The search for applicable theories of black family life. *Journal of Marriage and the Family, 40*(1), 117-129.

Allen, W. R. (1981). Moms, dads and boys: Race and sex differences in the socialization of male children. In L. E. Gary (Ed.), *Black men* (pp. 99-114). Beverly Hills, CA: Sage.

Alwin, D. F. (1988). From obedience to autonomy: Changes in traits desired in children, 1924-1978. *Public Opinion Quarterly, 52,* 33-52.

Anderson, E. (1989, January). Sex codes and family life among poor inner-city youths. *Annals of the American Academy of Political and Social Science, 501,* 59-78.

Anderson, E. (1990). *Streetwise: Race, class, and change in an urban community.* Chicago: University of Chicago Press.

Anderson, E. (1991). Neighborhood effects of teenage pregnancy. In C. Jencks & P. E. Peterson (Eds.), *The urban underclass* (pp. 375-398). Washington, DC: Brookings Institution.

Aries, P. (1962). *Centuries of childhood: A social history of family life.* New York: Random House.

Armor, D. J. (1992). Why is black educational achievement rising? *Public Interest, 108,* 65-80.

Asante, M. K. (1987). *The Afrocentric idea.* Philadelphia, PA: Temple University Press.

Aulette, J. R. (1994). *Changing families.* Belmont, CA: Wadsworth.

Austin, R. L., & Dodge, H. H. (1992). Despair, distrust, and dissatisfaction among blacks and women, 1973-1987. *Sociological Quarterly, 33*(4), 579-598.

Bachu, A. (1995). *Fertility of American women: June 1994* (U.S. Bureau of the Census, Current Population Reports P20-482). Washington, DC: Government Printing Office.

Baratz-Snowden, J. C. (1993). Opportunity to learn: Implications for professional development. *Journal of Negro Education, 62,* 311-323.

Bartz, K. W., & Levine, E. S. (1978). Childrearing by black parents: A description and comparison to Anglo and Chicano parents. *Journal of Marriage and the Family, 40,* 709-720.

Baumrind, D. (1968). Authoritarian versus authoritative parental control. *Adolescence, 3,* 255-272.

Beals, M. P. (1994). *Warriors don't cry: A searing memoir of the battle to integrate Little Rock's Central High.* New York: Pocket Books.

Bem, S. L. (1983). Gender schema theory and its implications for child development: Raising gender-aschematic children in a gender-schematic society. *Signs, 8*(4), 598-616.

Berns, R. M. (1993). *Child, family, community: Socialization and support* (3rd ed.). Fort Worth, TX: Harcourt Brace Jovanovich.

Berry, M. F. (1993). *The politics of parenthood: Child care, women's rights, and the myth of the good mother.* New York: Viking.

Billingsley, A. (1988). *Black families in white America.* Englewood Cliffs, NJ: Prentice-Hall. (Original work published 1968)

Billingsley, A. (1992). *Climbing Jacob's ladder: The enduring legacy of African-American families.* New York: Simon & Schuster.

Blake, W. M., & Darling, C. A. (1994). The dilemmas of the African American male. *Journal of Black Studies, 24,* 402-415.

Blassingame, J. W. (1972). *The slave community: Plantation life in the antebellum South.* New York: Oxford University Press.

Blau, Z. S. (1981). *Black children/white children: Competence, socialization, and social structure.* New York: Free Press.

Block, J. H. (1983). Differential premises arising from differential socialization of the sexes: Some conjectures. *Child Development, 54,* 1334-1354.

Blumer, H. (1969). *Symbolic interactionism: Perspective and method.* Englewood Cliffs, NJ: Prentice Hall.

Bowman, P. J., & Howard, C. (1985). Race-related socialization, motivation, and academic achievement: A study of black youths in three-generation families. *Journal of the American Academy of Child Psychiatry, 24,* 134-141.

Boykin, A. W., & Toms, F. D. (1985). Black child socialization: A conceptual framework. In H. P. McAdoo & J. L. McAdoo (Eds.), *Black children: Social, educational, and parental environments* (pp. 33-52). Beverly Hills, CA: Sage.

Branch, C. W., & Newcombe, N. (1986). Racial attitude development among young black children as a function of parental attitudes: A longitudinal and cross-sectional study. *Child Development, 57,* 712-721.

Brashears, F., & Roberts, M. (1996). The black church as a resource for change. In S. L. Logan (Ed.), *The black family: Strengths, self-help, and positive change* (pp. 181-192). Boulder, CO: Westview.

Bremner, R. (Ed.). (1970). *Children and youth in America: A documentary history* (Vol. 1). Cambridge, MA: Harvard University Press.

Brenner, D., & Hinsdale, G. (1978). Body-build stereotypes and self-identification in three age groups of females. *Adolescence, 13,* 551-561.

Brewster, K. L. (1994). Race differences in sexual activity among adolescent women: The role of neighborhood characteristics. *American Sociological Review, 59,* 408-424.

Brooks-Gunn, J., Klebanov, P. K., & Duncan, G. J. (1996). Ethnic differences in children's intelligence test scores: Role of economic deprivation, home environment, and maternal characteristics. *Child Development, 67,* 396-408.

Brown, P. (1996). Naming and framing: The social construction of diagnosis and illness. In P. Brown (Ed.), *Perspectives in medical sociology* (2nd ed., pp. 92-122). Prospect Heights, IL: Waveland.

Burgess, N. (1994). Gender roles revisited: The development of the "woman's place" among African American women in the United States. *Journal of Black Studies, 24,* 391-401.

Burton, L. M. (1990). Teenage childbearing as an alternative life-course strategy in multigenerational black families. *Human Nature, 1,* 123-143.

Burton, L. M., & Bengston, V. L. (1985). Black grandmothers: Issues of timing and continuity of roles. In V. L. Bengston & J. F. Robertson (Eds.), *Grandparenthood* (pp. 61-77). Beverly Hills, CA: Sage.

Busse, T. V., & Busse, P. (1972). Negro parental behavior and social class variables. *Journal of Genetic Psychology, 120,* 287-294.

Caldwell, J. C. (1996). The demographic implications of West African family systems. *Journal of Comparative Family Studies, 27,* 331-352.

Carr, P. G., & Mednick, M. T. (1988). Sex role socialization and the development of achievement motivation in black preschool children. *Sex Roles, 18,* 169-180.

Carrington, C. H. (1980). Depression in black women: A theoretical approach. In L Rodgers-Rose (Ed.), *The black woman* (pp. 265-271). Beverly Hills, CA: Sage.

Cazenave, N. A. (1981). Black men in America: The quest for "manhood." In H. P. McAdoo (Ed.), *Black families* (pp. 176-185). Beverly Hills, CA: Sage.

Chafetz, J. S. (1988). *Feminist sociology: An overview of contemporary theories.* Itasca, IL: F. E. Peacock.

Chase-Lansdale, P. L., Brooks-Gunn, J., & Zamsky, E. S. (1994). Young African-American multigenerational families in poverty: Quality mothering and grandmothering. *Child Development, 65,* 373-393.

Christmas, J. J. (1996). The health of African Americans. In A. Rowe & J. M. Jeffries (Eds.), *The state of black America 1996* (pp. 95-126). New York: National Urban League.

Clark, K. B. (1965). *The dark ghetto: Dilemmas of social power.* New York: Harper & Row.

Clark, K. B., & Clark, M. P. (1939). The development of consciousness of self and the emergence of racial identification in Negro preschool children. *Journal of Social Psychology, 10,* 591-599.

Clark, K. B., & Clark, M. P. (1947). Racial identification and preference in Negro children. In Committee on the Teaching of Social Psychology (Ed.), *Readings in social psychology* (pp. 169-178). New York: Holt.

Clarke, S. C. (1995). Advance report of final marriage statistics, 1989 and 1990. *Monthly Vital Statistics Report, 43*(12), 3-5 (published by the U.S. Department of Health and Human Services, Centers for Disease Control and Prevention).

Coleman, J. S. (1988). Social capital in the creation of human capital. *American Journal of Sociology, 94,* S95-S120.

Collins, P. H. (1987). The meaning of motherhood in black culture and black mother-daughter relationships. *Sage: A Scholarly Journal on Black Women, 4,* 3-10.

Collins, P. H. (1989). A comparison of two works on black family life. *Signs: Journal of Women in Culture and Society, 14,* 875-884.

Collins, P. H. (1990). *Black feminist thought: Knowledge, consciousness, and the politics of empowerment.* Boston: Unwin Hymen.

Comer, J. P., & Poussaint, A. F. (1992). *Raising black children.* New York: Plume.

Cooley, C. H. (1964). *Human nature and the social order.* New York: Schocken. (Original work published 1902)

Coopersmith, S. (1967). *The antecedents of self-esteem.* San Francisco: Freeman.

Crain, M. R. (1996). The influence of age, race, and gender on child and adolescent multidimensional self-concept. In B. A. Bracken (Ed.), *Handbook of self-concept: Developmental, social, and clinical considerations* (pp. 395-421). New York: John Wiley.

Cross, W. E. (1985). Black identity: Rediscovering the distinction between personal identity and reference group orientation. In M. B. Spencer, G. Kearse-Brookins, & W. R. Allen

(Eds.), *Beginnings: The social and affective development of black children* (pp. 155-171). Hillsdale, NJ: Lawrence Erlbaum.

Crouter, A. C., McHale, S. M., & Bartko, W. T. (1993). Gender as an organizing feature in parent-child relationships. *Journal of Social Issues, 49*(3), 161-174.

Danziger, S. K., & Radin, N. (1990, August). Absent does not equal uninvolved: Predictors of fathering in teen mother families. *Journal of Marriage and the Family, 52,* 636-642.

Darling-Hammond, L. (1995). Cracks in the bell curve: How education matters. *Journal of Negro Education, 64,* 340-353.

Davis, A. (1981). *Women, race and class.* New York: Random House.

Davis, A. (1993). Outcast mothers and surrogates: Racism and reproductive politics in the nineties. In L. S. Kauffman (Ed.), *American feminist thought at century's end: A reader* (pp. 355-366). Cambridge, MA: Blackwell.

Davis, A., & Dollard, J. (1940). *Children of bondage: The personality development of Negro youth in the urban South.* New York: Harper & Row.

Davis, A., & Havighurst, R. J. (1946). Social class and color differences in child-rearing. *American Sociological Review, 2,* 698-710.

Deater-Deckard, K., Dodge, K. A., Bates, J. E., & Pettit, G. S. (1996). Physical discipline among African American and European American mothers: Links to children's externalizing behaviors. *Developmental Psychology, 32*(6), 1065-1072.

deMause, L. (1974). The evolution of childhood. *History of Childhood Quarterly, 1,* 503-575.

Dembo, R. (1988). Delinquency among black male youth. In J. T. Gibbs (Ed.), *Young, black, and male in America: An endangered species* (pp. 129-165). Dover, MA: Auburn House.

Demo, D. H., & Hughes, M. (1990). Socialization and racial identity among black Americans. *Social Psychology Quarterly, 53*(4), 364-374.

Dennis, R. M. (1995). Social Darwinism, scientific racism, and the metaphysics of race. *Journal of Negro Education, 64,* 243-252.

Denzin, N. K. (1978). *The research act* (2nd ed.). New York: McGraw-Hill.

Dill, B. T. (1979). The dialectic of black womanhood. *Signs: Journal of Women in Culture and Society, 4*(3), 545-555.

Dill, B. T. (1988). Our mother's grief: Racial ethnic women and the maintenance of families. *Journal of Family History, 13*(4), 415-431.

Douglass, F. (1960). *Narrative of the life of Frederick Douglass an American slave* (B. Quarles, Ed.). Cambridge, MA: Belknap Press.

Downey, D. B., Jackson, P. B., & Powell, B. (1994). Sons versus daughters: Sex composition of children and maternal views of socialization. *Sociological Quarterly, 35*(1), 33-50.

Dressler, W. W. (1985). Extended family relationships, social support, and mental health in a southern black community. *Journal of Health and Social Behavior, 26,* 39-48.

DuBois, W. E. B. (Ed.). (1908). *The Negro American family* (Atlanta University Publications, No. 13). Atlanta, GA: Atlanta University Press.

Duneier, M. (1992). *Slim's table: Race, respectability, and masculinity.* Chicago: University of Chicago Press.

Dyson, M. E. (1993). *Reflecting black: African-American cultural criticism.* Minneapolis: University of Minnesota Press.

Ellison, C., & Sherkat, D. E. (1990). Patterns of religious mobility among black Americans. *Sociological Quarterly, 31*(4), 551-568.

Enger, J. M., Howerton, D. L., & Cobbs, C. R. (1994). Internal/external locus of control, self-esteem, and parental verbal interaction of at-risk black male adolescents. *Journal of Social Psychology, 134*(3), 269-274.

Fordham, S., & Ogbu, J. (1986). Black students' school successes: Coping with the "burden of 'acting white.' " *Urban Review, 18*(3), 176-206.

Franklin, J. H., & Moss, A. A. (1988). *From slavery to freedom: A history of Negro Americans* (6th ed.). New York: McGraw-Hill.

Fraser, N., & Gordon, L. (1994). A genealogy of dependency: Tracing a keyword of the U.S. welfare state. *Signs: Journal of Women in Culture and Society, 19*(21), 309-336.

Frazier, E. F. (1930). The Negro slave family. *Journal of Negro History, 15,* 198-259.

Frazier, E. F. (1949). *The Negro family in the United States.* Chicago: University of Chicago Press. (Original work published 1939)

Frazier, E. F. (1963). *The Negro church in America.* New York: Schocken.

French, V. (1995). History of parenting: The ancient Mediterranean world. In M. H. Bornstein (Ed.), *Handbook of parenting* (Vol. 2, pp. 263-284). Mahwah, NJ: Lawrence Erlbaum.

Fulbright-Anderson, K. (1996). Developing our youth: What works. In A. Rowe & J. M. Jeffries (Eds.), *The state of black America 1996* (pp. 127-143). New York: National Urban League.

Furstenberg, F. F., Jr. (1987). Race differences in teenage sexuality, pregnancy, and adolescent childbearing. *Milbank Quarterly, 65,* 381-403.

Gambetta, D. (1987). *Were they pushed or did they jump?* Cambridge, MA: Cambridge University Press.

Gans, H. J. (1995). *The war against the poor: The underclass and antipoverty policy.* New York: Basic Books.

Garbarino, J., & Kostelny, K. (1995). Parenting and public policy. In M. H. Bornstein (Ed.), *Handbook of parenting* (Vol. 3, pp. 419-436). Mahwah, NJ: Lawrence Erlbaum.

Gates, H. L. (1995). *Colored people: A memoir.* New York: Vintage.

Gibbs, J. T. (1988). Young black males in America: Endangered, embittered, and embattled. In J. T. Gibbs (Ed.), *Young, black, and male in America: An endangered species* (pp. 1-36). Dover, MA: Auburn House.

Giddings, P. (1984). *When and where I enter: The impact of black women on race and sex in America.* New York: Bantam.

Goldscheiter, F., & Waite, L. (1991). *New families, no families: The transformation of the American home.* Berkeley: University of California Press.

Gordon, S. (1986, October). What kids need to know. *Psychology Today,* pp. 22-26.

Gutman, H. (1976). *The black family in slavery and freedom, 1750-1925.* New York: Pantheon.

Hale, J. E. (1986). *Black children: Their roots, culture, and learning styles* (Rev. ed.). Baltimore: Johns Hopkins University Press.

Hammons-Bryner, S. (1995). Interpersonal relationships and African American women's educational achievement: An ethnographic study. *Sage: A Scholarly Journal on Black Women, 9*(1), 10-17.

Hampton, R. L., & Gelles, R. J. (1991). A profile of violence toward black children. In R. L. Hampton (Ed.), *Black family violence* (pp. 21-34). Lexington, MA: Lexington.

Harrington, M. (1962). *The other America: Poverty in the U.S.* New York: Penguin.

Harris, K. M. (1993). Work and welfare among single mothers in poverty. *American Journal of Sociology, 99*(2), 317-352.

Harris, K. M. (1997). *Teen mothers and the revolving welfare door.* Philadelphia, PA: Temple University Press.

Harry, B., Allen, N., & McLaughlin, M. (1995). Communication versus compliance: African-American parents' involvement in special education. *Exceptional Children, 61*(4), 364-377.

Harter, S. (1987). The determinants and mediational role of global self-worth in children. In N. Eisenberg (Ed.), *Contemporary topics in developmental psychology.* New York: John Wiley.

Haurin, R. J., & Mott, F. L. (1990). Adolescent sexual activity in the family context: The impact of older siblings. *Demography, 27*(4), 537-557.

Heath, S. B., & McLaughlin, M. W. (1993). Identity and inner-city youth. In S. B. Heath & M. W. McLaughlin (Eds.), *Identity and inner-city youth: Beyond ethnicity and gender* (pp. 1-12). New York: Teachers' College Press.

Hendry, L. B., & Gullies, P. (1978). Body type, body esteem, school, and leisure: A study of overweight, average, and underweight adolescents. *Journal of Youth and Adolescence, 7*, 181-195.

Hernandez, D. J. (1997). Child development and the social demography of childhood. *Child Development, 68*(1), 149-169.

Hernstein, R. J., & Murray, C. (1994). *The bell curve: Intelligence and the class structure in American life.* New York: Free Press.

Herskovits, M. J. (1958). *The myth of the Negro past.* Boston: Beacon.

Higginbotham, E. (1981). Is marriage a priority? Class differences in marital options of educated black women. In P. Stein (Ed.), *Single life: Unmarried adults in social context* (pp. 133-176). Ann Arbor, MI: Institute for Social Research.

Hill, R. (1972). *The strengths of black families.* New York: Emerson Hall.

Hill, R., et al. (Eds.). (1993). *Research on the African American family: A holistic perspective.* Westport, CT: Auburn House.

Hill, S. A. (1994). *The management of sickle cell disease in low-income African American families.* Philadelphia, PA: Temple University Press.

Hill, S. A. & Sprague, J. (1997). *Constructing gender in black and white families: The interaction of gender with race and class.* Presented at the annual meeting of the American Sociological Association in Toronto, Canada, August, 1997.

Hill, S. A., & Zimmerman, M. K. (1995, February). Valiant girls and vulnerable boys: The impact of gender and race on mothers' caregiving for chronically ill children. *Journal of Marriage and the Family, 57*, 43-53.

Holliday, B. G. (1985). Developmental imperatives of social ecologies. In H. P. McAdoo & J. L. McAdoo (Eds.), *Black children: Social educational, and parental environments* (pp. 53-69). Beverly Hills, CA: Sage.

hooks, b. (1981). *Ain't I a woman: Black women and feminism.* Boston: South End Press.

hooks, b. (1992). *Black looks: Race and representation.* Boston: South End Press.

Hunter, A. G., & Davis, J. E. (1992). Constructing gender: An exploration of Afro-American men's conceptualization of manhood. *Gender & Society, 6*(3), 464-479.

Hunter, A. G., & Davis, J. E. (1994). Hidden voices of black men: The meaning, structure, and complexity of manhood. *Journal of Black Studies, 25*(1), 20-40.

Hurst, C. E. (1998). *Social inequality: Forms, causes, and consequences* (3rd ed.). Boston: Allyn & Bacon.

Hymowitz, C., & Weissman, M. (1978). *A history of women in America.* New York: Bantam.

Ickes, W. (1993). Traditional gender roles: Do they make, and then break, our relationships? *Journal of Social Issues, 49*(3), 71-85.

Jarrett, R. L. (1994). Living poor: Family life among single parents, African American women. *Social Problems, 41*(1), 30-47.

Jones, C. L., Tepperman, L., & Wilson, S. J. (1995). *The futures of the family.* Englewood Cliffs, NJ: Prentice Hall.

Jones, D. J., & Roberts, V. A. (1994). Black children: Growth, development, and health. In I. L. Livingston (Ed.), *Handbook of black American health: The mosaic of conditions, issues, policies, and prospects* (pp. 331-343). Westport, CT: Greenwood.

Jones, J. (1985). *Labor of love, labor of sorrow: Black women, work and the family from slavery to the present.* New York: Vintage.

Joseph, J. M. (1994). *The resilient child: Preparing today's youth for tomorrow's world.* New York: Plenum.

Kami, C. K., & Radin, N. L. (1967). Class differences in the socialization practices of Negro mothers. *Journal of Marriage and the Family, 29,* 302-310.

Kaplan, E. B. (1997). *Not our kind of girl.* Berkeley: University of California Press.

Kardiner, A., & Ovesey, L. (1951). *The mark of oppression: Explorations in the personality of the American Negro.* New York: World.

Katz, M. B. (1989). *The undeserving poor: From the War on Poverty to the war on welfare.* New York: Pantheon.

King, D. K. (1988). Multiple jeopardy, multiple consciousness: The context of black feminist ideology. *Signs, 14*(11), 42-72.

Kitano, H. H. L. (1991). *Race relations* (4th ed.). Englewood Cliffs, NY: Prentice Hall.

Kohn, M. L. (1963). Social class and parent-child relationships. *American Journal of Sociology, 63,* 471-480.

Kohn, M. L. (1977). *Class and conformity: A study of values* (2nd ed.). Chicago: University of Chicago Press.

Ladner, J. A. (1971). *Tomorrow's tomorrow: The black women.* Garden City, NY: Doubleday.

Ladner, J. A., & Gourdine, R. M. (1984). Intergenerational teenage motherhood: Some preliminary findings. *Sage: A Scholarly Journal on Black Women, 1*(2), 22-24.

Landry, B. (1987). *The new black middle class.* Berkeley: University of California Press.

Landry, D. J., & Camelo, T. M. (1994). Young unmarried men and women discuss men's role in contraceptive practice. *Family Planning Perspectives, 26,* 222-227.

Leigh, W. A. (1996). US housing policy in 1996: The outlook for black Americans. In A. Rowe & J. M. Jeffries (Eds.), *The state of black America 1996* (pp. 188-218). New York: National Urban League.

Levin, J. S., Chatters, L. M., & Taylor, R. J. (1995). A multidimensional measure of religious involvement in African Americans. *Sociological Quarterly, 36,* 157-177.

Lewis, D. K. (1975). The black family: Socialization and sex roles. *Phylon, 36*(3), 221-238.

Lewis, O. (1959). *Five families: Mexican case studies in the culture of poverty.* New York: Basic Books.

Lichter, D. T., Cornell, G. T., & Eggebeen, D. J. (1993). Harvesting human capital: Family structure and education among rural youth. *Rural Sociology, 58*(1), 53-75.

Luker, K. (1996). *Dubious conceptions: The politics of teenage pregnancy.* Cambridge, MA: Harvard University Press.

Luster, T., & McAdoo, H. P. (1994). Factors related to the achievement and adjustment of young African American children. *Child Development, 65,* 1080-1094.

Marshall, S. (1995). Ethnic socialization of African American children: Implications for parenting, identity development, and academic performance. *Journal of Youth and Adolescence, 24*(4), 337-396.

Massey, D. S. (1990). American apartheid: Segregation and the making of the underclass. *American Journal of Sociology, 96*(2), 329-357.

McAdoo, H. P. (1985). Racial attitudes and self-concept of young black children over time. In H. P. McAdoo & J. L. McAdoo (Eds.), *Black children: Social, educational, and parental environments* (pp. 213-242). Beverly Hills, CA: Sage.

McAdoo, H. P. (1990). A portrait of African American families in the United States. In S. E. Rix (Ed.), *The American woman, 1990-1991: A status report* (pp. 71-93). New York: Norton.

McAdoo, J. L. (1981). Black father and child interactions. In L. E. Gary (Ed.), *Black men* (pp. 115-130). Beverly Hills, CA: Sage.

McAdoo, J. L. (1983). Parenting styles: Mother-child interactions and self-esteem in young black children. In C. E. Obudo (Ed.), *Black marriage and family therapy* (pp. 135-150). Westport, CT: Greenwood.

McAdoo, J. L. (1988). The roles of black fathers in the socialization of black children. In H. P. McAdoo (Ed.), *Black families* (pp. 257-269). Newbury Park, CA: Sage.

McCreary, D. R. (1994). The male role and avoiding femininity. *Sex Roles, 31*(9-10), 517-531.

McLanahan, S., & Sandefur, G. (1994). *Growing up with a single parent: What hurts, what helps.* Cambridge, MA: Harvard University Press.

McLeod, J. D., & Shanahan, M. J. (1996, September). Trajectories of poverty and children's mental health. *Journal of Health and Social Behavior, 37,* 207-220.

McLoyd, V. C. (1990). The impact of economic hardships on black families and children: Psychological distress, parenting, and socioemotional development. *Child Development, 61,* 311-346.

Mead, G. H. (1962). *Mind, self, and society.* Chicago: Chicago University Press.

Meltzer, B., Petras, J. W., & Reynolds, L. T. (1975). *Symbolic interactionism: Genesis, varieties, and outcomes.* London: Routledge & Kegan Paul.

Midgette, T. E., & Glenn, E. (1993). African-American male academies: A positive view. *Journal of Multicultural Counseling and Development, 21,* 69-78.

Mishler, E. G. (1986). *Research interviewing: Context and narrative.* Cambridge, MA: Harvard University Press.

Mott, F. L. (1990). When is a father really gone? Paternal-child contact in father-absent homes. *Demography, 27*(4), 499-517.

Moynihan, D. P. (1965). *The Negro family: A case for national action.* Washington, DC: Department of Labor.

Murray, C. (1984). *Losing ground: American social policy 1950-1980.* New York: Basic Books.

Murry, V. M. (1994). Socio-historical study of African American adolescent females' sexuality: Timing of first coitus, 1950 through 1980. In R. Staples (Ed.), *The black family: Essays and studies* (5th ed., pp. 52-65). Belmont, CA: Wadsworth.

Mutran, E. (1985). Intergenerational family support among blacks and whites: Response to culture or to socioeconomic differences. *Journal of Gerontology, 40,* 382-389.

Nobles, W. W. (1974). Africanity: Its role in black families. *Black Scholar, 5,* 10-17.

Nobles, W. W. (1985). *Africanity and the black family: The development of a theoretical model* (2nd ed.). Oakland, CA: Institute for the Advanced Study of Black Family Life and Culture.

Ogbu, J. U. (1978). *Minority education and caste.* New York: Academic Press.

Ogbu, J. U. (1997). African American education: A cultural-ecological perspective. In H. P. McAdoo (Ed.), *Black families* (3rd ed., pp. 234-250). Thousand Oaks, CA: Sage.

Ohuche, R. O., & Otaala, B. (1981). *The African child and his environment.* Elmsford, NY: Pergamon.

Oliver, M. L., & Shapiro, T. M. (1995). *Black wealth, white wealth: A new perspective on racial inequality.* New York: Routledge & Kegan Paul.

Page, C. (1996, August 7). Throwing out babies with the bath water. *Kansas City Star,* p. C9.

Pallas, A. M., Entwisle, D. R., Alexander, K. L., & Weinstein, P. (1990). Social structure and the development of self-esteem in young children. *Social Psychology Quarterly, 53*(4), 302-315.

Parcel, T. L., & Menaghan, E. G. (1993). Family social capital and children's behavior problems. *Social Psychology Quarterly, 56*(2), 120-135.

Parks, G. (1992). A choice of weapons. In J. David (Ed.), *Growing up black* (pp. 26-31). New York: Avon.

Pearson, J. L., Hunter, A. G., Ensminger, M. E., & Kellam, S. G. (1990). Black grandmothers in multigenerational households: Diversity in family structure and parenting involvement in the Woodlawn community. *Child Development, 61,* 434-442.

Peters, M. F. (1988). Parenting in black families with young children: A historical perspective. In H. P. McAdoo (Ed.), *Black families* (pp. 227-241). Newbury Park, CA: Sage.

Peters, M. F. (1997). Parenting of young children in black families. In H. P. McAdoo (Ed.), *Black families* (3rd ed., pp. 167-182). Thousand Oaks, CA: Sage.

Phinney, J. S., & Chavira, V. (1995). Parental ethnic socialization and adolescent coping with problems related to ethnicity. *Journal of Research on Adolescence, 5*(1), 31-53.

Pinkney, A. (1993). *Black Americans* (4th ed.). Englewood Cliffs, NJ: Prentice Hall.

Porter, J. R., & Washington, R. E. (1982). Black identity and self-esteem: A review of studies of black self-concept, 1968-78. In M. Rosenberg & H. B. Kaplan (Eds.), *Social psychology of self-concept* (pp. 224-234). Arlington Heights, IL: Harlan Davidson.

Powell-Hopson, D., & Hopson, D. (1990). *Different and wonderful: Raising black children in a race-conscious society.* New York: Prentice Hall.

Pyant, C. T., & Yanico, B. J. (1991). Relationship of racial identity and gender-role attitudes to black women's psychological well-being. *Journal of Counseling Psychology, 38,* 315-322.

Queen, S. A., & Habenstein, R. W. (1967). *The family in various cultures* (3rd ed.). Philadelphia, PA: J. B. Lippincott.

Razak, A. (1990). Toward a womanist analysis of birth. In I. Diamond & G. F. Orenstein (Eds.), *Reweaving the world: The emergence of ecofeminism* (pp. 165-72). San Francisco: Sierra Club Books.

Reddy, M. T. (1994). *Crossing the color line: Race, parenting, and culture.* New Brunswick, NJ: Rutgers University Press.

Reid, P. T., & Trotter, K. H. (1993). Children's self-presentations with infants: Gender and ethnic comparisons. *Sex Roles, 29*(3-4), 171-181.

Reinisch, J. M. (1990). *The Kinsey Institute new report on sex: What you must know to be sexually literate.* New York: St. Martin's.

Reiss, A. J., & Roth, J. A. (1993). *Understanding and preventing violence.* Washington, DC: National Research Council, Panel on the Understanding and Control of Violent Behavior

Robinson, T. L., & Ward, J. V. (1995). African American adolescents and skin color. *Journal of Black Psychology, 21*(3), 256-274.

Rogers-Dulan, J., & Blacher, J. (1995). African American families, religion, and disability: A conceptual framework. *Mental Retardation, 33,* 226-238.

Roschelle, A. R. (1997). *No more kin: Exploring race, class, and gender in family networks.* Thousand Oaks, CA: Sage.

Rosenberg, M. (1965). *Society and the adolescent self-image.* Princeton, NJ: Princeton University Press.

Rosenberg, M., & Kaplan, H. B. (1982). *Social psychology of the self-concept.* Arlington Heights, IL: Harlan Davidson.

Ruggles, S. (1994, February). The origins of African-American family structure. *American Sociological Review, 59,* 136-151.

Saluter, A. F. (1994). *Marital status and living arrangements: March 1993* (U.S. Bureau of the Census, Current Population Reports, Series P20-478). Washington, DC: Government Printing Office.

Sanday, P. R. (1981). *Female power and male dominance: On the origins of sexual inequality.* Cambridge, MA: Cambridge University Press.

Scanzoni, J. (1977). *The black family in modern society: Patterns of stability and security.* Chicago: University of Chicago Press.

Scheirer, M. A. (1984). Household structure among welfare families: Correlates and consequences. *Journal of Marriage and the Family, 45,* 761-771.

Scott, J. W. (1993). African American daughter-mother relations and teenage pregnancy: Two faces of premarital teenage pregnancy. *Western Journal of Black Studies, 17*(2), 73-81.

Scott, R. J. (1985). The battle over the child: Child apprenticeship and the Freedmen's Bureau in North Carolina. In N. R. Hiner & J. M. Hawes (Eds.), *Growing up in America: Children in historical perspective* (pp. 193-207). Chicago: University of Chicago Press.

Shujaa, M. J. (1992). Afrocentric transformation and parental choice in African American independent schools. *Journal of Negro Education, 61,* 148-159.

Sigelman, L., & Welch, S. (1991). *Black American's views of racial inequality: The dream deferred.* Cambridge, MA: Cambridge University Press.

Smith, R. C., & Seltzer, R. (1992). *Race, class, and culture: A study of Afro-American mass opinion.* Albany: State University of New York Press.

Smith, T. (1990). The polls—a report: The sexual revolution? *Public Opinion Quarterly, 54,* 415-435.

Sonenstein, F. L., Pleck, J. H., & Ku, L. C. (1991). Levels of sexual activity among adolescent males in the United States. *Family Planning Perspectives, 23,* 162-167.

Stack, C. (1974). *All our kin: Strategies for survival in a black community.* New York: Harper & Row.

Staples, R. (1984, October). The mother-son relationship in the black family. *Ebony, 39*(12), 76-78.

Staples, R. (1994). Substance abuse and the black family crisis: An overview. In R. Staples (Ed.), *The black family: Essays and studies* (5th ed., pp. 260-270). Belmont, CA: Wadsworth.

Staples, R., & Johnson, L. B. (1993). *Black families at the crossroads: Challenges and prospects.* San Francisco: Jossey-Bass.

Steinberg, L. (1992). Impact of parenting practices on adolescent achievement: Authoritative parenting, school involvement, and encouragement to succeed. *Child Development, 63,* 1266-1281.

Straus, M. A. (1994). *Beating the devil out of them: Corporal punishment in American families.* New York: Lexington.

Straus, M. A., Gelles, R. J., & Steinmetz, S. K. (1980). *Behind closed doors: Violence in the American family.* New York: Doubleday.

Sullivan, M. L. (1989, January). Absent fathers in the inner city. *Annals of the American Academy of Political and Social Sciences, 501,* 48-58.

Swidler, A. (1986). Culture in action: Symbols and strategies. *American Sociological Review, 51,* 273-286.

Taylor, R. J. (1986). Receipt of support from family among black Americans: Demographic and familial differences. *Journal of Marriage and the Family, 48,* 67-77.

Taylor, R. J., Chatters, L. M., & Mays, V. M. (1988). Parents, children, siblings, in-laws and non-kin as sources of emergency assistance to black Americans. *Family Relations, 37,* 298-304.

Taylor, R. J., Chatters, L. M., Tucker, M. B., & Lewis, E. (1990, January). Developments in research on black families: A decade review. *Journal of Marriage and the Family, 52,* 993-1014.

Taylor, R. L. (1994). Black youth in crisis. In R. Staples (Ed.), *The black family: Essays and studies* (5th ed., pp. 214-230). Belmont, CA: Wadsworth.

Thomson, E., Hanson, T. L., & McLanahan, S. S. (1994). Family structure and child well-being: Economic resources vs. parental behaviors. *Social Forces, 73*(1), 221-242.

Thornton, M. C., Chatters, L. M., Taylor, R. J., & Allen, W. R. (1990). Sociodemographic and environmental correlates of racial socialization by black parents. *Child Development, 61,* 401-409.

Tilly, L., & Scott, J. (1978). *Women, work and family.* New York: Holt, Rinehart & Winston.

Tolson, T. F. J., & Wilson, M. N. (1990). The impact of two- and three-generational black family structure on perceived family climate. *Child Development, 61,* 416-428.

Tower, C. C. (1996). *Understanding child abuse and neglect* (3rd ed.). Boston: Allyn & Bacon.

Ucko, L. G. (1994). Culture and violence: The interaction of Africa and America. *Sex Roles, 31,* 185-204.

Ulbrich, P. M., Warheit, G. J., & Zimmerman, R. S. (1989). Race, socioeconomic status, and psychological distress: An examination of differential vulnerability. *Journal of Health and Social Behavior, 30,* 131-146.

U.S. Department of Commerce. (1996). *Statistical abstract of the United States 1996* (116th ed.). Washington, DC: Government Printing Office.

U.S. Department of Education, National Center for Education Statistics, & Smith, T. M. (1996a). *The condition of education 1996* (NCES 96-304). Washington, DC: Government Printing Office.

U.S. Department of Education, National Center for Education Statistics, & Snyder, T. D. (1996b). *Digest of education statistics* (NCES 96-133; Production Manager, C. M. Hoffman; Program Analyst, C. M. Geddes). Washington, DC: Government Printing Office.

U.S. Department of Health and Human Services, Public Health Service, Centers for Disease Control and Prevention, National Center for Health Statistics. (1996). *Health United States 1995* (Pub. No. [PHS] 96-1232). Hyattsville, MD: Author.

Ventura, S. J., Martin, J. A., Taffell, S. M., Matthews, T. J., & Clarke, S. C. (1995). Advance report of final natality statistics, 1993. *Monthly Vital Statistics Report, 44*(3, Suppl.).

Wacquant, L. (1993). Urban outcasts: Stigma and division in the black American ghetto and the French urban periphery. *International Journal of Urban and Regional Research, 17,* 366-382.

Ward, J. V., & Taylor, J. M. (1994). Sexuality education for immigrant and minority students: Developing a culturally appropriate curriculum. In J. M. Irvine (Ed.), *Sexual cultures and the construction of adolescent identities* (pp. 51-68). Philadelphia, PA: Temple University Press.

Washington, B. T. (1992). Up from slavery. In J. David (Ed.), *Growing up black* (pp. 94-105). New York: Avon. (Original work published 1924)

Weber, M. (1964). *The theory of social and economic organizations* (T. Parsons, Ed.). New York: Free Press.

West, C., & Zimmerman, D. (1987). Doing gender. *Gender & Society, 1,* 125-151.

Whaley, A. L. (1993). Self-esteem, cultural identity, and psychosocial adjustment in African American children. *Journal of Black Psychology, 19*(4), 406-422.

White, J. (1974). Whatever happened to the slave family in the old South? *American Studies, 8,* 383-390.

Wilkinson, D. Y. (1974). Racial socialization through children's toys: A sociohistorical examination. *Journal of Black Studies, 5*(1), 96-109.

Wilkinson, D. Y. (1996). Integration dilemmas in a racist culture. *Society, 33,* 27-31.

Willie, C. V. (1985). *Black and white families: A study of complementarity.* Bayside, NY: General Hall.

Willis, M. G. (1989). Learning styles of African American children: A review of the literature and interventions. *Journal of Black Psychology, 16,* 47-65.

Wilson, M. N. (1989). Child development in the context of the black extended family. *American Psychologist, 44,* 380-385.

Wilson, M. N., Tolson, T. F. J., Hinton, I. D., & Kiernan, M. (1990). Flexibility and sharing of childcare duties in black families. *Sex Roles, 22,* 409-425.

Wilson, W. J. (1978). *The declining significance of race: Blacks and changing American institutions.* Chicago: University of Chicago Press.

Wilson, W. J. (1987). *The truly disadvantaged: The inner-city, the underclass, and public policy.* Chicago: University of Chicago Press.

Wilson, W. J. (1991, February). Studying inner-city social dislocations: The challenge of public agenda research. *American Sociological Review, 56,* 1-14.

Wilson, W. J. (1996). *When work disappears: The world of the new urban poor.* New York: Knopf.

Wu, L. L., & Martinson, B. C. (1993). Family structure and the risk of a premarital birth. *American Sociological Review, 58,* 210-232.

Yinger, J. M. (1994). *Ethnicity: Source of strength? Source of conflict?* Albany: State University of New York Press.

Young, V. H. (1970). Family and childhood in a southern Negro community. *American Anthropologist, 72*(2), 269-288.

Young, V. H. (1974). A black American socialization pattern. *American Ethnologist, 1,* 405-413.

Zelizer, V. A. (1985). *Pricing the priceless child: The changing social value of children.* New York: Basic Books.

Zinn, M. B., & Eitzen, D. S. (1987). *Diversity in families* (2nd ed.). New York: HarperCollins.

Index

About the Author

Shirley A. Hill is Associate Professor at the University of Kansas. She teaches classes on the family, social inequality, and health care. She is the author of *Managing Sickle Cell Disease in Low-Income Black Families* (1994) and has published research articles in other areas of interest, including motherhood among black women, coping with chronic illness, and gender inequality in health care. She is the mother of two children, and the grandmother of five children.